DUMBARTON OAKS
MEDIEVAL LIBRARY

Jan M. Ziolkowski, General Editor

SAINTS' LIVES

VOLUME I

HENRY OF AVRANCHES

DOML 30

Saints' Lives

HENRY OF AVRANCHES

VOLUME I

Edited and Translated by

DAVID TOWNSEND

DUMBARTON OAKS
MEDIEVAL LIBRARY

HARVARD UNIVERSITY PRESS
CAMBRIDGE, MASSACHUSETTS
LONDON, ENGLAND
2014

Library of Congress Cataloging-in-Publication Data

Henry, of Avranches, active 13th century, author.

    [Poems. Selections. English]

    Saints' lives / Henry of Avranches ; edited and translated by David Townsend.

    pages cm — (Dumbarton Oaks medieval library ; 30, 31)

    Includes bibliographical references and index.

    ISBN 978-0-674-05128-7 (v. 1 : alk. paper)

    ISBN 978-0-674-72865-3 (v. 2 : alk. paper)

    1. Christian saints—Poetry. 2. Latin poetry, Medieval and modern.

I. Townsend, David, 1955– II. Title. III. Series: Dumbarton Oaks medieval library ; 30, 31.

    PA8330.H3A2 2014

    871'.03—dc23   2013034085

Contents

Introduction

From at least the early 1220s until his death (presumably in 1262), Henry of Avranches was the most prolific and successful Latin versifier of his day. His patrons included highly placed English prelates, Pope Gregory IX, King Louis IX of France, and, continuously for the last twenty years of his life, King Henry III of England. A poetic debate with his rival Michael of Cornwall in 1254 to 1255 (of which only Michael's half survives) seems to have been staged formally in a series of celebrated public events. The various short occasional poems with which he is generally credited suggest an extraordinarily peripatetic career and an impressive range of further personal and professional associations. Writing two generations after the notable Latin epic poets of the late twelfth century, such as Alan of Lille, Walter of Châtillon, Joseph of Exeter, and John of Hauville, Henry stands near the end of the tradition of medieval Latin narrative verse on a grand scale, which had continued more or less uninterrupted, albeit with dramatic shifts of dominant genre and style, since the poets of late antiquity. It is easy to see how Henry so successfully sustained his career on his skills as a poet: he is virtually unsurpassable as a master of ingenious wordplay, delightfully complicated sound patterns, clever effects of arrangement, and appealingly vivid conceits.

Many details of Henry's biography depend on his authorship of specific works—a question in many instances insufficiently settled—and so further attention to his career follows somewhat later in this introduction. Henry's total surviving output consists for the greatest part of versified saints' lives, almost all of them based on identifiable prose sources. Seven of these *vitae,* as found in the principal manuscript of his works, are edited and translated in the present volumes: lives of Francis of Assisi; the eighth-century King Oswald of Northumbria; the seventh-century missionary Bishop Birinus of Wessex; the East Anglian hermit Guthlac; the ninth-century Edmund, king and martyr; the fictional martyr Fremund; and the martyred archbishop of Canterbury, Thomas Becket.

The Texts Presented in This Edition

The *Life of Francis* (Saint Francis of Assisi, the founder of the Franciscan order), is by any account Henry's magnum opus, an ambitious work divided into fourteen books and dedicated to Pope Gregory IX. Henry composed the poem between 1232 and 1234, and an anecdote preserved in the prose introduction that accompanies an adapted version in one manuscript (Versailles, Bibliothèque Municipale, MS 8) attests the attention its dedicatee gave it in a public reading and in subsequent conversation with its author.[1] Henry's poem versifies Thomas of Celano's first prose life of Francis, which Gregory had commissioned at the time of Francis's canonization in 1228. Henry's adaptation showcases his skills at their most polished in this performance for the most powerful patron of his career. The poem is rife with biblical allusions as well as with tags reminiscent of classical verse, and the hagiographical narrative is assimilated to conventions of epic diction and presentation. But Henry's playful, rhetorically ingenious wordplays and aural effects, a hallmark of his style here as elsewhere, are far from the classicizing aesthetic of much of the twelfth-century verse that constituted his most immediate literary context, for example and perhaps most notably, the *Alexandreis* of Walter of Châtillon. (Henry thus imports into the practice of quantitative Latin verse the over-the-top pyrotechnics of the rhythmical Latin verse most modern readers know best from the poems of the *Carmina Burana*.)

Henry positions his work explicitly in relation to Walter's poem, which was completed roughly a half century before Henry's and had achieved by his day a solid canonical position in the literary curriculum. The initial letters of Henry's fourteen books form the acrostic GREGORIUS NONUS (that is, "Gregory the Ninth"), in imitation of the acrostic initials of Walter's ten books, which similarly spell out the name of his patron. Henry prefaces each of his fourteen books with four lines of versified summary, also in imitation of Walter's practice (which itself emulates the versified summaries that often accompanied the text of classical epics in medieval manuscripts). The very fact that Henry begins his epic with the word *Gesta* (deeds) imitates Walter's opening—while his choice of the accompanying verb *cantabo* (I shall sing) recalls the opening words of Virgil's *Aeneid*, *"arma virumque cano."* In his prologue he compares Saint Francis to Julius Caesar and Alexander the Great as a hero even worthier of epic celebration than those predecessors, thus declaring an emulation both of Lucan's *Bellum civile* (celebrating Caesar) and Walter's latter-day poem.

Henry appears to have made some emendations to the poem some years after its presentation to Gregory IX. The version edited below reflects the later of two complete texts, that of Cambridge, University Library MS Dd.XI.78 (hereafter referred to as A), a manuscript that, as we shall see below, figures centrally in all studies of Henry's surviving poetry. Among these changes are a number of revisions that excise explicit references to Brother Elias of Cortona, one of Francis's early disciples, who was deposed as Minister General of the Franciscan order in 1239 and excommunicated by Pope Gregory in 1240.[2] In addition to these politic modifications, a number of significantly revised passages appear to reflect more intrinsically literary reconsiderations. The Cambridge version of the text carries an explicit ascription to Henry, as the earlier complete text in Assisi MS 338 (on which prior editions of the text have been based, and hereafter referred to as F) does not.

The remaining six *vitae* in the present edition all take as their subject English saints. The *Life of Oswald* dates from no earlier than December of 1226, no later than 1233, and probably from 1227, to judge from available information on the officeholders of Peterborough Abbey addressed in its prologue.[3] Unlike the *Life of Francis,* it is not based on a single clearly identifiable prose version of Oswald's biography, though it shares affinities with several. The version from the Cambridge manuscript edited below is considerably shorter than a second version found in Oxford, Bodleian Library, MS Bodley 40 (referenced in the notes to the texts as B), which includes several hundred lines narrating posthumous miracles of Oswald found already in Book Three of Bede's *Ecclesiastical History,* but largely omitted by the shorter version.[4] The shorter version found in the Cambridge manuscript probably reflects more closely the original version of the text as first presented to the community of Peterborough Abbey as patrons.

The *Life of Birinus,* a seventh-century missionary from Rome responsible for the conversion of Wessex (whose career is also first attested in Book Three of Bede's *Ecclesiastical History*), is dedicated to Bishop Peter des Roches of Winchester. In his prologue, Henry announces the text as the first installment of four *vitae* of Winchester saints that he will produce for Peter; but there is no evidence that he continued the series beyond this first installment. Since Peter departed for the Holy Land on Crusade during the summer of 1227, and Henry appears to have been resident at the papal curia in the early 1230s from shortly after Peter's return to England, the poem appears to date from before its patron's departure.[5] It seems, then, to be very close in date to the *Life of Oswald;* it might thus suggest a period of itinerant search for patronage among English prelates in the mid-1220s. Henry's text is clearly based, with noteworthy passages of his own free invention, on a prose life of Birinus produced during the great efflorescence of texts honoring pre-Conquest English saints in the generation following the Norman Conquest.[6] As with the *Life of Oswald,* a second copy of the *Life of Birinus* is extant in Oxford, Bodleian Library, MS Bodley 40.

The other four texts edited here are extant only in A. Henry dedicated his *Life of Guthlac* to Henry de Longchamps, abbot of Croyland from 1190 to 1237.[7] Abbot Henry advanced the prestige of his house through translation ceremonies of several local saints—Guthlac (the abbey's founder) in 1195, Neot in 1213, and Waltheof in 1219. He also commissioned both Peter of Blois's prose life of the saint and Henry's versified version, as attested by the notice of a monastic chronicle.[8] Henry based his poem directly on Peter's prose but also drew on the original eighth-century version of Guthlac's life by Felix of Croyland. The substantial scope of Henry's adaptation befits a text commissioned to take its place next to the newly completed prose version by Peter, one of the most prestigious prose stylists of his day. Henry assimilates his hagiographical material to the generic expectations of Latin epic, as throughout his hagiographical corpus, notably by adding epic similes and other amplifications to his source text (as at ll. 266–76, 1027–34, 1117–31) and in the arrangement of his prologue, which is closely modeled on that of the *Alexandreis*.[9] Abbot Henry's long tenure in his office makes a precise dating of the text more difficult, but it is most economical to assume that the *Life of Guthlac* forms part of a cluster, together with the *Life of Oswald* and the *Life of Birinus,* likewise composed for English monastic patrons, from the mid-1220s.

The next two *vitae* in this edition, the *Life of Fremund* and the *Life of Edmund,* also extant only in A, carry no dedicatory prologue like those of the preceding four texts and no particular clues as to their respective dates. They were presumably written for the monastic houses that possessed the relics of Henry's subjects: Dunstable Priory and the powerful abbey of Bury St Edmunds, respectively. Henry's apparently indefatigable search for patronage among English monastic foundations in the 1220s might perhaps have targeted Dunstable as part of the same series as the works already discussed; but Henry was in the continuous service of King Henry III by the time of a royal visit to the priory in 1247, and it is also possible that the king commissioned the *Life of Fremund* as a suitable gift to the community upon that occasion. Henry's version closely follows a prose life extant in Dublin, Trinity College, MS B 2 7, and printed by Horstmann in his edition of the *Nova legenda Anglie*.[10] Fremund was very much a local saint of entirely legendary status, and the only references to his veneration are associated with the Augustinian house of Dunstable, which beginning in 1203 held an annual three-day fair around the saint's feast on May 11.[11]

Henry loosely based his *Life of Edmund* on Abbo of Fleury's late tenth-century account, supplementing it from subsequent texts produced at Bury St Edmunds. It plausibly dates from the abbacy of Hugh de Northwold (1215–1228), whose interest in bolstering his house's strong hagiographical traditions might well have led him to commission a versified *vita* of the house's patron saint.[12]

The final text in this edition, the *Life of Thomas Becket,* both in structure and in style stands markedly apart from the mainstream of Henry's hagiographical work. It dates more or less certainly from 1222, to conclude from events it describes as recent, and was written either under the patronage of Archbishop Stephen Langton of Canterbury or in solicitation of it. Only the first 769 lines recount the biography of Thomas; the remainder of its 1860 lines leap forward by several decades to treat the struggles of Langton against King John for the autonomy of the English church from 1207 to 1214, the translation of the saint's relics in 1220, and a lavish banquet following that ceremony. We have no identified prose source for these latter sections, the last of which stands as an important witness in its own right to the 1220 ceremony, but the life of Becket proper is based on John of Salisbury's life of the saint. The present edition includes only the portion of the text that treats the life of Thomas itself, as adapted from John of Salisbury's prose.

The text contrasts starkly with the style common to Henry's other *vitae*. It exhibits none of the hallmark rhetorical facility and playfulness that characterize Henry's other saints' lives, above all the *Life of Francis*. The debt to John of Salisbury's prose is direct and obvious, but often by way of eccentrically contorted word order and anomalous grammatical usage, at consequent expense of intelligibility without comparison to the prose source. It is hard not to view the poem as an amalgam of sustained ingenuity and literary incompetence, and hard to imagine that it could have garnered much enthusiasm from Langton and his circle. Perhaps it represents an early effort by a poet who had not yet consolidated his hallmark style, but the sheer scope of the work argues against a youthful experiment; nor does it seem plausible that a writer would progress in a few short years to the style of the *Life of Oswald* and the *Life of Birinus*. One might alternatively question whether the work is by Henry at all. Such doubts, moreover, vividly instantiate a central problem in the study of Henry, the corpus of his poetry, and his literary biography: namely, that the canon of his works is less definitively established than most modern studies assume. So we turn now to the difficulties of this question.

The Canon of Henry's Works

Our knowledge of Henry's career and literary output depends substantially on Matthew Paris (ca. 1200–1259), the Saint Alban's monk, historiographer, and bibliophile whose personally compiled anthology of Henry's poetry, now preserved as Cambridge, University Library MS Dd. XI.78, stands as principal witness to the poet's work. Matthew assembled the manuscript from multiple smaller preexisting units, adding further material in his own hand and prefacing the whole with a contents list on a front flyleaf. At the top of the first folio of the manuscript proper, we read the notation, "Versus magistri H." (Verses of Master H.). Scholars have long identified this book with that referred to in a marginal notation of another of Matthew's manuscripts, a copy of his *Chronica maiora,* now Cambridge, Corpus Christi Library MS 16, which refers to "the book that brother Brother M. Paris has of the verses of Henry of Avranches."[13] MS Dd.XI.78 (A) contains nearly one hundred items in a wide range of genres. Virtually all modern work on Henry and his poetry rests on this identification.

Rubrics in the manuscript expressly attribute four items to Henry: a poem about the arrival of the relics of the Crucifixion at the newly built Ste-Chapelle in Paris in 1241, a versification of Aristotle's treatise *On Generation and Corruption,* a short debate-poem between a knight and a clerk, and the massive *Life of Francis,* edited below. A fifth poem, a short occasional piece to William of Trumpington, abbot of Saint Alban's, is attributed to Henry in another manuscript, Matthew's *Liber additamentorum,* now London, British Library, Cotton MS Nero D.I. Together, these five poems form the central core of Henry's canon, since they carry explicit contemporary attributions in the manuscripts. Of them, only the *Life of Francis* exists in further copies, Assisi MS 338, where the poem appears without attribution, and an adapted version in Versailles, Bibliothèque municipale, MS 8, where a prose prologue also attributes the poem to Henry. On the basis of just these five poems, we can see something of the range of Henry's work: they include short occasional verse, ambitious extended narrative, debate poetry (a genre of great medieval popularity, especially in the twelfth and thirteenth centuries), and technical subject matter that modern readers might think ill suited as a subject of verse. In them, Henry addresses a highly placed churchman, a pope, and a king of France. Two of the longest are versifications of identified prose works: *On Generation and Corruption,* based on Aristotle's treatise, and the *Life of Francis,* based on the first prose life of Saint Francis by Thomas of Celano, while the poem on the relics of the Crucifixion may perhaps have been based on an unidentified sermon. Hagiography dominates this core canon: the *Life of Francis* is longer than the four other attributions of this group combined.

Henry is universally acknowledged to have written a much broader body of surviving poetry than these five works. Most subsequent research into his oeuvre has been founded on the work of Josiah Cox Russell, who in 1935 published *The Shorter Latin Poems of Master Henry of Avranches relating to England.* Russell prefaces his study with a "Catalogue of the Poems attributed to Master Henry of Avranches." Russell includes the complete contents of A as items 1–93 in this list, as well as the complete contents of London, British Library Cotton MS Vespasian D.v, fols. 151–184, to which he elsewhere refers as "the second great collection" of Henry's works—an ascription later supported from evidence set forth by Peter Binkley.[14] Subsequent studies of Henry have often assumed the validity of Russell's work and so received the question of the poet's output as already largely answered, founded on the assumption that the contents of A can be individually ascribed to Henry without further inquiry, unless clear evidence suggests the contrary. But Russell's catalogue often rests on unsystematically presented evidence of widely disparate value. Uncritical acceptance of Russell's assertions runs the risk (all the greater since later work has contributed meticulous research into the historical context of a wide range of short occasional poems written for various patrons and addressees) of adding chapters to Henry's career without revisiting the possibility that some of the poems in question may plausibly not have issued from our Henry's pen in the first place.

The present edition is grounded in a self-consciously cautious approach to the question of Henry's canon, in the first instance because of a critical reassessment of the status of the Cambridge manuscript as Matthew Paris's anthology of Henry's poetry. The identification of A with that anthology is not in doubt, and Matthew Paris has added at the top of the first folio of the manuscript (after a contents list added at a late, but apparently not the final, stage of compilation) the notation, "Verses of Master H." But the complexity of the manuscript's many-staged compilation begs the question of how early in that process, and how exclusively, its contents were selected on a strict criterion of Henry's authorship, as the present editor has extensively argued elsewhere.[15] In brief, the codex as it stands was assembled from five smaller units, two of which were in turn assembled from originally separate materials, over an indeterminate period. Matthew was clearly the compiler of the manuscript as we have it, but from booklets of disparate origin. The assembly of medieval poetic anthologies very rarely took authorship as a prime category of selection, and it is entirely plausible to conclude from the evidence of an "archaeology" of the manuscript that Matthew came to think of the codex as a collection of Henry's verse only well into the ongoing process of assembly, on the basis of a strong representation of Henry's work, without at any point taking authorship as a principle excluding work by others.

As a consequence of these circumstances of compilation, studies of Henry can on the one hand never afford to dismiss the central importance of A as the principal repository of what we have of Henry's work, and of Matthew Paris as the principal agent of Henry's literary survival; but on the other hand, the evidence for authorship of every text in A needs to be assessed on its own merits, not taken for granted by virtue of the work's simple presence in A.

The order in which this edition presents the texts reflects descending certainty of attribution to Henry. It thus begins with the *Life of Francis*. The *Life of Oswald* and the *Life of Birinus* carry no explicit attribution, in either A or B, their other surviving exemplar, but each of these texts shares verbatim an extended passage also found in Henry's poem on the relics of the Crucifixion, which does carry an explicit attribution in A. The first volume of this edition includes these three texts.

The second volume comprises the four of our texts found only in A, where they carry no explicit contemporary attribution to Henry. But we have independent evidence, as noted above, that Henry composed a verse *Life of Guthlac* for the dedicatee of our text, and numerous stylistic affinities with the more certainly attributable *vitae* of the first volume confirm that attribution is altogether plausible. We have neither external confirmation nor manuscript attribution to confirm Henry's authorship of the *Life of Fremund* and the *Life of Edmund* and must rely on stylistic affinities alone to corroborate the simple fact of their presence in A. Such affinities are nonetheless strong.

The attribution of the *Life of Thomas,* however, is set against glaring stylistic inconsistency with the rest of these texts. As observed above, the characteristic topoi, rhetorical techniques, and close verbal reminiscences that variously knit the rest of the corpus are notably absent here. It is virtually only the text's position at the opening of Matthew's collection that supports the attribution. While Matthew Paris placed his notation, "Verses of Master H." on the opening leaf of the text (and of the manuscript), the *Life of Thomas* stands in such marked contrast to the style and structure of Henry's other hagiographic works as begs the question of shared authorship.

A also includes an account of visions after the death of Becket and a much shorter account of his life, as well as a version of the martyrdom of Saints Crispin and Crispinian, all written, like the *Life of Edmund* (but unlike the dactylic hexameter of the other six texts here edited), in elegiac couplets. While none of these shorter poems carries a contemporary attribution, the latter shows stylistic affinities with Henry's *vitae,* and aspects of its thought and vocabulary are reminiscent in particular of the *Life of Birinus.* An eighth surviving full-length verse *vita* of Hugh of Lincoln is very plausibly attributable to Henry; it survives in two manuscripts, London, British Library MS Royal 13 A IV and Oxford, Bodleian Library MS Laud 515.

Henry's Literary Biography: A Conservative Reconstruction

We come relatively late in this introduction to a brief and cautious sketch of Henry's career precisely because the textual evidence for attribution on which more elaborate deductions have depended remains equivocal. The shift from the awkward and abstruse composition of the *Life of Thomas* to the consolidated style of most of the hagiographical works might suggest (if that work is indeed by Henry) that Henry came to a literary maturity in the mid-1220s that allowed him to enjoy the patronage of a number of highly placed English churchmen before departing for the Continent. In the early 1230s his masterwork garnered the attention of Pope Gregory IX. A papal bull of 1234 mentions one Henry, canon of Avranches, presumably our poet. In 1241 or 1242, he wrote *On the Crown of Thorns* under the patronage of King Louis IX of France. By 1243 he had joined the court of King Henry III of England and received stipends under the express designation of "versificator" for some twenty years, as witnessed in the Court Rolls. He thus joined Henry

III's court as a poet of established international reputation, and the size of the payments at the outset of his tenure suggests high stature indeed: an entry dated March 30, 1244 orders a payment of six pounds for expenses from October 20, 1243 to April 5, 1244, and stipulates his receipt of twenty shillings per month "for as long as he remains in our service by our command." One entry in the Rolls, dated March 7, 1245, records payment for the lives of Saints Edward and George, which do not survive. Further payments are recorded for the summers of 1251 to 1253. A far more modest allowance granted in February 1255 "for as long as he shall live" suggests that he had by then reached pensionable age. His disappearance from those records suggests that he died in 1262, three years after the death of his great admirer Matthew Paris in 1259.

The gaps in these records have afforded several generations of researchers easy scope for speculation about the place of a range of shorter poems, mostly recorded in A and in Vespasian D.v. Details of such poems place their author(s) variously in Germany, England, France, and Italy between 1227 and 1251. Some short poems added at the very end of A, arguably simply as "fillers" that are hardly likely to have been included with a rigorous concern for uniformity of authorship, were the basis on which Russell asserted an early German phase of Henry's career and first suggested his identification with a Master Henry of Cologne already in England as a representative of Otto IV in 1214.[16] Later researchers, notably Konrad Bund, have built on this identification; but it not only assumes the prior demonstration of authorship but presupposes that Henry had already begun a significant diplomatic career well before writing an early and stylistically immature work starkly out of character with his later hagiography as well as with the poems at issue themselves. Bund further suggests that Henry was once again in Germany in the early to mid-1220s, which requires us to posit a return from England between the likely dates of the *Life of Thomas* and of the *Life of Birinus* and the *Life of Oswald* written later in the decade; whereas Russell attributes to Henry a cluster of short poems addressed to a range of English patrons from late in the second decade of the thirteenth century to early in the third. A period around 1238, as dean of Maastricht has also been posited.[17]

HENRY'S HAGIOGRAPHICAL CRAFT

As a versifier of earlier prose saints' lives, Henry participated in a tradition that reached back as far as Paulinus of Périgueux in the late fifth century and Venantius Fortunatus in the sixth, whose verse retellings of the life of Martin of Tours presuppose the authoritative prose *vita* by Sulpicius Severus. Such versifications necessarily engage (sometimes explicitly, sometimes only by implication) a principal tension in the self-definition of hagiography as a genre. The saint's life presents a model of Christian heroism, in contrast to secular norms of behavior and endeavor; and it espouses a register of language and style that admits of ready comprehension by the simple among the faithful, in keeping with Saint Augustine's prescription of *sermo humilis* as a quintessentially Christian rhetorical choice aimed at charitable attention to the needs of all for edification. The medieval composition of Latin narrative verse, for its part, rarely escaped the long shadow of the classical epics that remained nearly universally known and read as a staple of standard literary education. The contrast between the epics' celebration (or at least ostensible celebration) of individualistic martial heroism and their ornate rhetorical apparatus, on the one hand, and of the values, aims, and characteristic style of hagiography, on the other hand, demanded some response—more or less self-conscious, more or less explicit—on the part of verse hagiographers.

Henry's answer to this dynamic tension in his mature works was suave, playful, and self-assured. Several of his prologues share a characteristic topos by which he compares the spiritual exploits of his heroes to those of Hercules, Julius Caesar, and Alexander—and finds the latter heroes wanting by comparison. A less obvious implication of such openings is that, despite his protestations of humility, he is claiming his place as a rival to the poets who celebrated those secular heroes—including, most recently and most pointedly, Walter of Châtillon, whose *Alexandreis* had assumed a secure place in the literary canon to rival that of the classical epics in the fifty years since its appearance. Henry not only makes close reference to Walter's prologue in the *Life of Guthlac* but goes on to echo substantial episodes of that text, thus positioning his poem in sustained emulation. He begins the *Life of Oswald* with a close adaptation of the opening line of Ovid's *Metamorphoses* and goes on throughout the work to emphasize the transformations and continuities thematic to the miracles he narrates. The opening lines of the *Life of Birinus* incorporate both a citation from Ovid's *Tristia* and Horace's encapsulation of the *Iliad* in *Ars poetica* 137. The *Life of Hugh of Lincoln* (not edited here) begins by baldly appropriating the opening phrase of the

Aeneid. Henry's freely invented additions to his source texts include a range of extended similes modeled on those of classical epic, even as his frequent devotional exclamations and lengthy doctrinal excursus align him with indubitably hagiographical conventions.

Henry clearly intends to entertain his readers by clever performance and by display of broad erudition at least as much as to edify. Features of his verse pursue such goals in ways that reflect neither the agenda of mainstream hagiography nor the aesthetic canons of classicizing epic. Passages expounding illnesses and miraculous cures serve principally to showcase Henry's command of contemporary medicine and Aristotelian philosophy. Descriptions of healings that allow the beneficiaries to witness one another's cure—wherein the deaf hear the mute speak, the blind see the lame run—are a signature narrative ornament of several of the *Lives,* but these seem aimed more at demonstrating a virtuosic mastery of conceit than at inspiring heightened devotion in the reader. Other distinguishing features of Henry's highly ornamented style can unfortunately be conveyed only intermittently by direct prose translation. His love of wordplay, alliteration, assonance, and intermittent rhyme depends on specifics of his Latin vocabulary that an English rendering can only occasionally convey.

My debts of gratitude in the preparation of these volumes are many and various: to the Syndics of the University Library, Cambridge, for permission to edit these texts; to A. G. Rigg for first introducing me to the works of Henry of

Avranches over thirty years ago, for guiding my early study of Henry's works, and for collaboration in close study of Cambridge, University Library MS Dd.xi.78, the manuscript from which this edition was prepared; to the staff of the University Library, Cambridge, for their kind and expert assistance; to Robert Babcock, Raquel Begleiter, Sasha Benov, Rebecca Frankel, Ruth Harvey, Andrew Hicks, Danuta Shanzer, Elliot Wilson, and Michael Winterbottom, for the generosity with which they shared some hundreds of suggestions for improvement; to Emily Blakelock, for her thorough and shrewd attention to the work in progress; to Jonathan Silin for practical and emotional support that exceeds the limitation of any brief acknowledgment; to Bracket for (mostly) remaining off my keyboard during working hours.

To George, in abiding gratitude

Notes

1 Townsend and Rigg, "Medieval Latin Poetic Anthologies (V)," 385–86.

2 Ibid., 385.

3 Townsend, *"Vita Sancti Oswaldi,"* 6.

4 Ibid., 25–26.

5 Townsend, *"Vita Sancti Birini,"* 312–13.

6 Townsend, "Eleventh-Century Life of Birinus of Wessex," 129–59. The text was subsequently reedited, with a translation, by Rosalind Love, *Three Eleventh-Century Anglo-Latin Saints' Lives: Vita S. Birini, Vita et miracula S. Kenelmi and Vita S. Rumwoldi* (Oxford, 1996).

7 David Knowles, C. N. L. Brooke, and Vera C. London, eds., *The Heads of Religious Houses: England and Wales, 940–1216* (Cambridge, 1972), 42.

8 Russell and Heironimus, *Shorter Latin Poems,* 6, 105–8.

9 Adkin, *"Vita Sancti Guthlaci,"* 349–55.

10 Horstmann, *Nova legenda Anglie,* 2:689–98.

11 Townsend, *"Vita Sancti Fredemundi,"* 4.

12 Townsend, *"Vita Sancti Edmundi,"* 98–99.

13 Townsend and Rigg, "Medieval Latin Poetic Anthologies (V)," 353–54.

14 Russell and Heironimus, *Shorter Latin Poems,* 11; Peter Binkley, "Medieval Latin Poetic Anthologies (VI): The Cotton Anthology of Henry of Avranches (B.L. Cotton Vespasion D.v, fols 151–184." *Mediaeval Studies* 52 (1990): 221–54.

15 Townsend and Rigg, "Medieval Latin Poetic Anthologies (V)," 354, 386–90.

16 Russell and Heironimus, *Shorter Latin Poems,* 26.

17 Ibid., 20.

LIFE OF FRANCIS

Gesta sacri cantabo ducis qui monstra domandi
primus adinuenit tribuitque Minoribus artem:
neue (quasi lucens aliis sibimetque lucerna
deficiens) proprio uibraret lumina dampno,
5 actus premittens monitis exemplaque uerbis
carnem preceptis anime frenauit, et hostem
nutibus internis pessumdedit, et pede nudo
mundum calcauit. Ueteres iam Fama triumphos
seuiciis partos et materialibus armis
10 parcius extollat—plus enituere moderni!
Nam quid respectu Francisci Iulius aut quid
gessit Alexander memorabile? Iulius hostem
vicit, Alexander mundum, Franciscus utrumque,
nec solum uicit mundum Franciscus et hostem,
15 set sese, bello uincens et uictus eodem.

Inuocat auctor Franciscum

O Christi miles, qui solus stigmata Vite
morte triumphantis uiuens in mente latenter,
et moriens in carne palam, Francisce, tulisti!
Vatis opus tueare tui, celseque canendis
20 milicie titulis humilem dignere Camenam.

I shall sing the deeds of the holy commander who first discovered the art of taming monsters and passed it on to the
Friars Minor: putting actions before admonitions and ex- 5
amples before words lest (like a lamp shining for others but
failing itself) he should cast light to his own loss, he reined in
the flesh with the precepts of the spirit, destroyed the foe
by inward will, and barefoot trod down the world. Let Fame
now extol more sparingly old triumphs achieved by savagery
and material arms—the moderns have outshone them! For 10
in comparison with Francis, what did Caesar or Alexander
do that was worthy of memory? Caesar conquered the foe
and Alexander the world, but Francis both. Nor did Francis
conquer only the world and the foe, but also himself, con- 15
queror and conquered in the selfsame battle.

The author invokes Francis

Christ's soldier, O Francis, you who alone while living bore
secretly in your mind the stigmata of that Life which triumphs through death, and then when dying bore them
openly in your flesh! Look upon the work of your poet, and 20
judge his humble Muse worthy to sing the achievements of
your lofty combat.

Inuocat Papam Gregorium

Et tu, sancte pater, bone pastor, None Gregori,
qui pro peccato gregis orans, qui gregis horis
inuigilans tanti mensuram nominis imples,
da michi te placidum, precor, oblatamque libenter
25 suscipe dignanter minimam rem, maxime rerum.

[Liber 1]

Primus Franciscum scribit terrena sequentem,
donec eum dignacio nunc diuina flagellans
febre graui, nunc alliciens radiantibus armis,
conuertit uerique Boni succendit amore.

INCIPIT LIBER PRIMUS.

Francisci natale solum perfunditur huius
luce quasi solis, tantique refloret alumpni
illustrata nouis fulgoribus urbs ueterana
Assisium, que ualle tenus protensa Spoleti
5 pendet oliuifere conuexa cacumine rupis,
tecta subalternans a summis usque deorsum.

Invocation to Pope Gregory

And you, holy father, good shepherd, Gregory the Ninth, you who fulfill the measure of your name by praying for the sin of your flock, by keeping watch over the borders around the flock, be well-disposed toward me, I pray, O greatest of personages, and take up courteously this least of trifles willingly offered. 25

[Book 1]

The first book describes Francis chasing after earthly things, until divine favor, now scourging him with a severe fever, now enticing him with glittering arms, converts him and enflames him with love of the true Good.

HERE BEGINS BOOK ONE.

Francis's native soil is bathed in this man's light as in that of the sun, and the ancient city of Assisi flourishes once more by illumination with the new splendors of such a foster son. Spread out down to the valley of Spoleto, the town hangs 5 sloping from the top of an olive-bearing crag, its roofs in zigzags from the heights all the way to the bottom.

De parentibus eius

Mater honesta fuit pueri, pater institor, illa
simplex et clemens, hic subdolus et uiolentus.
O nostri monstrum figmenti! Quam male constat
10 inconstans ex oppositis essencia rebus!
Non excusandus per yperbaton: omnia turbat,
omnia confundit nostri preposterus ordo.
Imperio pars digna subest, et digna subesse
imperat in nobis, et uincit lubrica fortem,
15 terrea celestem, corruptibilisque perhennem.
    Forcior est sensus ratione, uidensque parentum
oppositos mores puer inter utrumque statutus
subsequitur peioris iter, mauultque patrissans
ire sinistrorsum per praua, per auia, quam per
20 directas methodos, per plana diametra uite
dextrorsum sincera sequi uestigia matris.
Proni sunt sensus in deteriora: deorsum
tendimus ex facili; grauis est ascensus ad astra.
    Inde fit ut prauum longe conuersus in arcum
25 nil anime uiuens indulgeat, omnia carni,
nil intellectu consideret, omnia sensu;
nil studio uirtutis agat, nil lumine mentis
inspiciat, nil consilio rationis honestet;
apparensque bonum plus existente sequatur,
30 plus et amet uictum quam uitam, plus sua quam se;
immo nec uictum nec uitam, nec sua nec se.

Of his parents

The lad's mother was an honorable woman, his father a huckster; she simple and gentle, he deceitful and violent. O monstrosity of our formation! How ill-constituted out of opposite substances is our inconstant essence! Our last-things-first order can't be excused by hyperbaton: it jumbles and confounds everything. The part of us that deserves to reign is subordinate, the part that should be subordinate holds sway in us; the inconstant part conquers the strong, the earthly conquers the celestial, and the corruptible conquers the eternal.

The senses are stronger than reason, and the boy, positioned between his two parents and seeing their contrasting characters, followed in the track of the worse. Taking after his father, he preferred to tread the left-hand path, off the road through wickedness, rather than to follow his mother's sincere footsteps to the right by a direct procedure along life's straight diameter. The senses are prone toward the degenerate: we easily head downward; the ascent to the stars is difficult.

So it is that, veering far off into an arc of wickedness, he conceded nothing to his soul in the manner of his life, granted everything to the flesh, considered nothing according to intellect, but everything according to the senses, did nothing in the zeal of virtue, scrutinized nothing by the light of his mind, bestowed no honor by the counsel of reason; he pursued an apparent good more than one which truly existed. He loved livelihood more than life, his possessions more than himself; or rather loved neither his livelihood nor life, neither his possessions nor himself. For that

Debet enim uel amor erroneus ille uel error
simpliciter dici quo decipitur quis habere
intendens odio quod amat, uel amare quod odit.
35   Iam lucri momenta sequens, iam fallere doctus
iamque rudimento patris coruptus auari
merces multiplicat, multos circumuenit, alte
se gerit, illecebris intendit, tempora perdit.
Mens tamen eius erat bona naturaliter omni
40   inpermixta malo, set conuersacio mores
plus sibi praua bonos conformat quam bona prauos.
Mitis enim, largus, clemens, affabilis, inter
ipsos excursus uicii uestigia quedam
uirtutis retinet non peruenientis in actum.

Quod in fine respexerit eum Dominus

45   Quinque fere lustris sic exspaciante iuuenta,
cum sit flagicium res exigitiua flagelli,
cedit eum qui noluerat sibi cedere, frenat
effrenem, domat indomitum mutacio dextre
Excelsi, dignata malis imponere finem.
50   Sicut enim dragme post tempora longa reperte
quando superficiem sepelit rubigo, moneta
vix apparet ibi, quo ne reprobetur oportet
purgari uicium rubiginis igne fabrili;
sic animam iuuenis tanta caligine mersam
55   ut uix diuine uideatur ymaginis umbra
undique noxa premit, quo ne dampnetur oportet
purgari nubem caliginis igne febrili.
O clemens dulcedo Dei, clemencia dulcis!

love should be called erroneous, or just plain error, by which one is deceived who is intent upon holding in hatred that which he loves, or upon loving what he hates.

Now chasing the promptings of monetary gain, now be- 35 ing taught deceit, now corrupted by the instruction of his greedy father, he compounded his profit, wheedled his way around many, bore himself haughtily, was intent on trickery, and wasted his time. Yet his mind was naturally good, en- 40 tirely unmingled with evil, but his wicked way of life shaped his good character more than his good habits influenced the wicked. Mild, generous, gentle, affable, he retained even among the attacks of vice certain traces of a virtue that as yet did not issue into action.

That the Lord in the end looked upon him

Since crime demands punishment, when his youth had pro- 45 gressed thus for nearly twenty-five years, the Most High saw fit to set a limit on evil and turned his right hand: he struck the one who did not wish to yield, bridled the unbridled, and tamed the untamed. When tarnish obscures the sur- 50 face of a coin rediscovered after a long time, the mintage is there scarcely visible, wherefore (lest it be rejected) the flaw of that tarnish must be purged by the refiner's fire. Just so, punishment from every side oppressed the youth's soul, which was plunged in such darkness that it scarcely seemed 55 a shadow of the divine image, wherefore (lest it be damned) the cloud of that darkness had to be purged by the fire of fever. O gentle sweetness of God, and sweet gentleness!

Cuius ut indignum seruum dignacio seruet
60 implicitum uiciis, intentum luxibus, odit
et de iure ferit, terret, premit, agit; at ipsum
corripiens odit ut amet, ferit ut medeatur,
terret ut erudiat, premit ut leuet, agit ut ungat.
Igne remulceri solet ignis adustio, uulnus
65 uulnere curatur, dolor est medicina doloris.
    Sic anime morbum Medico curante superno
seruum blandiciis ingratum uerbera iuste
inmoderata premunt, naturalemque calorem
ipsius per menbra fugans extraneus ardor
70 in cordis regione furit, uenisque minutis
succendente chymos generatur caumate causon,
interiorque calor dum flegma liquefacit extra,
supra sensibiles neruos aspergitur ille
algor et horripilat caput inducitque tremorem
75 quo paciens feruendo tremit feruetque tremendo.
Frigora namque stupent nerui desueta ferentes,
at postquam longa stupor assuetudine cessat;
tunc nerui resident, tunc et tremor ille quiescit.
Set feruor persistit adhuc uehemencia cuius
80 circa principium properat disoluere plus quam
consumat, circa finem consumere plus quam
dissoluat; toto rarescit corpore sanguis;
spiritibus uix est in quo consistere possint.
    Francisco quem tanta premunt incomoda uite
85 presentis spes nulla datur, uix illa future,
cumque laboranti timor incuciatur uterque,

In order to save an unworthy slave caught up in his vices 60
and intent upon indulgence, God's pleasure showed hatred
and rightfully smote, terrified, oppressed, and harried him;
showed hatred in order through correction to show love,
smote in order to heal, terrified in order to instruct, oppressed in order to raise up, harried in order to anoint. The
burning of fire is as a rule alleviated by fire, a wound is cured 65
with a wound, and pain is the medicine for pain.

When the Physician on high thus cured the disease of his
soul, immoderate blows rightly fell upon the slave whom no
blandishments made grateful. Heat from without, driving
off natural warmth throughout his limbs, raged around his 70
heart; it generated a severe fever, whose heat burned up the
humors in the shrunken blood vessels, and while the interior warmth turned the phlegm to liquid outside the body, a
chill was spread over his sensory nerves, made the hair of his
head stand on end, and induced a shivering with which the 75
patient shivered as he burned and burned as he shivered.
The nerves were dumbstruck to endure such unaccustomed
cold, but by long acclimation the stupor subsided; then his
nerves settled, then too his shivering grew quiet. But the
heat still persisted, whose vehemence at the start hastened 80
to dissolve more than it consumed, but near the end to con-
sume more than it dissolved. His blood grew thin throughout his whole body; the spirits had scarcely anywhere to
abide.

As such impediments to life pressed upon him, no hope 85
of this present life, and precious little of the one to come,
was granted Francis. Struck amid his labor with the fear of

ignarum quid agat uite deformiter acte
penitet et lacrimas inter suspiria fundit.

Quomodo Dominus eum per febrem
compugerit et a febre curauerit

Respiciens cordis gemitum pietate paterna
90   qui cor contritum non despicit alleuat egrum,
erigit elisum consolaturque gementem:
ad nutum Domini cessant incomada serui.
Nulla uoluntati diuine causa risistit,
spiritibusque simul accitis omnibus ad cor,
95   prefixo natura die sinthomata morbi
occursu uehemente necat, proprioque calore
membra fouens pulsum regit urinamque colorat.
    Eger alacressit tantique pericula uisus
euasisse mali Medicum laudare supernum
100   gaudet et autorem uite Dominumque fatetur.
Inde die quodam patrios egressus in agros,
dum nitidos cernit fluuios, dum florida prata,
dum uirides siluas, dum celsa palatia, sensu
philosophante stupet cur oblectemur in istis,
105   cum neque sit mundus set celum patria mentis.
Hoc inconueniens, hoc arbitratur iniquum,
quod trahat humanas mundana creacio mentes;
ut quid enim fatui terrena requirimus ista?
Quorum si floret decor arridetque uoluptas
110   et saciat sensum bonitas et inebriat usus,

either of these outcomes, not knowing what to do, he repented the misshapen life he had lived and poured out his
tears amid his sighs.

How the Lord pierced him with
fever and cured him of fever

He who does not despise a contrite heart raised up the sick   90
man, looking with a father's mercy upon the moaning of his
heart; he lifted up the one who had been struck and con-
soled him amid his moans: by the Lord's assent the servant's
troubles ceased. No cause resists the divine will, and as the
spirits were all summoned to the heart, nature with vehe-   95
ment onslaught slew the symptoms of the disease on a pre-
determined day. Easing the limbs with its own warmth, it
regulated the pulse and gave color to the urine.

   The sick man grew glad when he appeared to have escaped the perils of such an illness, and he rejoiced to praise   100
the Physician on high, and confessed him as originator and
Lord of his life. Going out thence one day into his native
fields, while he beheld the glittering streams, the flowering
meadows, the green woods, the lofty palaces, Francis was
dumbstruck to philosophize through his senses why we   105
should be delighted in these things, since not the world but
heaven is the native country of the mind. He thought it un-
suitable and unjust that the worldly creation should entice
human minds. For why do we foolishly seek after these
earthly things? If their seemliness flourishes and pleasure
smiles upon us, if their goodness sates the senses and their   110

non tamen ipsorum ducenda cupidine mens est:
nam fallax in eis decor et penosa uoluptas,
et mala consistit bonitas et inutilis usus.
Prouenit inde labor, metus et dolor. Absque labore
115 quis tulit, absque metu quis possidet, absque dolore
illa quis amittet? Nullus quacumque cuculla
uirtutem profitens, nisi qui contempnere mundum
norit, et eternis totos infigere sensus.
     Hiis argumentis utcumque probantibus ima
120 imum sortiri precium, suprema supremum,
ille memor uirge Domini, quo iure nocentem
strauerit et quanta pietate leuauerit egrum,
mutandos animi mores carnemque domandam
ducit, et antiquos uouet expurgare reatus.
125   Set noua concipiens antiqua recurrere sentit,
et simplex anime uarios natura tumultus
intra se paciens secum quasi disputat utrum
existant pluris res quas intelligit, an quas
sentit, et aduersus apicem racionis iniquas
130 agreditur lites anime pars infima sensus.
Sensu quid fiat attenditur et racione
quid mox eueniat. Sensus non peruenit usque
ad rerum fines; racio res iudicat ante.
Pretendit sensus epulas, pretendit amoris
135 illecebras, pretendit opes, et culmen honorum
et laudes hominum, procedere nescius ultra.
Pretendit racio uitam sine fine, superne
urbis delicias, paradisi gaudia, cantus
indiffinibiles et inenarrabile lumen.

use intoxicates, yet the mind should not be led on by desire for them: the beauty in them is deceptive and their pleasure full of pain, their goodness turns out badly and their use is useless. Labor, fear, and grief come thence. Who has ob- 115 tained those things without labor, who possesses them without fear, who will lose them without grief? None who professes virtue, whatever cowl he wears, save the one who knows how to despise the world and to fix all his senses upon eternal things.

When these arguments proved in all manner of ways that the lowest things garner the lowest price, while the highest 120 things garner the highest, he remembered the Lord's rod, remembered how rightfully it had laid him low in his guilt, and with what mercy raised him from his sickness; he judged that he must change the habits of his mind and tame his flesh, and he vowed to expurgate his old crimes.

But even as he conceived new endeavors, he felt the old 125 ones creep back. The nature of his soul in its simplicity, suffering various tumults within itself, disputed as it were as to whether the intelligible was worth more than the sensible, and sensation, the soul's lowest part, initiated an unjust 130 suit against reason's heights. Sensation attends to what is happening, reason to what will soon occur. Sensation does not arrive at the end of things; reason judges things beforehand. Sensation offers its banquets, offers the enticements 135 of love, offers riches, the heights of honor and the praise of men, but it does not know how to progress further. Reason offers life without end, the delights of the city on high, the joys of paradise, endless song and ineffable light.

140 Esse supradictis cum nulla proporcio rebus
    inter se ualeat, quantus furor est animarum,
    ut dubie conferre uelint eterna caducis,
    celica terrenis inmensaque gaudia paruis?
    Ex per se notis fit demonstracio propter
145 mundi contemptum. Cuius cum propter amorem
    nil persuaderi queat absque sophismate, iudex
    inconsultus adhuc Franciscus, in auia pernix,
    non interloquitur pro recta parte secundum
    allegata, set ad partem declinat iniquam.
150 Non tamen inponi laus aut infamia primo
    debet ab euentu, donec sententia totum
    iudicis affectum diffinitiua reuelet.
    Mens ita nunc eadem sursum, nunc acta deorsum
    cum noua proponat, tamen ad consueta recurrit
155 unde nichil firmum proponit, set quasi nauis
    turbine diuerso nunc sensus, nunc racionis
    fertur in oppositas regiones, nunc Aquilone
    flante uoluptatum, nunc Austro flante salutis.
    In labes labi leuis est labor. Ast ubi longa
160 conualuere mora seu more, resurgere fortes
    uix etiam possunt—assueta relinquere durum est.

Quomodo per uisionem armorum conuerterit eum Dominus

    Interea ciuis tota ditissimus urbe
    merce replens bigas et plaustra iugalia uersus
    Appuliam procingit iter, nulloque reuerti
165 se putat euentu, quin plurima lucra reportet.

Since there can be no proportion between these aforesaid things, how great is the madness of souls that they should doubtfully wish to compare eternal things to those that perish, heavenly to earthly, or great joys to meager? From self-evident axioms, there proceeds a proof in regard to contempt for the world. Since nothing can be persuaded because of love for the world without sophistry, Francis, as yet an uninstructed judge and swift to veer off the path, did not speak for the right side according to the allegations, but sided with the unjust party. Yet praise or blame ought not to be assigned at the first outcome, until a final opinion reveals the full sentiment of the judge. His same mind, now thus driven upward, now downward, though it proposed new intentions, still returned to what was accustomed, so that it proposed nothing firm, but like a ship was borne now on the maelstrom of the senses, now of reason, and was carried to opposite regions, according as the north wind of pleasures or the south wind of salvation blew. Light is the labor of lapsing into ruin. But where strong men have grown strong by long delay or by habit, even they can scarcely arise: it is hard to abandon what is familiar.

How through a vision of arms the Lord converted him

Meanwhile, the wealthiest citizen of the entire town, loading pushcarts and four-wheeled wagons with merchandise, fitted out an expedition toward Apulia and thought he had no chance of returning without hauling back enormous

Audito Franciscus eum debere lucratum
ire, magis solito flagrante cupidinis igne,
uult comes esse uie propter consorcia lucri.
    Omnibus aptatis ad iter spectantibus instat
170 hora recedendi, ducuntque crepuscula noctem
cuius in aurora mens una duobus eundi
perstat in Appuliam; recubant lentoque sopore
artubus inmisso mentes sua fata tuentur.
Sed quicquid de ciue Deus prouiderit illo,
175 ipsius circa Franciscum gratia ceptum
prosequitur pietatis opus, dignata mederi
cordis duricie capitisque tumultibus, in quo
sponte reuiuiscunt abscise semina pestis
iamque cicatrices redeunt in uulnera. Set qui
180 uina preinfudit oleum super adicit, et quem
ui pretemptarat dulcedine temptat, ut ipsum
blandicie moneant quem non mouere flagella,
et qui restiterat compulsus obediat ultro.
    Sensibus oppressis sompno dum libera rerum
185 perspicit euentus pure speculacio mentis,
extra se rapitur Franciscus, eique uidetur
quod domus ipsius sit plena quibuslibet armis,
ut puta loricis aceris candentibus usu,
ensibus extersis, et acumen habentibus hastis,
190 gemmatis galeis, clipeisque nitentibus auro.
    Tot preciosa uidens delectatusque uidendo
gaudet et obstupefit, nec enim robusta solebat
arma uidere domi, set quos aut Flandria molles

lucre. When Francis heard that he was going in order to heap up wealth, the fire of his greed flared even more than usual, and he desired to be a partner on the journey for the sake of partnership in gain.

When everything was readied that pertained to the journey, the hour of departure drew near, and the twilight shadows ushered in the night at whose dawn the two shared one mind of going into Apulia. They lay down as a gentle sleep crept upon their limbs, and their minds regarded their prospects. But whatever God had foreseen for that townsman, his grace toward Francis pursued the work of mercy already begun: he saw fit to heal the hardness of his heart and the confusion of his head, since in him the seeds of the excised disease flourished freely once more, and its scars opened again as wounds. But he who first poured on wine now added oil, and assayed with sweetness the one whom he had previously tried through force, that enticements might sway one whom scourges had not moved, and that he who had resisted under compulsion might obey freely.

When his senses were suppressed in sleep and his mind's free speculation clearly beheld the outcome of things, Francis was taken out of himself, and it seemed to him that his whole house was filled with all sorts of arms: breastplates shining from their use by a fierce warrior, polished swords, sharp spears, gem-studded helmets, and shields gleaming with gold.

Seeing so many precious objects and delighted at the sight, he rejoiced and was stupefied, for he was unaccustomed to seeing powerful weapons in the house, but rather the soft productions sent by Flanders and yellow-haired

mittit et inbelles aut flaua Britannia cultus.
195 Dum tacito secum scrutatur pectore, quis sit
armorum dominus responsum celitus audit,
"Te sociosque tuos Deus hiis insigniet armis."
    Inde nimis gaudens expergefit, et sibi letum
coniecturat iter. Set quo subtilius intra
200 se studet, hoc munus minus ad mundana referri
pensat et ad ueros pocius spectare triumphos.
Hinc ad bella parans se spiritalia mutat
propositum, nec in Appuliam decernit eundum—
ut quid enim, si lucra decet contempnere, propter
205 lucra laboraret? Mutatus quod uehementer
appreciatus erat contempnit, quod studiose
quesierat refugit, quod semper amauerat odit,
uimque sibi faciens, pensans quia uim paciatur
regnum celorum, sibimet contrarius ire
210 sustinet et multo prescriptos tempore mores
exuit et solitas reputat quasi stercora merces.

Quomodo in cripta deserta iugiter orando profecit

Cripta uetus multis iam desolata diebus
(ut fit in Ytalia) modicum distabat ab urbe.
Secreto consuetus eam Franciscus adire
215 feruidius solito semel et prolixius orat,
ut Dominus conuertat eum mentemque supernis
herentem numquam sinat ad terrena relabi.
Cuius in excelsis admissa peticio dextre

Britain's unwarlike artifacts. When he considered within his silent breast who was the master of these arms, he heard an answer from heaven: "God will deck you and your companions with these arms." ₁₉₅

Greatly rejoicing, he thereupon awoke and supposed that for him the journey would be a happy one. But when he inquired with subtler zeal within himself, he considered that this gift referred less to worldly matters but rather pertained to real victories. Hence, preparing himself for spiritual battles, he changed his intention and decided that he should not proceed to Apulia. For why, if it was fitting to despise gain, was he laboring for the sake of gain? He was transformed; he despised what he had vehemently valued, fled what he had zealously sought, hated what he had always loved; and using force against himself, in consideration that the kingdom of heaven suffers force, he undertook to go against himself, shed habits determined over a long time, and esteemed his usual merchandise as dung.

How in a deserted crypt he progressed in continual prayer

An old crypt now abandoned for many a day (as happens in Italy) lay some little distance from the city. Francis, being accustomed to go there in secret, prayed once more fervently and longer than usual that the Lord should convert him and never allow his mind, now that it clung to things above, to slip back to earthly concerns. His petition—

scripta Dei digito bullata caractare sancte
220 uiuificeque crucis superare uiriliter hostem
optinet et rebus non plus inhiare caducis.

[Liber 2]

*Alter prosequitur quibus assistentibus, in quo
bello, quos hostes quibus ille subegerit armis,
qualiter abiiciens pro Christo quicquid habebit
non exspectato male sit tractatus ab hoste.*

Rore suo deuota sibi precordia Sanctus
Spiritus humectat, quorum compunctio, tanquam
scopa domum mundans, tanto facit hospite dignam.
Miratur que semper erat spelunca latronum
5   facta domus Domini, cuius clemencia seruum
aduentu dignata suo nichil intus haberi
permittit quod dedeceat, set cordis opacos
illustrat thalamos et haras transformat in aras.
     Nec tamen aufertur scrupulus quin lubrica carnis
10   uota reuertantur quasi titillancia mentem.
Neue reuertendo quicquid peruertere possint
spirituale, timor Domini, primaria uirtus,
consilio reddit fortem, pietate scientem
ac intellectu sapientem. Spiritus ergo

admitted to heaven, written with the finger of God's right
hand and sealed with the mark of the holy and life-giving   220
cross—obtained the manful conquest of his foe and ended
his sighing after perishable things.

[Book 2]

*The next book tracks what enemies he subdued: with whose assis-
tance; in what battle; with what arms; and how, casting away for
Christ's sake everything he will possess, he was ill-treated by an
unlooked-for foe.*

The Holy Spirit moistened with his dew the heart devoted
to him: its compunction, like a broom cleaning the house,
made it worthy of such a guest. Amazement overtook what
had always been a den of thieves, which now became a house   5
of the Lord, whose mercy, having made the servant worthy
of his arrival, permitted nothing unseemly to be contained
within, but illumined the dark chambers of the heart and
transformed pigsties into altars.

Yet no scruple is removed without the shifty desires of
the flesh returning to titillate the mind. Lest by their return   10
those desires might pervert anything spiritual, the fear of
the Lord, first among virtues, rendered him strong of counsel, knowing in his piety, and wise of intellect. The Spirit

15 armat eum clipeo septemplice, monstraque septem
  stant ex aduerso piceis stipata cateruis.

  Prosequitur auctor .vii. uicia, premittens de Superbia

  Ex quacumque tumens uirtute Superbia, nullum
  dignatura parem, donis ingrata supernis.
  Concomitantur ei Tumor, Indignacio, Fastus,
20 preponensque suas aliis Elacio dotes,
  et minuens augendo suam Iactancia famam,
  et celeste nichil contemplans Gloria Mundi,
  laudis et humane uenatrix, florida mundo
  Ypocrisis fetensque Deo, ieiunia cuius
25 ficta papant lardum uirtusque sophistica sordet.
    Huius ubi regnum premit excellencia maior,
  succedit mentem succedens igne maligno
  spiritus Inuidie, que nulli parcat amico,
  affines gaudere dolens gaudensque dolore.
30 Nec desunt illi comites: Detraccio mordax,
  Arbitrium Mendax, Infamia ficta, Cachinnus
  nares corrugans, Liuorque ualencia carpens
  et reprobans laudanda, nephas reprobandaque laudans.
    Si minus Inuidie succedant prospera, surgit
35 Ira nichil moderans et inexorabile monstrum
  uix sibimet parcens. Cuius uexilla secuntur
  Impetus et Feritas desiderioque nocendi
  inuigilans Odium, scelerisque puerpera diri
  Pernicies nullas exauditura querelas,

therefore armed him with a seven-layered shield, while on   15
the other side stood seven monsters flanked by their pitch-
black cohorts.

The author treats the seven vices, beginning with Pride

Pride can swell forth from any virtue: it recognizes no equal
and is ungrateful toward all gifts from on high. Accompanying her are Conceit, Disdain, Arrogance, and Snobbery, who   20
places her own gifts before all others; Boastfulness who di-
minishes her own reputation by promoting it; Vainglory
who considers nothing of heaven; and that lavish huntress
of human praise, Hypocrisy, decked with flowers before the
world but stinking before God, whose pretended fasts are   25
fed on lard and whose sophistical virtue is tawdry.

When the royal rule of this vice is suppressed by something superior, the spirit of Envy succeeds her, enflaming
the mind with malignant fire. She spares no friend, grieving
when those near her rejoice and rejoicing when they grieve.
Nor does she lack companions: biting Detraction, Menda-   30
cious Judgment, counterfeit Infamy, Derision who wrinkles
up her nose, and Spite that pecks at everything of value,
reproaching what is praiseworthy, praising sin and what is
worthy of reproach.

If Envy's efforts succeed less prosperously, Wrath rises   35
up, an unopposable monster moderate in nothing, and
barely sparing even herself. Her banners are followed by
Attack, Ferocity, and Hatred, watchful in the desire to do
harm; Calamity, the mother of dire crime, deaf to all pleas;

40 et Furor incendens iram, Rabiesque furorem,
     et qui crudeles temerarius incitet Ausus
     insidias, armans aut in discrimina mentes
     aut in bella manus aut in conuicia linguas.
       Cumque sit Ira malum cuius nos penitet omnes,
45 quoquo prorumpant Ire primordia, finis
     vergit in Accidie uicium, que tedia rerum
     sentit et in nullo uirtutis peruiat actu.
     Accidie comites sunt postpositiua pudoris
     Garrulitas, et Torpor iners, et Sermo Sinister,
50 nocturnansque diem Sopor, et Lasciuia dampno
     temporis arridens, et presentiua futuri
     Sompnia iudicii uerosque probancia mortis
     argumenta metus, et Desperacio tristis
     haut metuens mortem sibimet concire cruentam.
55   Hic dolor Accidie solacia prima sororis
     querit Auaricie, que blandimenta dolenti
     noxia pretendens quod deficit ad racionem
     suppleat ad sensum, lucris eterna caducis
     dampna recompensans desperantemque superna
60 terrenis inhiare iubens animamque creatis
     oblectare bonis cui se negat ipse Creator.
      Sunt et Auaricie qui perfida castra sequantur
     Fraus, Dolus, Impietas, Homicidia, Furta, Rapine,
     Lucrandi sceleratus Amor, Mercacio Dispar,
65 Ambicioque tenax, Usuraque tempora uendens,
     et res celestes mercans Symonia scelestis.
      Accidie sic tristiciam compescere temptat
     questus Auaricie per delectancia uisum.

Fury that kindles wrath, and Madness that kindles fury, and   40
Recklessness who incites cruel plots, arming minds for
times of crisis, hands for war, and tongues for contention.

And since Wrath is an evil which we all regret, wherever   45
Wrath's beginnings burst forth, her end tips over into the
vice of Melancholy, which feels loathing for everything and
follows through with no virtuous act. Melancholy's companions are Garrulity that sets shame aside, sluggish Torpor,
Sinister Speech, and Slumber that turns day into night;   50
Wantonness that smiles at loss of time, Dreams that fore-
see future judgment—arguments confirming the true fear
of death—and sad Despair that fears not to bring a bloody
death upon itself.

Melancholy in her grief seeks first the solace of her sister   55
Avarice, who supplies to the senses what is lacking to reason, offering noxious blandishments to the one who grieves,
making recompense for eternal loss with perishable wealth,
bidding one who despairs of things above to pant after   60
worldly things and to beguile with created goods the soul to
which the Creator denies himself.

Those who also follow the treacherous encampment of
Avarice are Fraud, Deceit, Impiety, Homicide, Theft, Pil-
lage, wicked Love of Gain, Unfair Commerce, grasping Am-   65
bition, Usury that puts time up for sale, and Simony that
trades wicked things for heavenly.

Thus the profit of Avarice attempts to restrain Melancholy's sadness through things pleasing to the sight. But

Set quid agunt emplastra foris, cum seuiat intus
70 causa latens? Ideo Gula delectancia gustum
attrahit interius, nullo contenta paratu.
    Assistuntque Gule Modus Inmoderatus Edendi
Osque Molendinum, Dentes Mola, Venter Abissus,
cui quasi pertuso comittimus omnia sacco,
75 Cena Frequens, Facies Grauis, Eructacio cruda,
et cum pene crepat ad plura cibaria semper
Ingluuies inhyans, alienatiuaque mentis
Ebrietas siciendo bibens siciensque bibendo
et calices replens uacuos uacuansque repletos.
80 Cuius ut ad finem balbutit lingua, uacillat
gressus, hebet sensus, turgent precordia, languet
cor, marcet uultus: tunc primum meta bibendi
nausea letargum membris inducit onustis.
    Tot bona dilapidans Gula, cum non influat usque
85 ad proprios anime secessus, quomodo fiet
mentis et interni consolatiua doloris?
Prosilit ergo soror coniuncta propinquius et que
non homines extra faciat peccare set in se,
humani sensus inmutatiua Libido.
90 Cuius enim mox peniteat flagrat anxia uoto:
dum seruire parat, seuit; dum ludere, ledit;
si quem uult lenire, linit; si quem saciare,
sauciat: in primis Venus est, in fine uenenum.
    Plurima turba ruit post castra Libidinis: egros
95 millesies animos fastiditura Voluptas
et totidem placitura modis; Suspiria tractu
intercisa graui, Mendicantesque Fauorem,
Sermo Procax, Nutusque leues humilesque Susurri,
Ira superueniens Leuis ut grauiora reformet

what do these poultices accomplish externally, when a hid- 70
den cause rages within? And so Gluttony takes inside things
that delight the taste and is content with nothing spread before it.

Flanking Gluttony are Immoderate Eating, Mill-Mouth,
Grind-Tooth, Gape-Gut to whom we give everything as if
to a sack with a hole in it; Frequent-Food, Long-Face, crude 75
Belch, and ever-yawning Maw that fairly rattles over the
many dishes, and Drunkenness that alienates the mind from
itself, drinking amid thirst but still thirsting in drink, refill-
ing the empty cups and emptying them when refilled. At the 80
end of Drunkenness the tongue stammers, the gait grows
erratic and the senses dull, the diaphragm swells, the heart
languishes, the face droops. Then for the first time nausea
(drink's final destination) spreads lethargy over burdened
limbs.

Since Gluttony does not flow all the way to the soul's very 85
recesses as it demolishes so many good things, how will it
become a consolation for the mind's internal grief? Therefore Lust leaps forth, her more nearly joined sister, who
transforms men's senses and makes them sin not outside but
within themselves. She blazes forth, anxious because of a 90
vow that she soon repents: intending to serve, she rages, intending to play, she injures; if she wants to mollify anyone,
she smears him; wishing to satisfy, she wounds. At first she's
Venus, in the end she's venom.

A vast rout tumbles after Lust's encampment: Pleasure 95
that will shun ailing spirits a thousand times, and just as often will aim to please them; Sighs cut short with a heavy in-
take of breath, Beggars of Favor, Wanton Speech, frivolous
Nods and meek Whispers, Ready Anger that's swift to revise

100 federa, diuerso pellens fastidia uultu
    et rudibus lacrimis, uel Simplicitatis ymago
    uera uel apparens, pietatis uiscera pulsans,
    et Fantasma frequens, Desideriumque Placendi
    quas homini natura negat confingere dotes
105 sollicita sibi mente studens. Ex omnibus istis
    principium causamque trahens Amor Anxius amens
    prosilit, Anxietas, Amplexus et Oscula, molles
    Illecebre, Stimuli; fornax in fornice, fornix
    in fornace furens coniugalisque ruina
110 legis, Adulterium; naturalisque solutor
    federis Incestus, et Abusio turpior istis.

Quod tres Gracie tribus Furiis restiterint

    Contra Franciscum bellandi uota gerentem
    has introducunt pestes, Allecto, Megera,
    Tesiphone, quibus Eugiale, Phasitea, Prosigne
115 pro defensanda Francisci parte sorores
    opponunt totidem, meliori stirpe creatas.

Quomodo vii uirtutes de vii uiciis triumpharint

    Hec ad eum ueniens humilem facit, illa benignum:
    inde fit aduersi paciens cuiuslibet, inde
    feruens; hinc largus, hinc sobrius, inde pudicus.
120 Virtutes igitur uiciis dominantur in ipso
    et Carites Furiis, humilique Superbia cedit.
    Clemens Inuidiam, paciens eliminat Iram,
    feruens Accidie pedibus contagia calcat,

solemn compacts, and drives off aversion with varied ex- 100
pression and coarse tears; the real or seeming image of Simplicity, that knocks for access to pity's inward parts, frequent Fantasy, and Desire to Please, that with zealous mind 105
is eager to confect the endowments that nature has denied
a man. Drawing its origin and cause from all of these, Anxious Love springs forth in madness, along with Anxiety, Em-
braces and Kisses, soft Enticements, Incitements; Adultery,
that furnace raging in the brothel and brothel within the
furnace, the ruin of conjugal law; Incest, which dissolves the 110
bonds of nature, and Abuse that is even more shameful than
these.

That three Graces resisted the three Furies

Alecto, Megaera, and Tisiphone introduced these scourges
against Francis in his desire to wage war. Against them the
sisters Aglaia, Pasithea, and Euphrosyne set just as many,
created from a better stock, in order to defend Francis's 115
side.

How the seven virtues triumphed over the seven vices

One in coming to him made him humble, another made him
benevolent: through one he became patient in every adversity, through one fervent; through another generous, through
another sober, through another chaste. In him, therefore, 120
the virtues prevailed over the vices, the Graces over the Furies, and Pride yielded to the humble. Placid, he drove out
envy; patient, drove out Anger; fervent and generous, trampled the contagion of Melancholy and Avarice underfoot.

largus Auaricie. Gula sobrietate, Libido
125 uicta Pudore iacet, diuinarumque sororum
sacra supradictas debellant agmina pompas.

Quomodo spiritaliter fuerit armatus

Uirtutum princeps Caritas celestia tendit
arma uiro. Nequiens errare Modestia frenum
carnis equo firmat, duo cui calcaria totas
130 impingunt acies, Amor et Timor. Ocrea duplex
crura tuetur Opus et Contemplacio, pectus
Iusticie lorica tegit, laterique sinistro
appendet scutum Fidei. Paciencia curat
ceruici galeam uinclis annectere firmis.
135 Conus ibi Spes est crebroque refulgurat astro.
Hasta mouet belli primordia: fraxinus haste
Iudicium Rectum, cuspis Deuocio Feruens;
postquam fracta iacet propriis inpulsibus hasta,
acrius accenso belli discrimine dextra
140 fulminat ense Crucis seuas mutilante cateruas.
Taliter armatus nil tempore gessit ab illo
quod non milicie titulum pretendere certum
posset, et ex omni stetit acrior obice uirtus.

Quomodo uendens omnia que habuit
dederit propter Deum

Sic ubi sacra sacrum dedit inspiracio munus
145 spiritualis eques, ne forte superbia propter
uirtutes extollat eum, uel quisque latentum

Gluttony lay conquered by sobriety, Lust by Chastity, and   125
the holy ranks of those heavenly sisters warred down the
aforesaid retinues.

How he was armed in spirit

Charity, chief among virtues, dispatched celestial arms to
the man. Modesty, incapable of error, made fast its reins
on the horse of the flesh, whose two spurs, Love and Fear,   130
goaded with all their sharpness. The two greaves of Work
and Contemplation protected his thighs, the breastplate of
Justice covered his chest, the shield of Faith hung at his left
side. Patience took pains to fasten a helmet upon his neck
with firm bonds. Hope was the apex there, and shone with   135
many a star. A spear initiated the war: Right Judgment was
the spear's shaft, its point Fervent Devotion; once the war's
contest had been more fiercely kindled, after the spear lay
broken by its own force, his right hand flashed with the   140
sword of the Cross, which maimed those savage troops. So
armed, from that time hence he did nothing that could not
proffer the clear name of combat, and his virtue stood forth
the more keenly for every obstacle.

How, selling everything that he had,
he gave it away for God's sake

Thus, when sacred inspiration bestowed its sacred gift, this   145
spiritual knight concealed his intention, wishing to be a
hypocrite according to antiphrasis, lest pride should perhaps raise him up on account of his virtues, or lest anyone

conscius infusum premat extollendo uigorem,
esse per antifrasim cupiens ypocrita mentem
palliat: optat enim bonus esse timetque uideri.

150   Neu sua uota suis perpensa parentibus ipsos
commoueant aduersus eum, procingitur ac si
lucratiua uelit tractare negocia. Merces
colligit in summam, Fuligeneumque profectus
non solum quecumque tulit uenalia uendit,

155 set currus et equos; uix tot pedes era reportat.

Quomodo ad fabricam eccelsie Sancti
Damiani totam pecuniam dederit

Sic mercatoris curas exutus inanes,
cogitat in reditu quem tanta numismatis usum
massa sibi conferre queat, Christique figure
complantandus ubi deponat inutile pondus.

160 Hiis animum curis inuoluit, et ecce: reperta
Ecclesia Sancti Damiani uix pereuntem
conseruante statum subitamque minante ruinam
accedit ueteremque larem nouus introit hospes,
seque sacerdotis pedibus prouoluit, et offert

165 unde reedificat cellam iam pene ruentem.
   Illudi putat ille sibi quia uiderat illum
mercibus intentum desiderioque flagrantem
lucra reportandi, nec enim donanda uidentur
affectu subito tot parta laboribus era.

170 Nolens Franciscus reuocare quod obtulit instat

34

aware of them though they lay hidden should by praising him suppress the vigor instilled in him: for he desired to be good and feared to appear so.

And lest his desires, being known to his parents, should 150 move them against him, he vested himself as though he wanted to pursue some profitable business. He gathered merchandise into a heap, and having set forth toward Foligno he sold not only all his salable goods, but his wagons and 155 horses; on foot he could scarce cart back so much cash.

How he gave all the money for the fabric of Saint Damian's Church

Having thus shed a merchant's vain anxieties, he considered upon his return what use such a mass of coin might confer upon him, and where he might lay down that useless burden in order to be planted together in the image of Christ. He 160 immersed his spirit in these cares, and lo: having found the Church of Saint Damian barely clinging to its perishing state and threatening imminent ruin, he approached and entered that ancient precinct as its new guest, cast himself before the feet of the priest, and offered means by which he 165 might rebuild the now nearly collapsing chapel.

The priest thought he was being mocked, because he had seen him intent upon commerce and burning with the desire to bring home a profit, nor did it seem likely that cash gained by so many labors would be donated because of a sudden impulse. Francis insisted, not wishing to revoke 170

seque moraturum promittit honusque fenestre
inicit, et saxis allisa pecunia tinnit.
    Abiectis ita diuiciis sub paupere tecto,
haud aliter residet quam si nutritus ibidem
175 esset, et exiguo gaudet producere uitam.

Quomodo pater eius hoc audiens ad locum cucurrerit

Rumor adhuc dubius iam se diffundit in omnes
Assisii uicos. Veri tristantur amici,
ficti subrident. Audit pater ipse susurros,
istud opinari uix ulla uoce coactus
180 quod de Francisco perhibet derisio uulgi.
O linguas hominum, quas in conuicia pronas
aut furor aut liuor acuit! Franciscus honorem
et famam meruit uirtute, pudorque subire
audet honoris onus, partes infamia fame
185 uirtutisque uices uicium, nec dicitur error
esse quod aggreditur, immo demencia. Nullus
parcit amicorum quin illi detrahat: omnes
insanire ferunt, et fingit opinio causas.
    Sunt qui Lethei sumpsisse papaueris haustum
190 aut cerebrum gustasse cati succumue cicute
arbitrentur eum; nec enim contingere credunt
absque ueneficiis, ut quem sic gloria mundi
irretire solet sit nunc inglorius ultro.
    Sunt quibus apparet quod nunquam sic preciosis
195 uilia preferret, iocundis tristia, lucris
detrimenta, nisi Furiis agitatus Auernis
esset et arbitrio proprie racionis egeret.

36

what he had offered, promised to remain, and tossed his burden through the window; the money clattered when it struck the stones.

His wealth thus cast away beneath a poor roof, he resided no otherwise than if he had been reared there, and rejoiced to continue his life in poverty. 175

How his father, hearing of this, ran to the place

The still-dubious rumor spread through all the neighbor-hoods of Assisi. His true friends grew sad, the feigned ones smirked. His father himself heard the whispers, though 180 scarcely compelled by anyone's voice to believe of Francis what popular derision declared. O tongues of men, which either rage or envy sharpens in their readiness for insult! Francis merited honor and fame for his virtue, and shame presumed to take up the burden of honor, infamy the role of fame, and vice the turn of virtue, nor was what he had 185 undertaken called error, but rather madness. None of his friends refrained from disparaging him: they all reported that he raved, and opinion made up its own explanations.

There were those who supposed he'd drunk a draft of Le-the's poppy, or tasted cat's brain, or the juice of hemlock; for 190 they did not believe that this had happened without witch-craft, that one whom worldly glory usually ensnared should voluntarily reject glory.

There were those to whom it appeared that he would never thus prefer vile things to precious, sad to delightful, 195 loss to gain, were he not shaken by Hell's Furies and did he not lack the judgment of his own reason.

Sunt et qui dicant non sicut oportuit ipsum
a febre curatum, set posteriore frenesim
200 in cella genitam raptis humoribus usque
ad cerebrum quos reppulerat uehemencia cordis.
Hiis pater auditis quibus irridetur ubique
filius accense nullatenus imperat ire
quin roget affines consanguineosque furori
205 assentire suo, turbare ferociter audens
mansuetos homines habitatoresque quietis.
Nec minus incandet flagrante medullitus igne
quam uel Appollinea traiectus arundine Phiton,
uel sibi prelatam dedignans Pallas Aragnen.
210 Patris ut aduentum presentit filius, antri
ingreditur latebras quod ad hoc prouiderat; a quo
per mensem non egrediens consuetus ibidem
est orare libens et ieiunare coactus.
Deffertur quamcumque malo reuerencia patri,
215 non debet sapiens comittere se furioso.
At postquam collata sibi diuinitus esse
arma recordatus, se munera tanta timendo
demeruisse timet sparsasque recolligit iras.
Forcia gesturum tanto iam tempore tali
220 dilituisse specu pudet, humanumque timorem
excludit diuinus amor, quem pectore gestans
exilit in lucem seseque parentibus offert.
Affines ipsum consanguineique uidentes
mente grauem, uultu procliuum, fronte seuerum,
225 carne macrum, facie pallentem, crinibus hirtum,
uestibus abiectum, cernendo quod ipse sit alter,

There were those who said that he was not properly cured of his fever, but that an agitation was generated in the posterior chamber when the humors that the heart's force had repelled were carried all the way to his brain. 200

When his father heard the things for which his son was everywhere mocked, he checked his rage not at all, but bid his neighbors and kinsmen assent to his fury, fiercely daring to trouble mild men who dwelt in quiet. He blazed no less with fire flaming to his marrow than the Python pierced through with Apollo's dart, or Pallas outraged that Arachne should be preferred to her. 205

When the son anticipated his father's approach, he went into a hidden cave that he had prepared against this occurrence; not emerging from it for a month, he was wont willingly to pray there and under compulsion to fast. However reverence is paid to an evil father, a wise man ought not commit himself to one gripped by fury. But once Francis recalled the weapons that God had conferred upon him, he feared that by his fear he had lost the right to such gifts, and gathered again his righteous anger. 210 215

It shamed him that one who would undertake brave deeds had hidden for so long a time in such a cave, and divine love shut out human fear. Bearing that love in his heart, he came forth into the light and presented himself to his parents. 220

His neighbors and kin, seeing him grave of mind, downcast of eye, severe of countenance, thin of flesh, pale of face, unkempt of hair, abject of garb, perceiving that he was not 225

decernunt quod sit alius queruntque, "Quis hic est?"
uixque recognoscunt ueteris uestigia forme,
mirantesque quasi miserantes digna relatu
230 et maiora fide: Franciscum scilicet omnem
immutasse statum quo prefulgere solebat.
Ridiculi fatuique uirum sapienter agentem
irrident, fatuumque uocant, cenumque platee
mitibus inmites inmittere uultibus audent.

[Liber 3]

Tercius explanat que carcere uinctus ut amens
prebuerit uulgo spectacula, quomodo nullis
peruersus monitis exheredatus inique
sit patris arbitrio nudusque reliquerit urbem.

Exterus est ubi ciuis erat; uestigia cuius
nuper adorarunt caput eius nunc colaphizant
sutores et carnifices. Iniuria quem non
tanta molestaret, nullo causata reatu?
5 Set quicquid faciant, Franciscus ad omnia constans
perstat et equanimis quem nulla molestia, nullus
incuruare potest furor inferrique benigno
passio tanta nequit quin sit paciencia maior.
   Ipsemet accurrit pater obprobriisque flagella
10 addit eumque ligat quasi furem uel furiosum

himself, decided that he was someone else, and they asked, "Who is this?" They scarcely recognized the traces of his old appearance, marveling as though with pity over what is worthy to relate, and surpasses credence: namely, that Francis 230 had changed the entire state in which he had been accustomed to shine forth. Ridiculous and foolish men mocked a man who conducted himself wisely; they called him foolish and cruelly dared to cast upon his mild countenance the dirt of the street.

[Book 3]

The third book sets forth what a spectacle he presented to the populace when bound in prison as a madman; how, being corrupted by no entreaties, he was unfairly disinherited by his father's judgment and left the city naked.

He is a foreigner where he was a citizen; cobblers and butchers who recently worshipped the ground he walked on now cuff his head. Whom would such injury not trouble, which was occasioned by no offense? But whatever they do, Fran- 5 cis remains constant and calm in all things. Upon a man of goodwill whom no trouble, no rage can bend, such passion cannot be inflicted but that his patience is all the greater.

His father himself ran forward, added scourges to reproach, bound him like a thief or a madman, and shut him 10

recluditque domi, nec tractat amicius hoste.
Non tamen intendit penas inferre nociuas,
immo quibus castiget eum; set in istud agendo
errat et in foueam cecus iubet ire uidentem.
15 Vana relinquenti Francisco plurimus obstat
error amicorum, qui tanta pericula passo
precludunt aditum patrie portumque salutis.
    Pre cuntis pater eius eum sublime uolantem
ingressumque uias Domini quibus astra petuntur
20 et uerbis et uerberibus reuocare laborat,
uirtuti penas uicioque salaria spondens.
Franciscum nec uerba monent nec uerbera frangunt
propositumque patris tali sermone refellit.
    "Quid michi uis, decepte pater? Repetamne Carybdim
25 quam semel euasi? Vis ut qui uiuere possum
interitum subeam? Vis ut qui celibe possum
libertate frui Letheo carcere dampner?
Non decet ut generes inferno quem genuisti
mundo: constaret nimii generacio carnis
30 si generaretur per eam corupcio mentis.
Scis equidem quod in exilio consistimus omnes.
Inde uiam facimus patriamque requirimus, estque
exilium mundus, uia tempus, patria celum.
Ergo uide quantum delinquas, cuius ab usu
35 exilium patrie preponitur, et uia mete.
Cur thesaurizas ubi uix habitabis ad horam?
Ad quod opus tot queris opes? Vergente senecta,
expliciente uia, cumulare uiatica stultum est.

up in the house, treating him with no more friendship than he would a foe. Yet he intended not to inflict these penalties for harm's sake, nay rather, to chastise him. But in doing so he erred and, being blind himself, ordered a man who could see to proceed into the ditch. His friends' many errors opposed Francis as he abandoned vanity: to one who had endured such dangers, these men blocked access to his homeland and the port of his salvation.

Even as he soared on high and entered upon the Lord's paths that lead to the stars, his father labored above all to recall him by both words and blows, promising punishment for virtue and wages for vice. Words did not sway Francis, nor blows break him, and with such a speech he refuted his father's proposal:

"What, in your deception, do you want of me, father? Shall I seek again the Charybdis that I have once escaped? Do you want me to submit to death when I am able to live? When I am able to enjoy the liberty of the celibate, do you want me condemned to a hellish prison? It is unseemly that you should beget into hell the one whom you begat into the world. Birth in the flesh would come at too high a price, if through it were born the corruption of mind. You surely know that we are all in exile. We make a road thence and seek our fatherland; the world is exile, time is our path, heaven our fatherland. Therefore, see how great is your offense, since according to your practice exile is preferred to fatherland, and the path to the goal. Why do you store up treasure where you will scarcely dwell an hour? To what end do you seek such wealth? As old age draws near, as the road winds to its close, it is foolishness to pile up provisions.

Nam quod habere iuuat, habuisse pigebit: habere
40 est breuis utilitas; habuisse, perhennis egestas.
Ergo ne quid agas in detrimenta salutis,
parce magisteriis erroris et indue formam
discipuli. Fugienda prius sunt prospera mundi
quam fugiant. Dum tempus habes, mundoque Deoque
45 te recolas non posse frui, mundumque relinquens
supplantes illum, ne supplanteris ab illo.
Cum nichil inconstans fidei mereatur honorem
nullaque mundanis insit constancia rebus,
ex huiuscemodi tibi sit fiducia tanquam
50 nulla, set in Domino pocius confide: beatus
uir qui confidit in eo, quia non pacietur
defectum cuiusque boni uiuetque per euum.
Inde michi placuit mundana relinquere. Saltem
exemplo doceare mei. Si gloria mundi
55 sit tua, si totus soli tibi supplicet orbis,
ut facias silicesque loqui picasque silere,
hoc totum tibi non poterit prestare salutem.
Instat enim supprema dies que cunta repente
surripiat temetque tibi, nudusque redibis
60 inferiusque cades quo plus sublime uolasti.
Forte iugum Domini non lene putabis onusque
non leue, presertim quia deliciosus es. Absit!
Mundi delicias poteris desuescere Christi
assuescendo uias. Usus dediscitur usu."
65   Talia dicentem non inde remissius arctat
set magis astringit patris irrepressa seueri
asperitas monitusque sacros audire recusat.

What is pleasant to possess, you will regret having possessed: possession is a brief convenience; possession once over entails endless craving. So spare the instruction in error and put on the guise of a disciple, lest you work to the detriment of your salvation. The world's prosperity should be fled before it flees. While you have time, remember that you cannot enjoy both the world and God, and, forsaking the world, throw it down before it throws you down. Since the inconstant man in no way merits the honor of faith, and no constancy inheres in worldly things, let your trust in such be as nothing, but rather trust in the Lord: blessed is the man who trusts in him, since he will suffer no loss of any good and will live forever. And so it has pleased me to forsake earthly things. Be taught at least by my example. If the world's glory should be yours, if all the world should kneel down to you alone, so that you make stones speak and magpies remain silent, all this will not be able to offer you salvation. For the last day is at hand that will snatch away from you everything (even your very self!) in an instant, and naked you will return falling all the lower, the higher you soared. Perhaps you will not think the Lord's yoke easy and his burden light, especially because you are ensnared in pleasure. God forbid! You will be able to lay aside the custom of worldly pleasure by becoming accustomed to the ways of Christ. Habit is unlearned by habit."

His father's unbridled severity restrained him no more gently when he said such things, but rather bound him tighter; he refused to listen to these holy admonitions.

Pessimus errorum ruditas ignara doceri;
peruersam non ingreditur sapiencia mentem.
70 Sic proprios fines transcendit iniqua potestas
et non recta uolens uult cogere recta uolentem
esse sibi similem, set arene semina mandat.
Istud enim cauit nature cura benigne,
ne qua uoluntatem mutare coaccio posset.
75 Hoc in Francisco liquet exemplariter, in quem
omnia conspirant: patrie derisio, patris
ira, flagellorum districtio, carceris horror,
et matris lacrime. Per tanta resistitur uni
monstra uiro, quem ne uolet ad celestia liber
80 tot nituntur ad hec terrena reducere uinctum.
Set quadruplex uirtus conquadrans eius ad omnes
incursus animam nulla sinit arte moueri,
totque nichil faciunt secus aduersancia, quam si
formice totidem montem transferre pararent.
85 At quia temptari nemo permittitur ultra
posse, Dei nutu nati miserata labores
materna pietate parens absente marito
astrictum uinclis emancipat. Ille recedit,
non tamen ut profugus, nec enim procul aufugit, immo
90 ad cellam letus redit incolumisque propinquam,
unde uerecundum patris exturbauerat ira.
Percipiens pater in reditu quod soluerit uxor
uincula Francisci pietatem dampnat apertam
ut scelus occultum rixisque strepentibus auras
95 implet et uxorem blasphemat turpis honestam.

Ignorance that cannot be instructed is the worst of errors; wisdom does not penetrate a perverted mind.

So his unjust power exceeded its proper limits, and one who did not desire righteousness desired to force one who did so to be like him; but he was sowing seed in the sand. For the caution of a benevolent nature is wary of this: that any coercion should be able to change its will. An example of this is clearly evident in Francis, against whom all things conspired: his native land's derision, his father's wrath, the constraint of the lash, the horror of prison, and his mother's tears. Such great monsters threw up resistance against this one man; so many of them strove to lead him in chains back to these earthly things, lest he should fly away free to the things of heaven. But fourfold virtue, squaring off his soul against all incursions, allowed no stratagem to sway him, and so many adversities accomplished no more than if a like number of ants should attempt to move a mountain.

But because no one is allowed to be tempted beyond his capacity, his parent in maternal pity had mercy, according to God's will, on her son's troubles, and while her husband was away freed him from the fetters with which he was bound. He departed, but not like a fugitive, for he did not flee far, but rather returned joyful and unharmed to the nearby chapel whence his father's wrath had driven him in his diffidence.

His father, learning upon his return that his wife had loosed Francis's bonds, condemned her open piety as a clandestine offense, filled the air with raucous accusations, and shamefully cursed his upright wife.

Protinus arrepto repetens sacra limina cursu,
uincula Francisco parat et tormenta minatur.
Ille metu uacuus: "Pater, immo uitrice," dixit,
"ut quid uincla paras, tormenta minaris? Uterque
100 malleus incassum gelido dat uerbera ferro.
    "O furiis agitate senex, michi uera uidenti
certo, securo, quedam quasi nubila falsi
obiicis, erroris foueam mortisque timorem.
At mea non metuit tales constancia uentos.
105 Astat namque michi ueritas, uia uitaque Christus
a dextris ut non conturber, cuntaque falsa
hec ueritas, cuntos errores hec uia, cuntas
euacuat mortes hec uita. Quid ergo timerem?
Tu pocius timeas, cui preparat ulcio digna
110 supplicium, cuius aquilone cor (ut Pharahonis)
est induratum nulloque resoluitur austro,
qui tua non curas pensare nouissima, cuius
irretita suo precordia mundus amore
unguibus et rostro tenet eternumque tenebit.
115 Ergo, michi datus ad stimulum, plus, improbe, pugna,
plusque repugnabo; plus nitere plusque renitar,
maioremque dabit maior michi pugna coronam.
Nonne Deo plus quam tibi debeo? Vis ut omittam
propter te mandata Dei? Tu me genuisti;
120 ipse magis fecit quia uitam contulit: ipse
fecit nos, et non ipsi nos. Ipse redemit
in cruce suspensus, saluabit in ethere regnans
non omnes, set quos opus indicat esse fideles,
estque fides humana Deo res debita, cuius
125 omnes plasma sumus. Omnis qui credit in illum
non confundetur, set refert quomodo credat:

48

At once seeking again on headlong course that sacred threshold, he prepared shackles for Francis and threatened torments. But Francis, empty of all fear, replied, "Father—or rather stepfather—why prepare shackles and threaten torments? Either of these hammers strikes in vain upon cold iron. 100

"Old man, shaken as you are by fury, you cast falsehood's obfuscations in my way, the snare of error and the fear of death, but I see the truth in confidence. My constancy fears no such winds. Christ, the truth, the way, and the life indeed 105 stands at my right side, lest I be troubled: this truth cancels all falsehood, this way all errors, this life all deaths. What then should I fear? You, rather, should be afraid, for whom worthy vengeance prepares punishment, you whose heart is 110 hardened like Pharaoh's by the north wind, and is melted by no breeze from the south; you who are unconcerned to consider last things, and whose heart, ensnared by love of the world, the world holds and will eternally hold in its talons and beak. Therefore, you who are given to me as a goad, 115 fight on all the more, wicked one, and I shall resist all the more; strive further, and I shall strive further in response, for the greater combat will grant me a greater crown. Do I not owe more to God than to you? Do you want me to neglect God's commandments on your account? You begot me; he accomplished more, for he bestowed life upon me: 120 he made us, and not we ourselves. He redeemed us being hung upon the cross; reigning in heaven he will save not all, but those whom works show are faithful, and human faith is a thing due to God, whose creation we all are. Every one 125 who believes in him will not be confounded, but it matters

esse potest aliquis non mente set ore fidelis,
aut econuerso sit utroque, nec inde sequetur
quod sit uera fides in eis completa duobus.

130 Si quis enim recte uelit esse fidelis, oportet
ut ferat in manibus animam fideique probande
attestetur opus. Quid consulis ergo gerendum?
Per quod opus potero me demonstrare fidelem?
Insistamne foris circumueniamque fideles

135 ut soleo, nunc emptor opum nunc uenditor: emptor
omnia deprauans et uenditor omnia laudans?
Ars mercatorum dolus et fallacia. Dampno
alterius sibi lucra facit, uix parcit amico,
uix eciam fratri. Quem proximus ergo dolosum

140 sentit eumne Deo censebimus esse fidelem?
Absque fide nemo saluatur. Ut ergo sit in me
consummata fides et completiua salutis,
acquisita dolis possessio sit procul a me.
Perfecte fidei michi proueniente talento,

145 nil in quo delecter habet topazius, aurum,
argentumue. Super topazion et super aurum
et super argentum desidero tale talentum.
Tu si uis credas; si uis, incredulus esto.
Me qui gustaui diuine mel pietatis

150 a caritate Dei, cuius perfectio uera
in Christo Ihesu consistit, non homo siue
angelus auellet, non princeps siue potestas,
non spes siue metus, non celsum siue profundum,
non mors seu uita, non instans siue futurum."

155   Talia Franciscus rigido pronunciat ore.
Cuius ut omnino uidet irreuocabile uotum,
ad diuersa pater se transfert, et reuocare

how one believes: a man can be faithful of speech but not in mind; or contrariwise he may be faithful in both, yet it will not follow from this that true faith is accomplished in these two things. If anyone wishes to be properly faithful, 130 he must carry his soul in his hands, and his works must testify to the faith he must prove. What then do you advise me to do? Through what works shall I be able to show that I am faithful? Shall I stand outside and cheat honest men, as 135 I am accustomed, now a buyer of wealth and now a seller: a buyer denigrating everything, and a seller praising everything? The shrewdness of merchants is trickery and falsehood. It produces profit by another's loss, barely spares a friend, barely even a brother. Shall we suppose then that one 140 is faithful to God whom his neighbor experiences as a cheat? No one is saved apart from faith. So in order that faith may be perfected in me and may accomplish my salvation, may all possession gained by deceit be far from me. Since I have acquired the talent of perfect faith, topaz, gold, and silver hold nothing for me to delight in. I desire such a talent be- 145 yond topaz, beyond gold and silver. Believe or disbelieve it as you wish. I have tasted the honey of divine mercy: neither man nor angel, neither principality nor power, neither hope nor fear, neither heights nor depths, nor death nor life, nor present nor future, shall tear me away from the love of God, 150 the true perfection of which consists in Christ Jesus."

Francis declared such things with unwavering speech. 155 When his father saw that his resolve was entirely irrevocable, he took a different tack, and, being unable to recover

personam nequiens uult extorquere monetam.
Era fimo minus apprecians inmissa fenestre
160 tollit Franciscus patrique resignat auaro.
Nec desistit adhuc seuus pater; immo paterni
immemor affectus nato quia summa petenti
ima negat, patremque Deum cupientis habere
abnuit ulterius dici pater, et quia Christo
165 mente coherendo Christi studet esse coheres,
heredem non posse sibi succedere censet,
pontificique domum compellit adire repletam
ciuibus in quorum conspectu censibus, agris,
et patris laribus iurique renunciet omni.
170 Francisci uirtus patris indignata furori
non modo predictis omnino renunciat, immo
ex eius dono ne quid uideatur habere,
circa se palpat zonamque recingit, et omnes
exutus uestes eciam femoralia ponit.
175 Stat sine ueste palam nudoque simillimus Ade;
in causa tantum distat status huius et eius:
suffert iste libens quod sustulit ille coactus,
suffert hic propter meritum quod sustulit ille
propter delictum; tamen hic punitus ut ille,
180 set secus, eius enim patuere pudenda, set huius
nulla pudenda patent. Quid enim caro nuda pudendum
offerret cuius animam uestiuit honestas?

Francis's person, wanted still to extract his money. Prizing less than dung the cash that he had tossed in through the window, Francis took it up and surrendered it to his greedy sire. Nor did his savage father yet leave off; rather, forgetting paternal sentiment, he denied the lowest things to his son, because he sought the highest. He refused any longer to be called the father of one who wanted God as his father, and because, by cohering to Christ in his mind, Francis strove to be Christ's fellow heir, he decreed that Francis could not succeed him as heir. He prevailed upon the bishop to come to a house filled with the citizenry, so that in his sight Francis should renounce rents, fields, his father's home, and all his rights. Francis's virtue, indignant with his father's madness, not only entirely renounced these things, but even, lest he should seem to possess anything his father had given him, reached around himself and undid his belt. Having shed all his clothes, he laid aside even his undergarments.

In plain sight he stood without clothing, quite like Adam in his nakedness; only his state and Adam's were different in cause: the one willingly sustained what the other sustained under compulsion; he for merit's sake endured what the other endured because of sin. Yet Francis was punished like Adam, but differently, for Adam's shameful parts were exposed, but of this man no shameful parts were evident. For what could the naked flesh of one whose soul is clothed in honesty offer to view that would cause shame?

Que fuit hec uirtus? Mundum contempnere, mundo
reddere se contemptibilem, rerumque suarum
185   personeque sue nullis insistere curis,
irrisiua pati commenta, relinquere patrem
terrenum propter celestem. Tot facienti
ardua uirtuti nomen non sufficit unum.
Admirans tante uirtutis episcopus ausum
190   surgit et exutum blandis amplectitur ulnis
et circumponit clamidem uotisque fauorem
spondet et exequitur rebus promissa secundis.
   Sic Franciscus opes et uestimenta resignans
nilque tenere uolens per quod teneatur ab hoste,
195   iam nil in mundo preter celeste requirit,
et licet in terris existens ciuibus heret
ethereis plusquam terrestribus, ethereusque
in terris languet, terrestris in ethere uiuit,
mente colens celos pocius quam corpore terras.
200   Iamque Deum uidet in speculo facieque uideret
ad faciem, si grossicies intersita carnis
incluse sineret anime procedere uisum.
Nudus abit coram patre, coram presule, coram
omnibus Assisii conciuibus. At quia, cum sit
205   humidus in summo nullique resistat agenti,
cuntis mutatur contrarietatibus aer,
non est ambiguum quin corpora nuda secundum
formas immutet quibus inmutatur et ipse,
nostra nec assiduos patitur complexio motus.
210   Inde licet feruens considerat hanc racionem
seque sciens non posse diu subsistere nudum,
suscipit oblatas ueteres a paupere uestes.

What was this virtue? To despise the world, to render himself contemptible before the world, to dwell on no concern for his own possessions or person, to suffer mocking comments, to leave his earthly father for the sake of his heavenly father. A virtue that performs so many arduous tasks cannot be encompassed by a single designation. The bishop, admiring the daring of such virtue, rose and embraced the unclothed man with gentle arms, placed his cloak around him, promised to favor his vows, and followed up his promises with favoring actions.

Francis, thus renouncing wealth and clothing, and wanting to hold onto nothing by which the enemy might hold onto him, now required nothing in the world except what was heavenly; and though dwelling on earth, he clung more to the citizens of heaven than to those of earth. A man of heaven, he languished upon earth; a man of earth, he lived in heaven, inhabiting the heavens in his mind more than he did the earth in his body. And now he beheld God in a mirror—and would have seen him face to face, if the interposed grossness of the imprisoned flesh had permitted the soul's vision to advance. He went out naked before his father, before the bishop, before all his fellow citizens of Assisi. But because the air, since it is moist in the heights and resists no agent, is transformed by all contraries, there is no doubt that it transforms naked bodies according to the forms by which it is itself transformed, nor does our composite nature sustain continuous motions. And so he considered this argument despite his fervor, and knowing that he could not long survive naked, he accepted old clothes offered by a pauper.

Nil nisi semet habens abit, utque repatriet exul
exulat in patria, nullo cogente set ultro,
215 de felice miser factus, de diuite pauper,
immo de misero felix, de paupere diues.
Iamque fenestratos de sago gestat amictus
qui uestes gestare nouas de uellere molli
arte laboratas solet, et mutare secundum
220 tempora cindatis pennas cindataque pennis.

[Liber 4]

Insinuat quartus nunc furum nunc monachorum
quomodo seuiciam tulerit quantoque leprosis
prefuerit studio; qua sollicitudine circa
Assisium ueteres Christo reparauerit edes.

Gracia celestis uernam comitatur euntem.
Infinita tamen patitur quibus ipsa grauari,
etsi non frangi tua, Iob, paciencia posset.
Factus enim quasi scurra uagus cui mansio nusquam
5 certa datur, pauper et egens, neglectus et algens,
fessus et esuriens, aliis grauis et sibi uilis,
natali patrioque solo peregrinus et exul
fertur, ut in patria meliore domesticus esse
et ciuis certaque domo requiescere possit.
10 Deque tot aduersis aliquot referenda uidentur.

Possessing nothing except himself, he departed. Under no one's compulsion but of his own accord, he was an exile in his own country, in order that as an exile he might be repatriated, turned from a happy man into a wretch, from a rich man into a pauper—or rather, turned from a wretch into a happy man, from a pauper into a rich man. And now he wore coverings of coarse wool full of holes, though he was accustomed to wear new clothes of soft fleece skillfully worked, and to change according to the seasons feathers for silks and silks for feathers.

[Book 4]

The fourth book reports how he bore the cruelty first of thieves and then of monks, and with what zeal he took responsibility for the lepers; with what solicitude he repaired old buildings around Assisi for Christ's sake.

Heaven's grace accompanied its servant on his way, yet he suffered countless trials with which even your patience, O Job, might be burdened, though not broken. For being made like a wandering rascal to whom no sure abode was granted, poor and needy, neglected and cold, tired and hungry, a burden to others and vile in his own eyes, he was considered a foreigner and exile from the native soil of his father, in order that he might be a dweller and citizen in a better country and rest in a secure house. Of so many adversities it seems we ought to mention a few.

Tempore brumali quando producere noctes,
abreuiare dies solet obliquacio solis,
et que mille fuit distincta coloribus uno
terra colore nitet, cum nudam nix quasi lana
15 uestit eam, glaciesque quasi cristallus adornat;
quando uiatores gaudent candore uiarum,
limes ubique merus, nusquam pes humefit, omnes
densat aquas aquilo, calor acquisitus eundo
temperat hibernum frigus, frigusque calorem,
20 per nemus incedens Franciscus pectore toto
gaudet et exultat; mouet exultacio cantum.
Delectatur enim reminiscens quod fit iniquo
exemptus patris imperio lucrisque dolosis;
quod Christo seruus iam peruiet et sibi liber;
25 quod nudus ferale ferat quasi mulcebre frigus.
Nam quis tam rigidus, mutatum quin aliquando
a peiore statu se gaudeat ad meliorem?
Inde resultandi tot agens in pectore causas
Franciscus lingua Francorum psallere cepit.
30 Silua sonum geminans latronum pertulit aures.
Exiliunt inopemque uident; spes excidit, et se
illusos reputant indignanterque requirunt,
"Tu quis es?" Ille refert, "Christi sum preco. Quid ad uos?"
Preturbata leui flagrat iracundia uento
35 iniiciuntque manus in eum nil tale timentem.
Proch! furum feritas coram quibus ipse nec insons
nec uacuus cantare potest inpune uiator.
Immo luit grauiter, plenum niue trusus in antrum
quod cecinit uacuus. Quid si cecinisset onustus?
40 In niue Franciscus iacet illuduntque latrones,

In the winter time, when the angle of the sun is wont to draw out the nights and shorten the days, and the earth that was picked out with a thousand colors shines with only one —when snow like wool clothes its nakedness, and ice like crystal adorns it; when travelers rejoice in the whiteness of the roads, thresholds everywhere are clean and feet nowhere soggy, and the north wind solidifies all water, the heat worked up in traveling tempers winter's cold, and the cold tempers the heat—Francis as he passed through the forest rejoiced and exulted with all his heart; his exultation called forth a song. For he took delight in remembering that he had been freed from his father's unjust sway and treacherous wealth; that he traveled as Christ's servant but free as to himself; that, though naked, he endured the savage cold like something pleasant. For who is so unbending that he would not rejoice to be changed at some point from a worse state to a better? And so, considering within his breast these causes for exultation, Francis began to sing in the Frankish tongue. The forest redoubling the sound struck the ears of bandits. They sprang forth and saw a pauper; hope eluded them; they thought themselves mocked and indignantly demanded, "Who are you?" He replied, "Christ's herald. What is it to you?" Their wrath blazed forth, aggravated by a light breeze, and they laid hands upon him, who feared no such thing. Shame on the savagery of thieves, before whom neither the innocent nor the destitute wayfarer can sing with impunity! Rather, he paid dearly, dragged into a snow-filled cave because he sang empty-handed—what if he had sung laden down with wealth? Francis lay in the snow and the

"Ecce tuus lectus! Iaceas ibi rustice Christi
preco. Tuum meruit ea lectisternia carmen."
Ille nichil contra, set eis abeuntibus exit
speluncam tumulumque niuis, quo pene sepultus
45   fine tenus latuit. Set quem diuina tuendum
assumpsit pietas, in eum non proficit hostis.
Excuciensque niues quibus omni parte globatis
et uestes omnes et barba comeque rigebant,
gaudet se furum sic euasisse furorem,
50   amissamque uiam repetens et carmen omissum
laude Creatoris sinuosa repercutit antra
et Christi resonare docet misteria siluas.
        Hic ubi cantando nemoris peruenit ad horam,
inde monasterium modico discrimine distans
55   intrat et hospicii petit assequiturque quietem.
Dumque quies motus releuat nocturna diurnos,
humidior uentus apperitiuusque pororum
nudat humi faciem, lateque liquefacit auster
compactas aquilone niues glaciemque resoluit.
60   Undique torrentes abeunt totosque per agros
expaciantur aque quas et niuis et glaciei
congeries liquefacta parit: collisa trahuntur
saxa trabesque natant auulsaque robora siluis.
Terra negat gressus humecta medullitus, omnis
65   limes fit limus, omnis uia deuia, pontes
occulit effluxus, aut obruit impetus unde.
Nec subito cessant tales excurrere riui,

brigands mocked him: "There's your bed! Lie there, yokel herald of Christ. Your song deserves this bedding." He answered not at all, but when they departed he left the cave and the mound of snow, where until that point he lay nearly buried. But the foe achieved nothing against him whom divine mercy had taken under its protection. Shaking off the snow that clung to him on all sides and stiffened all his clothes, his beard and hair, he rejoiced to have thus escaped the thieves' fury. Seeking once more the road he had left and his interrupted song, he again made the winding caverns echo with praise of the Creator and taught the forest to resound with the mysteries of Christ.

When he came singing to the edge of the wood, he entered a monastery that stood at some little distance in order to seek and obtain the quiet of lodging. And while the quiet of night brought respite from the day's emotions, a damper wind that opened the pores laid bare the face of the ground. Far and wide the south wind melted the snow that the north wind had compacted, and loosened the ice. Torrents ran off in all directions, and over all the fields spread the waters brought forth from the conglomeration of snow and ice as it melted. Colliding stones were borne along. Timbers floated together with oaks torn out of the forest. The earth, sodden to its depths, prevented travel, every path turned to mud, every track became trackless, the flow concealed the bridges, or else the force of the wave collapsed them. Nor did such streams immediately stop running, for their

successiuus enim stipata liquefacit actus
corpora; set sicut liquefiunt, sic et ab ipsis
70 eliciuntur aque. Non ergo repente residit,
immo diu talis replet exundacio terras.
Quid Franciscus agat, quem ueste ciboque carentem
nec monachi remanere sinunt nec tempus abire?
Articulos utrobique graues fert eius egestas,
75 aduersantur enim rigor hospitis et furor aure.
Dirior est hospes, set durior ingruit aura.
Inde prior claustri quasi dissimulare coactus
indignum patitur, patitur tamen ut miser hospes
interceptus aquis, cum nusquam possit abire,
80 operiatur ibi donec pertranseat unda.
Dum sic Franciscus cogente perhendinat austro,
debile cilicium quod longa retexerit etas
decidit in partes nec filis fila coherent.
Sindone contentus residet quasi lusor ad ignem,
85 dumque fouet uentrem, tergum gelat et uice uersa,
afflictusque fame grauius quam frigore, panem
appositum decies uno consumeret esu.
De brodio non est sibi spes, ubi condiat offas,
nam consueuit eo pocius deuocio fratrum
90 impinguare sues; humanaque quomodo uestis
donaretur ei cui porci cena negatur?
Omne genus culpe monachus comittit auarus.
Relligionis enim districte quando professor
uergit in accidiam, nichil est quod abhorreat. Omne
95 attemptat facinus postquam deliquid in uno.
Tuta creature datur excellencia nulli,
set quo nobilior, quanto declinat ab alto.

continuing force turned solid bodies to liquid; but just as
they melted, so also from these even more water came forth.   70
Such a flood, then, did not recede swiftly but long occupied
the land. What could Francis do, whom the monks didn't
allow to remain, nor the weather allow to depart without
clothing or food? His poverty endured grave crises on every
side, for the severity of his host and the fury of the wind op-   75
posed him. His host was fiercer, but the wind fell on him
harder. Thus the prior of the cloister, being compelled as it
were to dissimulate, suffered it as an indignity (but suffered
it nonetheless) that his wretched guest should shelter there
until the wave passed on, since being cut off by the waters   80
he could nowhere depart. While Francis sojourned thus under the south wind's compulsion, the tattered hair shirt woven long before fell away in pieces, nor did one thread of it
cling to another. Content with a sheet, he sat like a gambler
before the fire; while he warmed his belly, his back grew   85
cold, and vice versa, and since he was afflicted more by hunger than by cold, ten times he consumed in a single gulp the
bread set before him. He had no hope of broth to immerse
the morsels, for the brothers' devotion was inclined instead
to fatten their swine; how might human clothing be granted   90
one to whom a pig's fodder is denied? An avaricious monk
commits every sort of sin. For when one who professes a
strict religion veers toward melancholy, nothing daunts him.
He assays every wickedness once he sins in one respect. Se-   95
cure perfection is granted to no creature, but it lapses from

Plus horroris habet nature gloria quondam
Lucifer angelice: nunc est quem monstra perhorrent.
100 Et rebus qui prefuerit mortalibus, Adam,
quando mori meruit, meruit turpissimus esse,
sicut adhuc perhibet humani funeris horror.
A simili monachus quem sacra professio membris
pretulit ecclesie, cum uergit ad infima, tanto
105 prauior est aliis quo sanccior esse tenetur.
   Postquam nix austri solisque soluta uapore
in riuos abiens glaciesque fatiscere cepit,
et Franciscus aque crementa residere uidit,
arripiens iter, immo fugam, quasi dama cruenta
110 fertur, non curans quo uadat, dummodo uadat.
Non adeo leti fugerunt de synagoga
Paulus Hebreorum, de carcere Petrus Herodis,
seque magisterio patris manibusque latronum
non adeo nuper fuerat gauisus ademptum,
115 nec falsos leuiore fugit conamine fratres
quam uel Lothophagos uel inhospita monstra Ciclopes
uel cantus olim Sirenum fugit Ulixes.
Cumque monasterio modicum speraret abesse,
Eugubium nudus ueniens amicitur amici
120 ueste noua ueteris, quo possit honestius ire
commodiusque pati quodcumque minabitur aura.
   Passus egestates pro Christi nomine tantas,
semper et assidue uultu persistit eodem,

the heights in proportion to its nobility. Lucifer, that glory of a once angelic nature, is all the more horrible: now monsters shudder at him. And Adam, who was master over 100 mortal beings, when he merited death also merited to be most vile, as the horror of a human corpse still demonstrates. Likewise, a monk whose holy profession has placed him over the members of the Church is that much more wicked than others, when he bends toward the depths, by 105 such degree as he is held to be more holy.

After the warmth of the sun and the south wind melted the snow, which ran off in rivulets, and the ice began to crack open, Francis, seeing the floodwaters subside, took his leave, or rather his flight—and was carried along like a 110 bloodied doe that cares not where it goes, so long as it goes. Paul did not flee the Hebrews' synagogue so joyfully, nor Peter Herod's prison; not so much had he previously rejoiced at being delivered from his father's authority and the hands of the bandits, nor did he flee those false brothers 115 with lighter exertion than Ulysses once fled the Lotus-Eaters or those inhospitable monsters, the Cyclopes, or the songs of the Sirens. And when he thought he was some little distance from the monastery, coming naked to Gubbio, he was dressed in the new clothing of an old friend, that 120 he might progress more respectably and endure more easily whatever menace the wind would offer.

Having suffered such deprivations in the name of Christ, ever steadfast, he persisted with the same countenance, all

quanto pauperior extra, robustior intus,
125 primaque dilatat eius paciencia famam,
intuitu cuius primum comittitur illi
cura leprosorum, quos sollicitudine tanta
nemo procurauit, et quorum tecta uidere
uix tulerat quamcunque procul distancia. Sternit
130 lectos, extergit saniem, fricat ulcera, tangit
ora lauatque pedes, corrosa putredine menbra
palpat, et affectus refugos insistere cogit.
    Neue sacri lateat quanto flagrarit amoris
igne, uiam carpens occurrit forte leproso,
135 leprosumque norans accedit et oscula sese
forcior infigit semesis cancere labris.
Nec solum circa leprosos sedulus, immo
circa mendicos omnes pietate profusus
subsidiis lapsus hominum releuare studebat:
140 consiliis curas, blandimentisque dolores,
rebus egestates, uerbis fastidia, donis
iacturas, epulisque famem, laribusque laborem,
presertim profugis, pupillis et uiduabus,
corde pio miserens: profugorum sicut asilum
145 et pupillorum sicut pater, et uiduarum
sicut sponsus erat, faciens satis unus ad omnes
ultra quam posset se dilatare facultas.
Unde placere Deo se uult elemosina soli,
inde Deo populoque placet famamque meretur
150 sponte set assequitur inuitus et inde cauendum
ducit ne presens adimat sibi fama futuram.

the stronger within the poorer he was without, and his
patience at the outset spread abroad his reputation. Upon 125
first sight of him he was charged with the care of lepers, for
whom no one provided with such solicitude, and whose
abodes no one had endured to look upon from however far
a distance. He made their beds, wiped away their clotted 130
blood, rubbed their ulcers, touched their faces and washed
their feet, massaged limbs consumed with rot, and compelled their fleeing sensations to remain stable.

Lest it should go unseen with what a flame of sacred love
he burned, he chanced to come upon a leper on his way. Rec- 135
ognizing him for what he was, he approached and, summoning up his courage, planted a kiss upon those lips half eaten
away by the cancer. Not only was he attentive to lepers,
but, being profuse in his pity toward all the poor, he was
concerned to relieve men's declining fortunes with his aid,
their cares with his advice, their sorrows with his soothing 140
words, their neediness with material goods, their aversion
with words, their losses with gifts, their hunger with banquets, their labor with lodging, having pity in his pious heart
especially for refugees, orphans, and widows: he was like an
asylum to refugees, a father to orphans, a spouse to widows, 145
a lone man sufficient for all beyond the scope of his capabili-
ties. While his alms were intended to please God alone, as
a result of them he pleased both God and the people and
spontaneously earned his reputation—but pursued it un- 150
willingly and so deemed it dangerous that his present fame
should rob him of fame to come.

Set preter morem pariente recentia casu
accidit ut cuidam semel exprobraret egeno.
Deinde recordantem pro quanti nomine regis
155   quam supplex mendicus eum quam parua rogasset
munera penituit non indulxisse roganti.
Neue malum uicii generare frequencia posset,
hoc in corde suo posuit semperque premendum
uouit, ut ulterius se quid dare posset habentem
160   nemo repulsandus peteret pro nomine Christi.
Hoc nusquam patitur a corde recedere uotum,
et manus inperio non ausa resistere cordis
affectus scriptos in mente sigillat in actu.
     Sic hominem iustum disciplineque capacem
165   prouehit oppositis diuina uocacio causis.
Iustus namque suo defectu proficit, audens
labi; contempnens excedere fit sceleratus.
Mox ubi conteritur temerarius ausus ad usum,
lapsus ad ascensum, contemptus ad agnicionem,
170   excessus facit ad meritum, scelus ad pietatem.
Sic in Francisco sese contraria causant,
cuius (ut Antei) uirtus geminata cadendo.
Tunc melius pugnat cum iam superata uidetur
exemploque sui docuit Franciscus ut omnem
175   abiiciant lapsum quoscumque redarguit unus.
     Interea cellam predictam que fugituro
mundum Francisco concessit prima penatem,
iam perstare diu nec conuersantis egestas
plurima, nec rerum demolitiua uetustas,
180   nec fundatoris permittit inercia primi.
Fundamenta labant humecta perhennibus ymbris;

But contrary to his habit, as chance gave rise to new circumstances, it happened that he once rebuked a certain
needy man. Then, as he recalled how humbly the beggar entreated him, and for how little, and in the name of how great   155
a king, it grieved him that he had not shown generosity to
his petitioner. Lest a repetition of this vice should beget
evil, he set this in his heart and vowed always to impress it
there: that henceforth no one should be repulsed who asked   160
him in Christ's name when he had anything he could give.
Nowhere did he permit this vow to vanish from his heart,
and his hand, not daring to oppose his heart's command,
sealed with its deeds the sentiments he had written in his
mind.

Thus God's call advances through the action of contrar-   165
ies a just man who accepts discipline. For being just, he
profits by his own failings when he dares to fall; disdain-
ing transgression, he becomes a sinner. Then when soon he
grows contrite, rash daring proves useful, his fall effects his
ascent, his contempt knowledge, his transgression merit,   170
and his sin piety. So in Francis contraries produced one another, and his virtue, like that of Antaeus, was doubled by
falling. Virtue fights better when it appears already to be
vanquished, and by his example Francis taught that those   175
whom one lapse accuses should reject every lapse.

Meanwhile, neither the great poverty of its incumbent,
nor corrupting antiquity, nor the indifference of its original   180
founder would much longer allow the aforesaid chapel to
survive that had first given Francis shelter as he prepared to
flee from the world. Foundations damp with constant rain

fluxibus ex tecto muri compage soluta
in partes abeunt: tecti pars pendet in alto,
pars in humum prostrata iacet, subitoque perire
185 horret et ex toto proponit abire sacerdos.
Cuius ne fuerit Franciscus inutilis hospes,
disponit quod proposuit cellamque reuisit
que labens et egens ueterana iacebat et ima;
set ueniens firmat labentem, ditat egentem
190 uir Domini, renouat ueteranam, subleuat imam.
    Hic locus est in quo dominarum fulget honestas;
hic uidue cum uirginibus laudabile gaudent
obsequium prestare Deo, quas nomine Clara,
clarior effigie, clarissima moribus ut fax
195 scintillas, ut stella faces, ut Sinthia stellas
laude preit, meritis excellit, scemate uincit.
Luce tamen uaria resplendet laus aliarum,
quas et debilitas sexus et inercia sensus
et generis mundanat apex et gracia forme;
200 set nec debilitas fortes nec inercia doctas
esse uetat, nec apex humiles, nec forma pudicas.
    Tales de mundo Dominus mediante uocauit
Francisco, sexu fragiles set pectore fortes,
sensu serpentes set simplicitate columbas,
205 sese indicibus ysopos set origine cedros,
partim formosas set ob omni parte pudicas.
    Sic ubi propositum Franciscus fine beato
consumauit, opus templumque quod egerat intus
spirituale, foris manuale nitescere uidit.

were crumbling; walls whose mortar had disintegrated from the runoff of the roof were coming apart in sections: part of the roof hung overhead, part lay flat on the ground, and the 185 priest, dreading that he faced a sudden death, resolved to leave altogether. Lest he should prove to have been a useless guest, Francis undertook what earlier he'd intended, and once more visited the chapel, which lay collapsing, needy, ancient, and lowly. But on his arrival the man of the Lord 190 stabilized its collapse, endowed its neediness, renovated its antiquity, and raised up its lowliness.

This was the place in which the honor of the nuns shone forth: here widows and virgins rejoiced to offer praiseworthy service to God. Clara—brighter in her appearance, brightest in her character—surpassed them in praise, excelled them in merit, vanquished them in appearance as a torch does embers, as a star a torch, as the moon the stars. 195 Yet still the others' praise shone forth with varied light. The weakness of their sex, the sluggishness of their senses, the loftiness of their birth, and the grace of their appearance drew them to the world, but neither did their weakness prevent them becoming strong, nor their dullness from learning, nor their lofty birth from humility, nor their beauty from modesty.

The Lord summoned such women from the world with Francis's assistance, weak as to their sex but strong of heart, serpents in their knowledge but doves in their simplicity, hyssop in their outward appearance but cedars according to 205 their origin, comely in some part but modest in every part.

Thus when Francis had brought his intention to a blessed completion, he beheld shining forth externally through the effect of his hands the spiritual work and temple that he had

210 Ad cellam secus Assisium que pene iacebat
diruta se transfert, sua cepta relinquere nusquam
incompleta uolens, laceramque redintegrat edem.
    Cella supradictis contermina nomine Porti-
Ungula, sub titulo Sancte fundata Marie,
215 iam senio confecta graui, facit undique rimas,
fit stabulum bobus, ara porcis, hospita nimbis,
peruia grandinibus cuntisque domestica uentis.
Set matrem Domini toto Franciscus amore
amplectens eius cellam sic uisitat ut se
220 excellat ueterana nouam, uicioque senecte
prima iuuentutis uirtus redit; ex ruditate
causatur species, ex dampno prouenit usus.

[Liber 5]

Quintus agit Christi preceptum quomodo complens
contentus tunica, precinctus fune trinodi,
prodierit subitus nulloque docente magister,
imbueritque suos dulci nouitate sequaces.

Omnibus hec prelata locis, nec sepe recedit
inde set immotus stabilisque perhendinat, edes
instaurans, ortos plantans, tenuique dieta
uitam sustentans, non qualia ferre solebat
5 indumenta ferens, set qualia sunt heremitis.

72

undertaken within. Desiring to leave nowhere incomplete   210
what he had begun, he betook himself to a chapel near
Assisi which nearly lay in ruins, and restored the damaged
building.

A chapel abutting the aforesaid, called the Portiuncula
and founded under the name of Saint Mary, now destroyed   215
by oppressive age, gaped with cracks on every side, having
become a roost for owls, a manger for pigs, a hostel for the
clouds, open to the hail and a home for every blast of wind.
But Francis, embracing with all his love the Mother of the
Lord, so visited the chapel that in its age it surpassed a new   220
structure, and the original virtue of its youth returned amid
the defects of its age; from its rusticity beauty was created,
and usefulness from its damage.

[Book 5]

The fifth book tells how he immediately went forth to fulfill
Christ's precept, content with a robe, girded with a triple-knotted
cord, a teacher though none instructed him, and how he instilled in
his followers a sweet renewal.

This chapel he preferred to all places, nor did he often depart thence, but remained unmoved and stable, reconstruct-
ing buildings, planting gardens, sustaining his life on a
meager diet, wearing clothing unlike what he was accus-   5
tomed to wear, but rather such as pertained to hermits. And

Dumque moratur ibi, quodam sibi tempore lectum
hoc euuangelium cupiens attendere, "Misit
Ihesus discipulos" et cetera, post celebratum
rite ministerium supplex humilisque rogauit
10   ut dignaretur sibi declarare sacerdos
uerba Redemptoris euuangeliumque diei.
Exponens euuangelii precepta sacerdos
singula prosequitur seriatim: quomodo mittens
discipulos Dominus contentos iusserit illos
15   simplicibus tunicis excalces ire, nec aurum
ferre uel argentum, nec zonam siue monetam
nec peram siue baculum. Dum sedulus aures
inclinat Franciscus ei, directus in illum
Spiritus est Domini, totumque carismate replet
20   pectus et archanum docet ad celestia callem.
       Nullus adhuc illo celestia calle petebat
quem feruore nouo Franciscus adinuenit, almis
intentus desideriis ut adimpleat omnem
iusticiam; nec uult aliquid glossare, set ipsum
25   prosequitur textum uerbisque fideliter heret.
In plerisque tamen ualet allegoria; set ipsam
littera precellit, ubi nulla parabola mentem
palliat auctoris, set rem sua uerba loquuntur.
       Auditis igitur quecunque poposcerat edi,
30   iamque suo melius sapiens interprete, ne sit
auditor uerbi tantum set factor, "Oportet,"
inquid, "ut hoc faciam quod Christus precepit. Hoc est
quod uolo, quod uoueo, quod totis opto medullis."
Dixerat, et preter tunicam reponit amictus

while he sojourned there, he desired on one occasion to attend to this Gospel passage as it was read to him: "Jesus sent
forth his disciples," etc. After the due celebration of the
Mass, he humbly entreated the priest to explain to him the   10
words of the Redeemer and the gospel of the day. The priest
followed through each of the gospel's commands, expounding them in sequence: how the Lord, sending forth his disciples, bade them be content with simple tunics and go un-   15
shod, carrying neither gold nor silver, neither girdle nor
coin, neither purse nor staff. While Francis zealously inclined his ears to him, the Spirit of the Lord was sent into
him, filled all his breast with grace, and taught him the se-   20
cret road to heaven.

No one as yet sought the heavenly places on that road
which Francis in his fresh fervor had discovered, intent in
his pious desires to fulfill all justice; nor did he wish to gloss
anything, but pursued the text itself and clung faithfully to   25
its words. Though allegory is valuable in many respects, still
the letter surpasses it, where no parable veils the author's intention, but rather his words speak forth the substance.

When he had heard everything he asked to be uttered,
and now wiser than his interpreter, in order not to be a mere   30
hearer of the word, but its doer, "It is fitting," he said,
"that I should fulfill what Christ has commanded. This is
my desire, this is my vow, this is what I wish in my very marrow." He had spoken, and he laid aside all the clothing

35 quotquot habet; non zona nitens accingere renes,
    non baculus fulcire gradum, non calceus ultra
    conseruare pedem solito permittitur usu,
    componitque sibi tunicam crucis instar habentem,
    ut tali signo domitos eliminet hostes.
40 Sustinet et laqueum pro zona ferre, nec ausus
    ulciscenda Deo peccata relinquere, factus
    ipse sui pro se, contra se, testis et actor
    et iudex, legum non impediente statuto:
    postquam discussit racionum pondera, sese
45 dampnat, et illecebre passos incendia lumbos
    tanquam latrones suspendit fune trinodi.
        Discipulis iniuncta Ihesu reuerenter adimplens
    discipulus fit et ipse Ihesu populique magister
    aduersus Furias certamen inire uolentis;
50 milicieque noue referente stipendia Christo,
    quam miserabiliter spoliat deuocio carnem,
    tam mirabiliter uestit sapiencia mentem,
    neue Ihesu frustra fuerit precepta secutus,
    mente recompensans habitus quos corpore perdit.
55 Res licet ignote sint illi fons Pegaseus
    Parnasusque biceps, subito fit dogmate summus.
    Nam causa meliore Sacri perfunditur igne
    Pneumatis, unde solet prodire sciencia uocum.
    A nullo doctus multos docet; alta loquentem
60 et quasi trans hominem noti quem tempore nullo
    discipulum uidere stupent audire magistrum,
    concluduntque, "Nichil didicit; nichil ergo docebit."
    Sic inferre locus presumit ab usibus; usu

he had, except for his tunic; neither was a gleaming sash al-   35
lowed as usual to gird his middle, nor staff to support his
step, nor shoe any longer to protect his foot, and he donned
a tunic that bore the image of the cross, that by such a sign
he might drive off his conquered foes. He also suffered him-   40
self to wear a noose in place of a sash. Not daring to leave
his sins for God to punish, he became both for and against
himself witness and advocate and judge, and no statute of
law could impede the decision. After he had examined the
weight of the arguments, he found himself guilty, and with   45
a triple-knotted cord hanged his private parts like bandits
when convicted of suffering the flames of lust.

Reverently fulfilling Jesus's commands to his disciples, he
became himself a disciple of Jesus and teacher of a people
who desired to join battle against the Furies; as Christ paid   50
the wages of this new warfare, his wisdom clothed his mind
just as wonderfully as his devotion wretchedly despoiled his
flesh, so that he might not follow Jesus's precepts in vain, if
he should restore in his mind the habits he had destroyed in
his body. Though the fount of Pegasus and twin-peaked Par-   55
nassus were unknown to him, all of a sudden he became the
acme of doctrine. For he was suffused with a better cause,
the fire of the Holy Spirit, from whom knowledge of tongues
is wont to proceed. Though taught by none, he taught many;
those who knew him were dumbstruck to hear as a teacher
—speaking of lofty matters, and as though transcending hu-   60
manity—one whom they had never seen as a disciple. And
they drew the conclusion: "He has learned nothing; therefore he will teach nothing." Just so, an argument presumes

autem nature si procedatur, habebit
65 tunc locus ille locum; si uero fefellerit usus,
fallet et ille locus, ut ubi miracula fiunt.
Hinc rerum causas hominum presumpcio reddit
inperceptibiles. Non exteriore magistro
erudiendus eget quem Spiritus erudit intus.
70 A quo Franciscus blande suscepta diserte
dogmata distribuit. Quod enim Deus edocet in cor
blandius ingreditur et ab ore serenius exit.
 O secreta Dei mortalibus abdita cuntis!
Qui modo propter eum terrena reliquerat, ecce
75 peruersos conuertit, ubi peruersus et ipse
uix eciam sese conuerterat, estque magister
egregius coram conciuibus et coalumpnis,
inter quos ydeota fuit, ueramque sophiam
acquisisse stupent, quem delirare putabant.

Quis ei modus exstiterit salutandi

80 Ingrediens quamcumque domum premittit in ipso
introitu, "Pax huic domui." Pax eius ad omnes,
iste salutandi suus est modus: hanc et honestis
et reprobis optat, hanc ciuibus et peregrinis
nunciat, hanc sexus utriusque fidelibus orat.
85 Discretus uir in Asisio, uestigia tanti
esse uidens imitanda uiri, comune ferendum
paupertatis honus ducit mundique fugaces
aspernatur opes, ne conculcetur ab hoste
sese conculcans, et egens imitatur egentem.

78

to make inferences from prior experiences; and if it proceeds from the experience of nature, then that argument will have its place, but if the experience has been deceptive, then that argument will deceive as well, as when miracles occur. Hence human presumption renders the causes of things imperceptible. He whom the Spirit instructs within has no need of instruction from an exterior teacher. Francis eloquently dispensed the doctrines he humbly received from the Spirit. For what God taught him passed more humbly into his heart and more serenely came forth from his mouth.

O secrets of God, hidden from all mortals! Behold, he who now had abandoned earthly things for God's sake converted the perverse, when he himself in his perversity had scarcely converted himself, and he became an outstanding teacher before his fellow citizens and associates, in whose eyes he was a fool, and they were dumbstruck that he whom they thought was raving had acquired true wisdom.

Of his manner of salutation

On his first entrance to any dwelling he said, "Peace be upon this house." His peace was for all, this was his manner of salutation: he wished this for the honorable and for the reprobate, he announced it to citizens and to foreigners, he prayed for this for the faithful of either sex.

A distinguished man in Assisi, seeing that he should follow in the footsteps of so great a man, thought that he should share the burden of his poverty and the world's fleeting wealth should be scorned, trampling himself lest he be trampled by the enemy; by his own need he imitated the needy man.

90   Francisci facit hospes idem, uir magnus in urbe
      Assisii diuesque penu Bernardus et agris.
      Actus namque sacros excellentemque tuendo
      Francisci uitam perpendit quanta salutis
      detrimenta sue tulerit terrena sequendo.
95   Non semel aut raro set sepius et quasi semper
      psalmis intentum sacrisque laboribus audit
      implicitum: non mensa uacat, non ipsa quieti
      debita nox a laude Dei Sancteque Marie.
      Prudens ut serpens, uigil ut draco, certat utroque
100   prudens serpentem, uigil oppugnare draconem
      Franciscus. Miratur eum desistere nunquam
      hospes et in lecto nichil indulgere sopori.
      Arcet enim fumos ascendentesque uapores
      communis uas particule, nullaque repleri
105   cella breuis patitur causa faciente soporem.
      Cumque renitentes occuli luctamine longo
      tandem coguntur succumbere, lingua susurrat
      semisopita preces; uixdum sopita quiescit.
      Hac exemplari Bernardus ymagine ductus
110   lorica fidei mentem premunit et armis
      iusticie, milesque nouus feruenter in hostem
      militat antiqum, Francisci castra secutus.
      Tanti (nec mirum) ducis emulus omnia uendit
      et dat pauperibus, euuangeliceque repertos
115   fert habitus et ei comes indiuisus adheret;
      partaque de mundo talis uictoria multos
      prouocat exemplis ad spiritualis amorem
      milicie, uirtusque trahit spectata sequaces.

Francis's host, a great man in the city of Assisi, Bernard, 90
rich in property and fields, did the same. Indeed, beholding
Francis's holy deeds and excellent life, he considered what
detriment he suffered to his salvation by pursuing earthly
things. He heard him intent upon the psalms and involved
in holy works, not once or rarely, but often, and nearly al- 95
ways: the table was not empty of praise of God and of Saint
Mary, nor even the night that was owed to rest. Prudent as a 100
serpent, watchful as a dragon, Francis strove in both fash-
ions, in his prudence to oppose the serpent, in his watchful-
ness the dragon. His host marveled that he never ceased and
in no way indulged in sleep when in his bed. For the vessel
of the common ventricle kept at bay the fumes and rising
vapors, and the small chamber permitted itself to be filled 105
with nothing that might bring on sleep. And when his resis-
tant eyes were at last compelled through long struggle to
succumb, his half-dozing tongue still mumbled its prayers;
it scarcely rested even in slumber. Led on by this exemplary
image, Bernard fortified his mind with the breastplate of 110
faith and the weapons of justice, and, following Francis's encampment, fought fervently as a new soldier against the ancient foe. Vying with such a leader (and no wonder), Bernard
sold everything and gave to the poor, took up the ways he 115
had discovered from the gospels, and clung to him as an in-
separable companion; by their examples, such a victory won
from the world summoned many to a love of spiritual combat, and their virtue attracted as followers those who observed it.

Eius enim zelo ciuis conuertitur alter,
120 uir simplex metuensque Deum, qui tempore multo
constanter certans et tandem uincere certus
uana relinquendi reliquis exempla reliquit.
Quintus et eiusdem capiens insignia pugne
aduersus Furias Egidius egide pectus
125 versicolore tegit, ubi ueri solis ab orta
luce crucis nimium fideique refulgurat aurum,
mundicie bissus, pressurarumque iacinctus.
Uno premissis adiecto, septimus arma
suscipiens eadem frater Philippus in ipso
130 accesssu toto mutatus pectore, que non
audiuit loquitur, que nescit edocet. Omnes
mirantur quorum reficit cor, inebriat aures
qui neutrum didicit set nuper egebat utroque.
Tyrones istos Franciscus ut et prothomiles
135 et princeps certare iubet, factisque tenorem
indicit uerbisque modum neutrisque probari
uirtutem perhibet, nisi discutienda supremo
iudice mens adeo primos compescere motus
certet ut ex primis non sit paritura secundos;
140 succensosque uiros celestis amore triumphi
omne genus belli quo spiritualia possunt
monstra triumphari docet; indiciisque priorum
exemploque sue uirtutis concio fratrum
sub tanto duce proficiens ad gaudia celi
145 non reputat mundi condignos esse labores.

Another citizen was converted by his zeal, a simple, God-   120
fearing man who strove constantly over a long time, and, being at last sure of conquest, left examples for others of how
to abandon vanity.

Egidius, the fifth who took the insignia of that same battle against the Furies, clad his breast in a varicolored aegis,   125
on which in the dawning light of the true Sun there shone
beyond measure the gold of the cross and of faith, the white
of purity, and the red of persecutions.

When yet another had been added to the aforesaid,
Brother Philip was seventh to don the same arms. Trans-   130
formed in his whole breast from his very arrival, he spoke
what he had not heard and taught what he had not known.
All whose hearts he restored and whose ears he intoxicated
marveled at one who had recently lacked all such learning
and knowledge.

Francis, as first soldier and chief among them, ordered   135
these fresh recruits into combat; he declared that their intention would be proven by their deeds, their measure by
their words, but he contended that their virtue was proved
by neither, unless the mind, which must be examined by the
supreme Judge, strove so to restrain its first impulses that
from them it should not bring forth their successors. To   140
men kindled with love of heavenly triumph he taught every
sort of warfare by which spiritual monsters could be overcome; and the assembly of the brothers, by the tokens of
their elders and the example of his own virtue, progressing
under such a great leader toward the joys of heaven, consid-   145
ered the labors of this world of no account.

At quia tam paucos trahit in certamina contra
tot Furias et monstra uiros, sibi celitus optans
ostendi dux ille sacer pluresne sequaces
esset adepturus, in uerba precancia totus
150 exit et expletur penetrans oracio celos
presentemque Deum directa mente tuetur.
In quo dum mentis acies defixa moratur,
Sanctus ei lumen infundit Spiritus, in quo
innumeros fratres ex omni gente futuros
155 tanquam presentes uidet existenter et audit.
Omnes Francisci gestantes arma magistrum
rectoremque uocant, patrem dominumque fatentur.
Letus in aspectu talis tanteque cohortis,
mentis ab excessu redit ad se sensilibusque
160 fratribus enarrat seriatim quomodo fratres
uiderit archetipos ipsius signa sequentes,
immo secuturos; tot enim sacer eius habebit
ordo professores, pars mundi nulla uacabit.
Talia mansuetus blando pater ore profatur,
165 cuius adhuc anime quedam complexio uisus
heret ymaginibus, uariasque recurrere formas
sentit et auditis tinnire tumultibus aures.
Neue putetur idem sopor esse, duobus ydeas
sensibus impressas non obliuiscitur, immo
170 circa communem fit adhuc mutacio sensum.
Gaudia concipiunt solito maiora Minores
quos pater exhilarat presens fratresque futuri.
Neue futura profans id adinuenisse putetur,
multa futurarum de se presagia rerum

But because he drew so few men into combat against so many Furies and monsters, that holy chieftain wanted it revealed from heaven whether he would gain more followers. He burst out in all his being into words of supplication and completed a prayer to pierce the heavens; with mind intent, he beheld God's presence. While the focus of his mind remained fixed upon God, the Holy Spirit poured into him a light in which he genuinely saw and heard as though present innumerable future brothers of every nation. Bearing Francis's arms, they all called him master and governor, confessed him their father and lord. At the sight of such a great band, he joyfully returned to himself from the abstraction of his mind and in sequence told the brothers he could see before him how he had seen that these archetypal brothers were following his banners, or rather would follow them in the future; for his holy order would have so many adherents, and no part of the world would be without them. 150 155 160

The gentle father declared such matters with mild voice, while an intimation of the vision still clung in images to his soul, and he felt the various shapes recurring once more and his ears ringing with the commotion he had heard. Lest it should be thought mere slumber, he did not forget ideas impressed upon him by two of his senses; rather, a transformation continued to occur linked with the shared sensations. 165 170

The Friars Minor rejoiced more than usual, being made glad by their present father and their brothers to come. Lest in declaring future events he should be thought to have made them up, he expounded many omens of things to come

175 pandit et hec iterum prenunciat abdita fati:
"Poma prius nobis predulcia, deinde remisse
dulcia, filioli; demum ponentur amara:
dulcia quando recens laudabitur ordo; remisse
dulcia dum pseudo paciemur scandala fratrum;
180 prorsus amara licet redolencia, quando per orbem
diffusi fratres populis fastidia gignent."

    Vir bonus interea uiteque probabilis alter,
ut fieri melior in Christo possit et eius
uita probabilor, accedit et arma capescens
185 forcia bella gerit sub forcia bella gerente
Francisco, milesque sacer sub principe sacro.
Sic ubi completus est octonarius, omnes
conuocat et binos mittit Franciscus in orbem,
ut doceant artem bellandi quam didicerunt,
190 precipiens ut, quicquid eis contingere possit,
fortes in bello pacientes sint in agone,
constantes in proposito, non prospera captent,
non aduersa tremant, set suspicione notantes
prospera, suscipiant aduersa libencius: absque
195 aduersis equidem nemo riget, absque rigore
nemo bellatur, sine bello nemo triumphat,
et regnum celi non prouenit absque triumpho.

    Verbaque conuertens ad eos, "Attendite," dixit,
"que uestri sit condicio, nec credite uitam
200 hic aliud quam miliciam, bellumque perhenne
indixere sibi partes utrimque rebelles.
De celis anime, de terris corpora: cum sint
ex hiis compositi naturis, de leuitate
est anime motus ad speram, de grauitate
205 corporis ad centrum. Set utro pars utraque motu

concerning himself, and again he announced in advance 175
these hidden decrees of fate: "First sweet fruits will come to
us, my little sons; then ones not so sweet; and at last the bitter will be served: the sweet fruits when the new order is
praised; the not-so-sweet when we shall suffer the scandals
of false brothers; and finally the bitter, though fragrant, 180
when the brothers, dispersed throughout the world, will en-
gender aversion among the nations."

Meanwhile, another good man of approved life came forward in order to become even better in Christ and his life
more worthy of approbation. Taking up arms, he waged 185
fierce battles under Francis, who was doing likewise, a holy
soldier under a holy prince. When a band of eight was thus
complete, Francis called them together and sent them out
into the world in pairs to teach the art of the warfare they
had learned, charging them that, whatever might happen to 190
them, being strong in battle they should be patient in combat, constant in resolve, nor should they grasp after prosperity, nor tremble at adversity; but taking note of prosperity
with suspicion, they should more gladly embrace adversity:
for without adversity no one has rigor, without rigor no one 195
does battle, without battle no one triumphs, and the kingdom of heaven does not arrive without triumph.

And directing his words to them, he said, "Attend to your
condition, and do not suppose that your life here is anything 200
other than warfare, as long as your rebel parts have declared
lasting war on each other from either side. Your souls are of
heaven, your bodies of earth: since men are composed of
these natures, the soul because of its lightness moves toward
the sphere, but the body, because of its heaviness, toward 205
the center. But whether either part, progressing by either

progrediens ad utram pertingere debeat horam
compositi stat in arbitrio: cui fauerit, illa
forcior est aliamque trahet. Nam sicut utrumque
est in composito componens, sic erit extra.
210 Ergo si motus anime preiudicet, ambo
consistent sursum; si corporis, ambo deorsum.
Ista duo sunt unus homo; spes inde quibusdam
est ut conueniant. Set que conuencio Christi
ad Belial? Proprio pars nititur utraque motu;
215 neutra trahi nisi uicta potest. Est ergo studendum
ut melior dominetur ibi peiorque dometur
et compellatur non carni spiritus, immo
spiritui seruire caro. Quod quinque ministri
corporis affectant, anime fidissima consors
220 uix racio conscire uelit mentemque iacentem
erigat et nulla recreet dulcedine sensum.
Set paupertatis quodam quasi fune trahatur
carnali caro mole carens, animeque uigorem
et motum sortita sue, celestibus illam
225 sectando studiis terrenaque nulla petendo.
Sobrietatis enim paupertas libera sedes,
uirtutum secura quies, nec pondere rerum
deprimitur, nec furta timet, nec inania captat,
attamen est multis onerosa. Set in profitente
230 miliciam Christi non est paciencia fortis
quam fortuna mouet. Tener est cuicumque uideri
paupertas res dura solet. Sub pondere tali
nemo uacillabit si duxerit ultro ferendum:
quo modo uult ita quisque potest gaudere pusillo.
235 Hoc tamen in primis graue, set prescripta relinquid
sobrietas habitum generatque frequencia mores.

motion, should reach either goal, depends upon the free will
of the composite: whichever the free will favors, that is the
stronger and will draw along the other. For just as each com-
ponent is within the composite, so it will be externally. If, 210
then, the soul's motion has its prerogative, both will rise;
but if the body's, both will descend. These two things are a
single human being; and so there is hope for some that they
should be in agreement. But what agreement exists between
Christ and Belial? Either part strives according to its own
motion; neither can be drawn along unless it is vanquished. 215
Strive, therefore, that the better may there dominate and
the worse be subdued, and that the spirit not be forced to
serve the flesh but rather the flesh be compelled to serve the
spirit. What the body's five ministers pursue, reason, the
soul's faithful consort, should desire though with difficulty 220
to comprehend, should raise up the prostrate mind, and
should restore the senses without sweetness. But let the
flesh, lacking its carnal mass, having acquired the vigor and
movement of its soul, following it with heavenly zeal and 225
seeking nothing earthly, be drawn along, as it were, by poverty's rope. For poverty is the free seat of sobriety, the secure repose of virtues, nor is it oppressed by the weight of
things, nor does it fear theft nor grasp after inanities, yet it
is burdensome to many. But in one who professes the war- 230
fare of Christ, no fortune sways firm patience. Anyone to
whom poverty seems a harsh thing is weak. No one will waver beneath such a weight if he considers that it should be
borne freely: thus each man is able to rejoice in that little he
has, in such way as he desires. This is nevertheless burden- 235
some at first, but the sobriety I have enjoined abandons

Cumque pusillanimes de paupertate querantur,
non in pauperie set in ipso paupere peccant;
quam nisi quisque ferat, inuitus nec feret impos.
240 Si toleraret egens, tolerabilis esset egestas
quantalibet, nullusque potest existere pauper
tam paciens, quin sit paupertas plus pacienda.
Libera namque quies ibi libertasque quieta
fortune non distrahitur leuitate, set orat
245 et contemplatur, solius sola supremi
inspectiua boni, solis intenta supernis.
Hanc uobis adhibete ducem, preferte magistram,
et facies uestre non confundentur. Ab ipso
namque Deo iuste datur, ut quos gloria mundi
250 delectare nequit, delectet gloria celi."

[Liber 6]

Sextus dispersos per mundi climata fratres
mirificis precibus reuocantem scribit in unum,
quo per apostolicum sua confirmante statuta
succreuit nomenque nouum nouus ordo recepit.

Recta resistendi uiciis precepta docente
Francisco, fatis animas exponere iussi
in tria sex abeunt mundi confinia bini
et bini. Franciscus eis benedicit, et ipse
5 in quartum contentus abit comilite solo.

habit, and repetition builds character. And though the weak
may complain of poverty, they sin not in regard to poverty
but against the poor man himself; unless each bears his poverty, neither will the powerless bear it unwillingly. If the   240
needy man bore it, any need would be bearable, and no pauper is so patient, but that his poverty should be borne more
patiently. There, indeed, fortune's inconstancy does not re-
move free rest and restful freedom, but these qualities pray
and contemplate, considering only the supreme Good, in-   245
tent only on the things above. Cling to poverty as your
guide, make of her your teacher and your countenance will
not be confounded. For she is rightfully bestowed by God
himself, in order that the glory of heaven may delight those   250
whom the world's glory cannot."

[Book 6]

*The sixth book describes how, by his miraculous prayers, he called
his brothers back together when they were dispersed through the
world's far climes, and how, when he confirmed his statutes by apostolic decree, the new order grew and received a new name.*

When Francis had taught them the correct precepts for re-
sisting vice, and had bidden them to expose their souls
to the fates, they departed two by two to three corners of
the world. Francis blessed them and himself departed to   5
the fourth, content with a single fellow warrior. Who may

Prelia quis numeret quibus in diuersa profecti
uirtutum pedibus uiciorum colla prementes
contriuere caput serpentis ubique reperti,
omnes ad mortem peccati fune trahentis?
10 Set quos Franciscus tenere dilexerat egre
passus abesse diu: rogat ut per climata mundi
dispersos qui discipulos collegit in unum
matris ad exequias sparsos quoque congreget istos.
Vota uiri mouere Deum: simul et semel omnes
15 et sine condicto redeunt quos Spiritus idem
colligit in punctum longo licet orbe remotos.
Mirari non sufficiunt que causa reuerti
tam subito compellat eos. Franciscus et ipse
obstupet effectum cui causam prebuit orans.
20 Visibus alternis hii gaudent huius, hic horum,
et quid pertulerint in itu redituque loquuntur.

Quomodo quattuor uiri habitum eius susceperint

Innocuuos uictus et spiritualia fratrum
gaudia zelantes nullo turbanda tumultu
quatuor accedunt diuersi, qui sub eodem
25 arma capessentes ductore, nociuaque mundi
blandimenta sequi renuentes, bella malignis
indiciunt Furiis stolideque silencia carni.

Quomodo ipse omnes indifferenter admiserit

Cum tot apostolici numerum complente senatus
Francisco sociis, rumor diffunditur, et sunt
30 tempora qui dicant instare nouissima mundi

number the battles in which those men, having set out for
their diverse destinations, trampled the neck of vice under
the feet of virtue, crushing, wherever they found it, the head
of the serpent who with the rope of sin drags all toward
death? But Francis ill suffered the long absence of those 10
whom he had loved tenderly. He entreated him who gathered his disciples together to attend a mother's funeral also
to bring together these who were scattered throughout the
world's climes. The man's prayers moved God: all at once
without any prior agreement they returned, (for the Spirit 15
gathered them to a single point) though they were far removed across the earth. They could not wonder sufficiently
what had caused them so suddenly to return. Francis as well
was himself dumbstruck at the effect, though his prayer had
afforded the cause. They rejoiced to see him, and he them in 20
turn, and they spoke of what they endured on their journey
and return.

How four men assumed his habit

Four men, all zealous though diverse, acceded to the blame-
less livelihood and spiritual joys of the brethren that no tumult will shake. Taking up arms under the same leader, 25
scorning to follow the world's noxious blandishments, they
declared battle against the malignant Furies and imposed silence upon the stubborn flesh.

How he admitted them all without distinction

As Francis completed with so many men the number of the
apostolic senate, rumor spread, and there were those who 30
said that the world's last times were at hand, the end of

cuius inauditus finem prenunciat Ordo.
Set cor Francisci dilatant gaudia quando
quilibet accedens uiciis indicere bellum
agreditur. Non condicio, fortuna uel etas
35 ulla recusatur; ueniens admittitur omnis
et sine delectu bonus et malus, altus et ymus,
rusticus et miles, ignobilis et generosus,
clericus et laicus, rudis et discretus, egenus
et diues, seruus et liber, sanus et eger,
40 affectuque mero Franciscus suscipit omnes.
Eius eos documenta trahunt, exemplaque uite
irreprehensibilis uerbis adhibencia pondus.

Quomodo precepta Ordinis in scripta redegerit

Neue per ambages eius doctrina uagetur,
fratribus instituit presentibus unde futuris
45 eniteat quid agant, quicquid decernit agendum
in scriptis redigens, euuangeliique tenore
sic fieri debere docens. Ne uero uideri
possit inauditi temerarius Ordinis actor
et quasi presumens de se nimis ardua, quicquid
50 dictat apostolico uult perpetuare registro.

Quomodo uenientem ad papam Iohannes de Sancto
Paulo uoluerit a proposito reuocare

Cumque gubernaret pater illustrissimus orbem
qui priuatiue nocuus proprieque uocari
utilis ecclesie meruit pater, ardua calcans,

which was presaged by this unheard-of Order. But joy
swelled Francis's heart when each one came forward to declare war on vice. He refused no condition, fortune, or age. 35
Everyone who came was admitted, the blamelessly good and
the wicked, the lofty and humble, peasant and knight, com-
moner and blueblood, cleric and lay, bumpkins and the distinguished, needy and rich, slave and free, healthy and sick,
and with pure affection Francis received them all. His teach- 40
ings drew them in, and the example of his irreproachable
life, which added weight to his words.

How he committed the precepts of the Order to writing

In order that his teaching should not waver ambiguously, he
told his present brothers what they should do to make that 45
teaching clearly known to those to come, committing everything to writing that he judged they should perform, teaching that it ought to be so done in the spirit of the Gospel.
But lest he should seem the presumptuous instigator of an
unheard-of Order, like one who takes on himself things too
lofty, he wished everything he prescribed to be perpetuated
by apostolic writ. 50

How Giovanni di San Paolo wanted to deflect him
from his intention as he approached the pope

When that illustrious father was governing the world who
by antiphrasis might be called harmful, and who properly
can be called a father useful to the Church—he trampled
down the lofty, raised up the lowly, terrified the kings of the

pressa leuans, qui reges terre nominis umbra
55   terruit, Ecclesie mundum subiecit, et ensem
Cesaris ense Petri domuit memorandus in euum,
tanti Francisco placuit patris auspice, ductu,
consilioque super dictis procedere rebus;
quoque statutorum grauitas autentica summam
60   perpetuet, Romam proficiscitur, a memorato
patre petiturus ut discuciendus ab ipso
sedis apostolice nouus impetret Ordo fauorem.
Aggrediensque uiam quosdam de fratribus ipsis
assumit comites; quibus ingredientibus urbem
65   existens uir sanctus ibi, Guido nomine presul
Assisii, querit que Romam causa uidendi
ipsos impulerit, perpensaque complacet illi
causa. Timebat enim ne se transferre pararent
consiliumque suum rebus concedit agendis.
70   Deinde Sabinensis pater antistesque Iohannes
de Sancto Paulo, quo nullum curia de tot
magnis totque bonis maiorem uel meliorem
tunc habuit, clementer eos confortat, honeste
suscipit, humane tractat, reuerenter honorat.
75   Set metuens ne forte cadant humanitus, ex quo
Ordinis exciderit nouitas et feruor in auras
exspirans euanuerit, suadere laborat
ut non circueant nostri contagia secli,
immo monasterii latebras eremiue subintrent.

earth with the very shadow of his name, subjected the world   55
to the Church, and by Peter's sword subdued the sword of
Caesar (a deed to be remembered forever)—it pleased Francis to proceed in the aforesaid matters under the auspices,
leadership, and counsel of such a father. That the weight of
authority might perpetuate the sum of his statutes, he set   60
out for Rome to request the said father to examine the new
Order, so that thus it might gain the favor of the Apostolic
See. Setting out on the road, he took some companions
from among the brothers. As they entered the city a holy   65
man dwelling there, the bishop of Assisi, Guido by name,
asked what purpose had brought them to visit Rome, and
their reason pleased him once he had learned it. Indeed, he
feared that they were preparing to postpone, and he offered
his advice how to proceed with matters. Then Giovanni di   70
San Paolo, father and bishop of Sabina—the Curia then had
none greater or better than him, among so many great and
good men—comforted them with kindness, received them
honorably, treated them with humanity, and honored them
with reverence. But fearing that things should perchance   75
turn out according to human nature—as a result of which
the Order's novelty might fall away and its fervor vanish
into thin air—he labored to persuade them that they should
not frequent the contagions of our present age but should
enter the refuge of a monastery or the desert.

Quomodo Franciscus predicti persuasionem refellerit

80   Franciscus "Quid," ait, "uir magne, uir inclite, claustris
aut heremis herere mones, quos puplica mundi
cura petit? Qui nec tantummodo ferre tenemur
pro nobis, uerum pro fratribus arma tuendis,
uis ut omittamus medicinam pestibus orbis
85   ferre salutiferam, soli saluere uolentes?
Communi propriam scelus est preferre salutem.
Set reparare reos et condescendere lapsis,
hic meus est labor, hec mea crux quam baiulo: Christum
sic affecto sequi, nec eum secus esse sequendum
90   ex ipsis euuangelii considero uerbis."
Tanto Francisci motus feruore, Iohannes
ad faciem pape quem consultare uolebat
introduxit eum. Fratres comitantur euntem,
aduentusque sui causas referentibus aptas
95   prouenit ex facili pape fauor. Omnia cedunt
ad uotum nullamque ferunt omnino repulsam.

Quomodo propositum a papa optinuerit

Sic impetrato quicquid duxere petendum,
restat ut abscedant, et papa licentiat ipsos
et benedicit eis, iniungens ut gradiantur
100   quo passu cepere gradi terrasque per omnes
doctrinam Christi promulgent, et uiciorum
fluctibus absorptos uirtutum naue reportent.

How Francis refuted the aforesaid man's persuasions

"Great and excellent man," said Francis, "why do you urge us
to cling to cloister or retreat, when the care of all the world
lays claim to us? We who are constrained to bear arms not
only for ourselves, but in order to watch over our brothers—
do you want us not to apply saving medicine to the world's
diseases, in desire for our own salvation alone? It is a sin to
prefer one's own salvation to that of the community. But to
restore the guilty and bend down to those who have fallen—
this is my work, this is the cross that I bear: that is how I aspire to follow Christ, nor, from the words of the Gospel, do
I judge that he is to be followed otherwise." Moved by Francis's great fervor, Giovanni brought him into the presence of
the pope whom he wished to consult. His brothers accompanied him as he went, and they easily obtained the pope's
favor when they explained the due reasons for their coming.
Everything turned out according to their desire, and they
experienced no rebuff at all.

How he obtained the desired outcome from the pope

When they had obtained everything they saw fit to request,
it remained for them to depart, and the pope gave them license and blessed them, charging they should walk the path
they had begun to tread, publish Christ's teaching through
all the earth, and carry back on the ship of virtue those
swamped in the waves of vice.

Quo merito Dominus dederit ei
graciam coram magnis

Vere Franciscum summo diuina fauore
gracia prosequitur, cuius succedere dono
105 miratur sibi tam propere tot prospera. Iure
iurando fecit Deus illum crescere. Non est
inuentus similis illi protendere legem
Excelsi, seruire Deo, contempnere mundum,
preesse sibi, prodesse suis, conuertere prauos,
110 emendare bonos, operari quicquid oportet.

Quomodo cum fratribus suis ad propria redierit

Exhilarat tanti Franciscum iussio patris,
a quo dimissus sanctorum limina Petri
uisitat et Pauli fratresque rediuit ouantes.
Alternoque uie releuant sermone laborem:
115 quam placide tractarit eos clemencia pape,
quam ferale suo moderamine quemque moueri,
quam sit iocundum fratres habitare sub uno.
Dumque diem fallunt et multa loquuntur eundo,
inperceptibili motu pars multa diei
120 transit, et ingeminat motusque calorque laborem,
membraque debilitat resolucio multa uaporem.
Fessi considunt in humum quos hora laborque
extenuans et causa fames urgencior istis
ad refocillandas animas inuitat. At ipsum
125 quo recreentur abest propter deserta locorum.
Set quia deesse nequit diuina fidelibus uncquam
cura suis, uir adest ex cuius munere leti

For what merit the Lord gave him grace
in the presence of great men

Divine grace truly followed Francis with its highest favor, by whose gift he marveled that so many successes so swiftly 105 came about for him. God made him to increase according to his oath. None was found like him in promulgating the law of the Most High, in serving God, despising the world, governing himself, being of service to his own, converting the depraved, making the good better, and doing whatever was 110 fitting.

How with his brothers he returned home

The command of so great a father gladdened Francis. Dismissed by him, he visited the shrines of Peter and Paul and returned to his joyful brothers. They lightened the labor of the journey with conversation: how peaceably the pope's 115 clemency had treated them; how fatal it is for each man to be moved by his own governance; how pleasant it is for brothers to dwell together in unity. While they beguiled the day and talked of much as they continued, a great part of the day passed in unobtrusive motion, the heat generated by 120 movement doubled their labor, and much weakness disabled their limbs and their respiration. Exhausted, they sat down on the ground when the hour, their debilitating labor, and hunger (a still more pressing cause) invited them to refresh their spirits. But the very thing that might have restored 125 them was lacking in the wilderness. Yet since divine providence can never desert its faithful ones, a man stood near at hand, of whose gift they joyfully received bread; then still

panem suscipiunt; incognitus ille recedit.
Illi uero stupent et ad ulteriora superne
130 munera sperandum bonitatis uoce fideli
admonet alterutrum, quibus est fiducia summi
certa boni, spem preterito faciente futuri.

Qualiter inde propter loci decorem recesserit

Panem qui superest fragmentaque lecta reseruat
extenso spelunca sinu, paucisque diebus
135 conuersantur ibi pariter nec abire placeret.
Set species suspecta loci, quem densa uirore
gramina perpetuo decorant, quem mille colorum
flores uermiculant, illectis ne racionem
sensibus impediat, prohibet residere uolentes.

Quomodo conuerterit Paterenos

140 Suscipit optatos uallis dilecta Spoleti.
Hic Paterinorum multos seduxerat error,
set Christi Franciscus oues ad ouile reducit,
erudiensque rudes sedet excellenter in ore
ipsius uerbum Domini, quasi iaspis in auro,
145 ros in agris, flos in uirgultis, ignis in aula,
diuinaque fide mentes ut iaspis adornat,
ut ros humectat, ut flos delectat, ut ignis
illustrat, captosque sua dulcedine sensus
mulcet, et humani penetrat penetralia cordis.

unknown, he went away. They were stupefied, and each with
faithful voice admonished the other to hope for further gifts   130
of the goodness on high, since the past gave hope for the future to those who have sure trust in the Supreme Good.

How he departed because of the beauty of the place

A cave provided storage in its deep interior to the bread and
remaining gathered fragments, and for a few days they dwelt   135
there together, nor would it please them to depart. But the
dangerous beauty of the place, which was adorned with
thick grass of perpetual verdure and dotted by flowers of a
thousand colors, forbade them despite their desire to remain, for fear it should get in the way of their reason by enticing their senses.

How he converted the Patarenes

The beloved valley of Spoleto received them as ones for   140
whom it longed. Here the error of the Patarenes had seduced many, but Francis led Christ's sheep back to the
sheepfold, and the word of the Lord, instructing the uneducated, sat excellently in his mouth, like jasper in gold, dew
on the fields, a flower on its bush, fire in the hall. Like jasper
he adorned their minds with godly faith, like dew he moistened them, like a flower beautified them, like fire enlight-   145
ened them. He soothed senses captivated by his sweetness
and penetrated the inner reaches of the human heart.

Quomodo dedicerit eos orare

150 Inde probabilius conpuncti forcius instant
ut qui tam celebrem didicit diuinitus artem
in fratres admittat eos, partemque ferendi
concedens oneris partem concedat honoris.
Ille suis insignit eos insignibus. Ordo
155 crescit in inmensum, set adhuc sine nomine res est.
Uult ergo suus huic opifex imponere certum
nomen et instituit dicatur ut Ordo Minorum,
et merito: quis enim minor illo quem neque potus
aut cibus inpinguat, nec diplois aut toga densat,
160 nec decus aut dicio sublimat; qui sibi cuntos,
se nulli, preferre studet, qui uilia mundi
apprecians preciosa sibi uilescere cogit,
qui, ne deficiat in Christo, defuit in se?
Tales Franciscus recte uocat ergo Minores;
165 ianua celestis maioribus est nimis arcta.

Quomodo propter uerbum agasonis reliquerit domum suum

Postquam per nomen nouus hic innotuit Ordo,
Franciscum sociosque suos utcumque fouebat
stramine tecta putri deserta domuscula, tynos
pretendens graciles. Paucis statura diebus
170 paupertasque suis cultoribus ipsa placebat,
donec preteriens onerati ductor aselli
rusticus inferret fatuo fastidia uerbo.
Poscere qui latebras pluuia uehemente coactus
affuit, et proprium sic est affatus asellum,

How he taught them to pray

Those thus more laudably touched by compunction force- 150
fully pressed him, once he had divinely taught them so illustrious a skill, to admit them as brothers, and to grant them a
share of his honor by granting them a share in bearing his
burden. He marked them with his insignia. The Order in- 155
creased immensely but still was without name. And so its
framer wanted to give it a fixed name and declared that it
should be called the Order of Minors, and rightly so: for
who is less than he whom neither drink nor food fattens, to
whom neither mantle nor toga gives substance, whom nei- 160
ther beauty nor authority elevates; who strives to place all
before himself and himself before none, who at once values
the world's vile things and holds its precious treasures vile in
his own eyes, and who fails in himself lest he should fail in
Christ? Such men Francis therefore rightly called the Minors; the door of heaven is too narrow for those greater. 165

How he left his dwelling because of a donkey-driver's quip

After the new Order became known by its name, an abandoned shack roofed with rotten thatch sheltered Francis
and his companions in some wise, extending over them its
flimsy timbers. Its condition and its very poverty pleased 170
those who dwelt there for a few days, until the rustic driver
of a loaded ass made it distasteful to them with his foolish words. Being compelled to seek shelter from the driving rain, he approached and thus addressed his own ass:

175 "Intra securus, Brunelle, iuuabimus istam
quandocumque domum," quasi diceret, "hii quoque fratres
intendunt cumulare domos." Promissa perosus
edita Franciscus intellectumque latentem,
ad loca se tranfert non sollicitanda procaci
180 uoce uiatorum, soliteque domestica paci.

[Liber 7]

Septimus ostendit fratres orare docentem;
quantus eis apparuerit uigilantibus absens;
quam uilis mundo curauerit esse; quis ipsum
martyrii feruor tumidis commiserit undis.

Interea supplex instat deuocio fratrum
ut Franciscus eos informet qualiter orent.
Ille satisfaciens precibus clementer honestis:
"Peccatis," ait, "et uiciis inuoluimur omnes.
5 Ergo supernorum debens oracio niti
uestra patrociniis proprio non euolet ausu
ad superos, immo mediatrix Virgo Beata
ad Christum, Christus ad Patrem sit mediator.

Salutatio Beate Virginis

"Virgo salutetur sermone uidelicet isto.
10 'O pia Mater, aue Maria karismate plena,
sit Dominus tecum. Benedicta super mulieres

"Enter this house in confidence, Brunellus. In due time we 175
shall be of assistance to this house," as though he were saying, "These friars too intend to accumulate houses." Loathing the utterance and its hidden meaning, Francis conveyed
himself to a place untroubled by the chattering voice of 180
travelers and suited to his accustomed tranquility.

[Book 7]

*The seventh books shows him teaching the friars how to pray; in
how great a form he appeared to them, though absent, while they
kept watch; how vile he strove to appear to the world; what a fervor for martyrdom committed him to the swelling waves.*

Meanwhile the brothers' suppliant devotion insisted that
Francis should instruct them how to pray. Gently consent-
ing to their worthy entreaties, "We are all," he said, "envel-
oped in sin and vice. And so let not your prayer, which 5
should rely on the suffrage of those above, fly forth to
heaven on its own presumption. Rather let the Blessed Virgin be your mediator before Christ, and Christ before the
Father.

A salutation to the Blessed Virgin

"Greet the Virgin with these words. 'O gentle Mother, hail 10
Mary, full of grace, the Lord be with you. Blessed are you

tu uentrisque tui fructus benedictus.' Et istum
sermonem tociens deuocio uestra reuoluat,
hec ut prima sue recolentes gaudia matris
15   gaudia uos faciat perferre nouissima Christus.
Matre salutata, deinceps hac uoce rogetur
Christus: 'Adoramus te, Christe, superna regentem
et terrena, tibi benedicimus, O Crucifixe,
qui cruce sanasti cruciatus, qui reparasti
20   morte tua mortale genus.' Mediantibus istis,
hac prece pulsetur Patris indulgencia summi:

Oracio dominica

"'O sine patre Pater noster, uis insita celis
imperiosa, tue deitatis sanctificetur
nomen, et adueniat regnum, fiatque uoluntas
25   in terra sicut in celo. Cotidianum
panem da nobis hodie dimitteque nobis
sicut nos aliis, set et in temptamina ne nos
inducas fragiles, immo mala cunta repellas.'"

Quomodo cuiusdam fratris uanum timorem sedarit

Has aliasque preces quibus est clemencia summi
30   exoranda Patris fratrum deuota docetur
simplicitas, que tanta fuit ne uerba putarent
ulla sacerdotis grauitate carencia ueri.
Accidit inde semel, dum confessurus adiret
presbiterum quidam de fratribus, ille sacerdos
35   dixit ei, "Caueas ne sis ypocrita, frater."
Illius uoti plus de se quam sibi credens
ingemuit merore graui nullumque dolori

above women and blessed the fruit of your womb.' Your devotion should repeat these words some number of times, so that Christ may cause you to experience latter joys as you recall these first joys of his mother. When you have greeted his mother, beseech Christ in these words: 'We adore you, O Christ, who rule heaven and earth, we bless you, O crucified one, who, being crucified, have healed by means of the Cross and have restored by your death a race doomed to death.' Then through their mediation entreat the exalted Father's mercy with this prayer:

The Lord's Prayer

"'Our Father without father, your kingly power is lodged in heaven. May the name of your Godhead be sanctified, may your kingdom come, and your will be done on earth as in heaven. Give us today our daily bread, and forgive us as we forgive others, but do not lead us in our weakness into temptations, but rather ward off all evils.'"

How he stilled one friar's groundless fears

He taught the brothers these and other prayers, with which to win the mercy of the exalted Father. Their devout simplicity was so great that they thought the words of no priest could lack the weight of truth. Hence it happened once, when one of the friars went to a priest in order to confess, that the priest said to him, "Beware, brother, lest you be a hypocrite." Supposing that that admonition was uttered more specifically about him than simply addressed to him, he moaned with profound sorrow. He laid no word of a

apposuit uerbum consolatoris amici,
pro certo quin ypocritam se crederet, ex quo
40 ille uideretur sic astruxisse sacerdos,
donec Francisci finem facundia nugis
poneret, et uanum faceret residere timorem.

Quomodo ad omnes se habebat

Eius enim placore sui rigidissima sermo
corda penetrabat, prebens releuamina lapsis,
45 spem miseris, lumen cecis, solacia mestis.
De quo ne fratrum dubitaret opinio quanti
esset apud Dominum, signo didicere superno.

Quomodo fratres eum sub specie ignis uiderint

Nocte fere media, cum sol altissimus umbras
contrahit antypodum, procul absistente magistro,
50 pars fratrum sopita iacet, pars orat, et ecce:
igneus inspicitur dimissus ab ethere currus,
cui globus insidens quasi sol micat, undique uibrans
orbiculare iubar, qui fratrum disgregat ad se
directos uisus nimioque reuerberat igne.
55   Excitat alterutrum; quibus ad spectacula sese
mira cohortatis, fit questio quid sibi currus
hic uelit. In primis uariatur opinio; demum
esse notant animam Francisci, quam spera signat
perfectam, currus agilem, splendorque beatam,
60 unde timent uacuos ne forte reliquerit artus.

friendly consoler over the pain, that he should not with certainty think himself a hypocrite, from that time on when   40
the priest appeared to have so admonished him, until Francis in his eloquence set a limit on this foolishness and made
his baseless fear subside.

How he conducted himself toward all

Indeed, his speech in its mildness pierced even the most unbending hearts, offering alleviation to the fallen, hope to the   45
miserable, light to the blind, solace to those in sorrow. The
brothers learned by a sign from above not to doubt how precious he was before the Lord.

How the brothers saw him in a semblance of fire

Nearly at midnight, when at the antipodes the sun at its
highest contracts its shadows, when their master was far off,
some of the brothers lay sleeping, some prayed, and lo! a fi-   50
ery chariot appeared to be sent down from above, in which a
globe shone like the sun, scattering its curving brilliance, se-
questering the brothers' focused gaze to itself, and flashing
with immoderate flame.

They roused one another. When they had directed each   55
other to the miraculous sight, the question arose as to what
the chariot might portend. Opinion at first was varied; finally they recognized the soul of Francis, which the sphere
signified in its perfection, the chariot in its agility, the splendor in its blessedness, so that they feared he might have   60
abandoned his mortal limbs.

Cumque prophecie datus illi spiritus esset,
celitus agnoscens et quos predestinet et quos
presciat eterni series firmissima fati,
ut reprobos reprobet, electos eligat, omni
65 insudat studio. Similes sibi iungere gaudens,
dissimiles uitare studens, et utrosque magistrans,
neutros aspernans, colit hos et sustinet illos.
Attendens frater Richerus quod neque fati
consilium nec mentis eum secreta laterent,
70 excessus recolendo suos quos gesserat olim,
quos et eum conscire timet, uix sperat ut eius
optatum plene queat impetrare fauorem.
Talem Franciscus Richeri ne uideatur
ignorare metum, "Quid," ait, "Richere, uereris?
75 Non te detestor, quicquid deliqueris, ex quo
delicti te penituit ueniamque mereris.
Ne dubites quin firma michi sit gracia tecum."
Quoque suos posset magis inuitare sequaces,
est eadem uirtus diuerso prodita signo.
80 Collectis iterum multis, abscente magistro,
fratribus ad synodum, iussus benedicere frater
Antonius, ponens hoc thema, "Ihesus Nazarenus,
Rex Iudeorum," toto celestia corde
intendens occulos leuat in sublime manusque
85 in cruce distensas Franciscum cernit habentem.
Quod ne credatur ausu simulasse nefando,
celitus infusa quadam dulcedine fratrum
mira coadstantum replet exultacio mentes.
Sic tunc, sic iterum, sic per diuersa frequenter
90 signa representans absentem non quasi uilem,
non quasi terrenum, set iam quasi regna tenentem

And since he had been given from heaven the spirit of prophecy to recognize whom the unmovable sequence of eternal fate predestined and whom it foreknew, he labored with all zeal to reproach the reprobate and to choose the elect. Rejoicing to join those like him to himself, taking care 65 to avoid the others, and instructing both, spurning neither, he fostered the latter and endured the former. Friar Richerus, aware that neither fate's counsels nor the mind's secrets were hidden from Francis, recalling the transgressions that 70 he had once committed, and which he feared that Francis knew, scarcely hoped that he could obtain fully the favor he desired. In order not to appear ignorant of Richerus's fear, "What, Richerus, do you dread?" he asked. "I do not curse 75 you, however you have sinned, since you repent of your offense and deserve pardon. Have no doubt that my favor toward you stands firm." That he might better invite his followers, the same virtue was declared with yet another sign.

When many brothers were again gathered at a synod 80 in their master's absence, Friar Anthony was enjoined to preach, taking as his text, "Jesus of Nazareth, King of the Jews." Focusing with all his heart on heavenly matters, he raised his eyes on high and beheld Francis with his hands stretched out on the cross. That he might not be thought to 85 have feigned this in wicked presumption, a heavenly sweetness perfused the minds of the brothers who were present, and wondrous exultation filled them. Thus at that time, thus once again, thus through various frequent miracles, 90 divine mercy portrayed its servant, when he was absent, not as abject, not as earthly, but glorified him like one

glorificat diuina suum clemencia seruum,
cui uisum mundo nichil est inmundius, et cui
nil proprium preter nil proprietatis habere.

95   Set quamuis carni nichil indulgere uolentem
carne semel uesci febris imperiosa coegit.
Mox ubi conualuit epulum gustasse cruentum
penituit, penamque sibi prouidit, et uni
districte fratri laico precepit ut eius

100 iniceret collo funem traheretque per urbem
Assisii, clamans preconis uocibus, "Ecce,
O ciues, parasitus edax, ypocrita tristis,
qui coram uobis ieiunia laudat et odit
qui pingues pullos auidam congessit in aluum."

105 Exequitur iussus hoc ordine singula frater;
mirantur ciues et dicunt, "Pro semel esis
carnibus affligi sic sustinet iste; uel ergo
sancti sunt fatui, uel nos gens digna perire!"

Quomodo se coram magnatibus uituperari preceperit

Hoc quoque Franciscus fratri preceperat uni,
110 inter magnates ut quandocunque receptus
esset honorifice, ne forte superbia mentem
ipsius efferret, conuicia diceret illi
frater et alpigenam mercatoremque uocaret.
Non pretermittens quin quantumcunque seuera
115 eius adimpleret frater precepta, sedenti
inter honoratos nulla racione pepercit.
Retribuens illi propter maledicta fauorem,
propter probra decus, propter conuicia laudem,
dicere Franciscus consueuerat, "Approbo, frater,

who held sway over kingdoms, to whom nothing seemed filthier than the world, and who possessed nothing of his own, except to possess nothing. But at one time an over- 95 whelming fever compelled him to eat flesh, even though he desired in no wise to indulge the flesh. Upon his recovery, he soon repented that he had tasted that bloody banquet, and set a penance for himself. He strictly charged a lay brother to cast a rope around his neck and drag him through the city 100 of Assisi, shouting with a herald's voice, "Behold, O citizens, a voracious parasite, a sorry hypocrite, who in your presence praises fasts and expresses hatred for any who has packed away fat fowls in his greedy belly." The brother given this or- 105 der carried it out in every detail; the townsmen marveled and said, "This man is prepared to be chastised thus for eating meat once; so either the saints are fools, or else we are a race that deserves to perish!"

How he commanded that he be reviled before the great

This too Francis had commanded one brother: that when- 110 ever he was received with honor among great men, in order that pride might not lift up his mind, that brother should speak reproaches against him and call him a merchant from the Alps. Omitting nothing from the fulfillment of his commands, however harsh, the brother spared him not at 115 all when he sat among the illustrious. Francis rewarded his curses with favor, his reproaches with honor, his abuse with praise, and was accustomed to say, "I agree, brother,

120 omnia que dicis: nec enim decet ut tolerare
filius ista Petri de Bernardone recuset."
Hiis aliisque modis fugit inpudibundus et effrons
humanam quecumque solent attollere mentem;
exspectansque diem Domini que corda reuelat,
125 nullo pertrahitur uoto bona queque gerendi
humano placitura die. Talisque uacando
milicie gestis, sextum compleuerat annum,
nil preter celeste gerens; fortunaque forti
una manet nullasque uices excercet in illum
130 quin indistanter casus interuolet omnis.
    Tempora parua uiro celesti longa uidentur,
seque parum censet tot profecisse diebus,
cui licet assidue uisum sit triste iocari,
tristarique iocus, pasci ieiunia, pastus
135 ieiunare, quies sudare, quiescere sudor.
Non tamen est contentus eo, quin prelia carni
ulteriora sue moueat, propriique cruoris
inpensa certare uelit pro nomine Christi.
Mortis enim desiderio flagrat anxia mentis
140 nobilitas, tedetque more. Neu principis ira,
lictoris feritas aut cause desit honestas,
propositi mens est ut transfretet et reuocandis
predicet ydolatris credi quid oporteat, unde
uel tantum mundo uiuentes (quod quasi mors est)
145 Christo lucretur, uel mundo perditus ipse
cum Christo uiuat (quod solum uiuere uerum est).
Martirio cupiens ita consummare labores,
Parthorum partes proponit adire. (Set intus
Ecclesie flagrante domo, quid quereret extra

with everything you say; nor is it seemly that the son of   120
Pietro de Bernardone should refuse to endure these things."
In this and other ways he fled shameless and barefaced
whatever usually raised up the human mind; and awaiting
the day of the Lord that lays hearts bare, he was swayed by   125
no desire of pursuing whatever "goods" that are pleasing in
these days of humankind. He had completed a sixth year en-
gaging in deeds of such combat, doing nothing but the work
of heaven. A single fortune awaits a brave man and works no
vicissitudes against him but that every circumstance passes   130
by like every other in his eyes.

Short seasons seemed long to that man of heaven, and he
thought that he had accomplished too little in so many
days—even though to him it seemed a sad thing to jest continuously, and sport to mourn; seemed a fast to feast, and a   135
feast to fast; to whom rest seemed labor, and labor rest. Yet
he was not thus content, without waging even further battles against his flesh and wishing to strive at the cost of his
own blood for the name of Christ. Indeed, the nobility of
his mind blazed anxiously with desire for death, and he tired   140
of delay. Lest the wrath of a prince, the savagery of an executioner, or the honor of his cause should be lacking, his mind
proposed to sail abroad and preach to idolaters what they
ought to believe, in order to call them back to the faith, so   145
that he might either gain for Christ those who lived for the
world alone (which is a kind of death), or else, being lost to
the world, might himself live with Christ (which alone is
true life). Thus desiring to crown his labors with martyrdom, he proposed to approach the territory of the Parthians. (But since the house of the Church is in flames within,

150 qui custodit eam? Fidei doctore diserto
     plus Ytalus quam Parthus eget. De plebe loquendo,
     non dico de nobilibus. Fallacia Parthum
     unica seducit, Italum non una set omnis.
     Parthus ab antiquo susceptum scisma tuetur,
155 Ytalus admisse fidei precepta repellit.
     Unius hereseos inuente tutor habetur
     Parthus; adinuentor Ytalus triginta duarum.
     Estque quid hos faciat peccare licencius illis:
     Parthi sunt serui; libertas est Ytalorum.
160 Non ipsi uel primicias in lege statutas
     uel decimas debere Deo; sine uindice peccant.
     Nam si Sanctus eos Pater excomunicet, aut si
     yracundus eis Augustus bella minetur,
     inde nichil curant, neutrum reuerenter, utrumque
165 addixere iugo, prescripseruntque tributum.
     Plebis enim tot ibi sunt milia, quot numerare
     nemo queat, miles quiuis et rusticus idem:
     uim quia miles habet, dominos quia rusticus odit.
     Set taceo; quedam narrari uera uerentur.)
170   Simplicitas autem Francisci sustinet omnes,
     nullius uicii, nullius conscia culpe,
     astutosque uidens, credit quia sint sapientes,
     Ytalie ciues nec credit egere magistro.
     Quocirca Syrios cupiens conuertere, nauim
175 ingreditur. Ventus surgit contrarius, equor
     incipit esse fretum, uia desinit esse salubris.
     Aura fatigatos Geticas appellit ad horas.
     Prestolatus ibi Zephirum, detentus ab Euro,
     tandem Franciscus Boream insurgere sentit.
180 Iamque redire parat, cum non procedere possit.

why should he who guards it seek further afield? Italy more   150
than Parthia is in need of an eloquent teacher of the faith.
While I speak of the common people, I say nothing of the
nobility. A single falsehood seduces the Parthian; not one
but every falsehood seduces the Italian. The Parthian cher-
ishes a heresy received of old; the Italian rejects the precepts   155
of the faith he has received. The Parthian is considered the
protector of one heresy previously contrived; the Italian the
deviser of thirty-two. And there is something that makes
the one people sin with less restraint than the other: the
Parthians are slaves, but liberty belongs to the Italians. They   160
claim to owe God neither the first fruits established in the
Law, nor tithes; they sin with impunity. For if the Holy Father should excommunicate them, or if Augustus in his
wrath should threaten war, they care nothing for it, they
treat neither with reverence, they consign both to the yoke,   165
and set their own tribute. For so many thousands of the
common people are there as none can number; knight and
peasant are just the same, because the knight has power, and
the peasant hates his masters. But I fall silent; some truths
blush to be told.)

Francis's simplicity, being innocent of vice or guilt, en-   170
dured them all, and, seeing shrewd men, believed (because
supposing them wise) that the citizens of Italy were not in
need of a teacher. Therefore, in his desire to convert the Syr-
ians, he boarded a ship. A contrary wind blew up, calm water   175
began to seethe, and the route stopped being propitious. A
breeze drove the exhausted men to Thracian shores. Awaiting the West Wind, held back by the East, Francis at last felt
the North Wind rise up. And now he prepared to return,   180

Christus enim serui uotum, licet utile, propter
utilius reuocat, euuangelicique magistrum
eloquii Parthis negat, Ausoniisque remittit.

[Liber 8]

Indicat octauus Damiate quomodo feruens
ad conuertendos Nilum transiuerit hostes;
qualiter, in reditu uolucres affatus, earum
in laudem Domini siluestria soluerit hora.

Vota retardari non absque grauamine summo
passus et infectis elementa resistere ceptis,
nauim Franciscus uentis dare uela parantem
cernit et Anchoniam nautas properanter ituros.
5 Poscentem reuehi renuunt admittere naute,
non pro defectu nauli, pro pondere nauis,
pro feritate uirum, set pro defectibus esce
que uix sufficiat ipsis in puppe uehendis.
Ille nichil metuens, Christo prestante ducatum,
10 et nauim tacite nautis absentibus intrans,
inferius latet inter equos, ubi diues egenis
danda recondiderat alimenta, suoque clienti
dixerat ut, quociens uescendi tempus adesset,
assignaret eis quodcumque requireret usus.

since he could not move forward. For Christ called back his servant from his purpose, though it was a useful one, for the sake of one more useful still: he denied the Parthians that master of evangelical speech and sent him back to the Italians.

[Book 8]

The eighth book tells how at Damietta he crossed the Nile in fervor to convert his foes; how upon his return he addressed the birds and incited their forest haunts to praise of the Lord.

Not without deepest sorrow did Francis suffer that his intentions were checked, and that the elements opposed his unfinished undertakings. He saw a ship preparing to set its sails to the wind, and its sailors ready to hasten to Ancona. The sailors refused to admit him when he asked to be taken ₅ back, not for lack of fare, for the weight of the ship, nor for the rudeness of the men, but for lack of food, which scarcely sufficed even for those whom the boat was to convey. Fearing nothing, silently entering the ship under Christ's guidance while the sailors were away, he hid below among the ₁₀ horses, where a rich man had stowed food to be given the poor, and told his servant that as often as mealtime approached, he should distribute to them whatever need required.

15   Pontilege redeunt, auellitur anchora, tractis
     funibus, attollunt depressi uela rudentes.
     Prima locum puppi cedit ratis, ultima prore.
     Ingentes replet aura sinus, sub pondere malus
     accrescente gemit detrimentumque minatur.
20   Remigii puppis moderamine recta uolantem
     consequitur proram, uelocior alite nauis
     sulcat aquas, proprioque fere perit obruta uento.
     Iamque uidebatur leucas peragrasse ducentas,
     cum totus subito tenebris obducitur aer.
25   Accelerant nubes, insurgunt undique uenti,
     incipit undarum fieri collisio; nusquam
     equor, ubique fretum; fluctus ardere uidentur.
     Curritur ad funes, dimittunt carbasa naute.
     Set malo circumpositis insibilat aura
30   funibus, et uento ruit impetuosior unda.
     Eiciuntur aque, proiectaque mordet harenas
     anchora, set nauim uenti nichlominus unam
     exagitant omnes, et nunc impellitur Euri
     turbine, nunc Zephiri, nunc Austri, nunc Aquilonis.
35   Nunc supra nubes exurgit, nunc in abissum
     decidit, et portum cupit unum set timet omnem.
     Ille nec ad tempus mare turbat et aera densat
     et nautas terret et nauim girat in orbes
     turbo procellarum. Set donec nulla supersit
40   repressura famem toti substancia naui,
     quid faciant? Restat uia longa, uiatica nulla,
     naufragium prope, terra procul, mors undique certa,
     naufragiique timor, licet intentancia mortem,
     detrimenta famis facit apparere minora.

The seafarers returned, anchor was weighed, the ropes 15
drawn in, and tautened lines raised the sails. The back of the
dock yielded to the stern, the front to the prow. The breeze
filled the huge sails, the mast groaned at the growing burden
and threatened to fail. Under the rowers' guidance, the stern 20
followed straight after the flying prow, the ship cut the water swifter than a bird and nearly capsized, overturned by a
wind in its own favor. And it was now seen to have traversed
two hundred leagues when suddenly the whole sky was covered in shadow. The clouds hastened on, the winds rose on 25
all sides, and the waves began to collide. Nowhere was the
water calm, but everywhere roiling; the waves seemed like
flames. They ran to the lines; the sailors brought down the
sails. But the wind hissed against ropes wrapped around the
mast, and the waves fell with more force than the blast. The 30
water was bailed out, and the anchor, cast overboard, bit at
the sand, but nonetheless the winds all rocked the lone ship.
Now it was driven by the whirling East Wind, now by the
West, the South, the North. Now it rose above the clouds, 35
now fell into the abyss, desired but a single landfall, and yet
feared all. For no short time that maelstrom of storm-blasts
stirred the sea, thickened the air, terrified the sailors, and
spun the ship in circles. But what might they do, until there
remained nothing on the entire ship to repress hunger? A 40
long journey lay ahead without provisions, shipwreck was
imminent, land far off, death certain on all sides, and fear of
shipwreck made hunger's dearth appear the less, even
though it too threatened death. For the nearer every sort of 45

45 Mortis enim quanto genus omne propinquius instat,
   maior eo timor incutitur, totumque cor ad se
   conuertens, alias iubet euanescere curas.
   Nulla tamen possit tempestas tam diuturnam
   dissimulare famem. Set adhuc ibi sola superstes
50 Francisco fratrique suo data porcio uictus
   omnes sustentat, omnes alit, omnibus unam
   distribuit Franciscus eam; tantillaque tantas
   sufficiens releuare fames mirantibus illis
   persistit, nec in assiduo consumitur esu.
55 Quomodo prouenit diuinitus ut saciaret
   milia quinque Ihesus, panes tantummodo quinque
   apponens piscesque duos, partesque (stupente
   geometro) totis maiores esse probaret,
   dum tredecim sportas replerunt fragmina, nullam
60 uero duo pisces et panes quinque replessent:
   sic facit eiusdem diuino gracia signo,
   ut multis diuisa sui substancia serui
   inconsumptibilis maneat maiorque supersit.
      Iam compressa silent uentorum iurgia, nubes
65 pretereunt, nebule subsidunt, nubila cedunt.
   Prosperior nautis datur aura, serenior aer,
   cercior ars, leuius moderamen, amicius equor.
   Vela tument, mare detumuit, ciciusque putato
   Anchonie portus infixa naue tenentur.
70 Gaudent appulsi terris quos longa procella
   terruerat, uictusque breues et utramque salutem
   Francisci meritis asscribunt. Nunc animarum
   custodem recolunt seruatoremque fatentur
   seque recognoscunt per eum subsistere saluos.

death loomed, the greater the terror that struck them and, turning the heart's entirety toward itself, bade other cares vanish. Still, no storm could make them ignore such long-enduring hunger. But a single remaining portion of food, 50 given to Francis and his brother, sustained and nourished them all, as Francis distributed it to everyone. So small a portion sufficed to relieve such great hunger; to their astonishment, it endured and was not consumed despite the continual eating. In such wise it happened that Jesus divinely 55 satisfied the five thousand, though setting out but five loaves and two fishes, and proved (to the geometer's stupefaction) that the parts were greater than the whole, when 60 the fragments filled thirteen baskets, whereas the two fishes and five loaves had not filled a single one: so by divine miracle the same one's grace caused his servant's substance, though divided among many, to remain unconsumed, and even more was left over.

Now the winds' close-packed battles were silenced, the clouds passed on, the mists subsided, the fog gave way. A 65 more favorable breeze was granted the sailors, clearer air, surer skill of sailing, lighter steerage, a friendlier main. The sails swelled, the sea settled, and, swifter than thought, they gained the port of Ancona, the ship held fast within. They 70 whom the long gale had terrified rejoiced to strike land, and they credited to Francis's merits their short rations and their salvation in body and spirit. Now they venerated the guardian of their souls, confessed him as their savior, and recognized that by his doing they were saved.

75 Crebrescit totam Francisci fama per urbem.
 Visuri faciem facientis signa per orbem
 conueniunt ciues auditurique loquentem,
 ex quibus ipse sui multos insignibus armat.
 Set nec amor populi, nec consolacio fratrum,
80 nec dulcor patrie facit euanescere uotum
 martirii, quo tota flagrat deuocio mentis.

Quomodo uolentem transire
Marrochium Dominus reuocauerit

 Marrochium transire parans iter arripit. Ingens
 impedit inceptum, licet approbet, et quia multis
 rectorem prouidit eum, ferale salubri
85 febre retardat iter, indignantemque reuerti
 cogit et inuitum diuina potencia seruat.
 Compulsus redit Assisium, Christique coaptat
 milicie quoscumque potest, certoque ducatu
 dirigit ad brauium cuntos sua signa sequentes.
90 Set necdum preter hec omnia mortis honeste
 refrigessit amor quem preconceperat. Immo
 se naui, nauim uentis comittit et undis,
 et uentos undasque Deo, moderamine cuius
 excipit incolumem portu Damiata cupito.
95 Christicolis contra gentiles et uice uersa
 magnus ibi conflictus erat, Damiataque stabat
 belli causa mouens preciumque futura triumphi.
 Nec seuas miscere manus uel cominus ense
 exerto poterant pugnare, set eminus arcu,

Francis's fame was celebrated throughout the city. The 75
people assembled to behold the face of one who had performed such miracles throughout the world, and to hear
him speak; many of them he armed with his trappings. But
neither the love of the people, nor the consolation of his 80
brethren, nor the sweetness of his homeland, caused his desire for martyrdom to vanish: with it blazed the whole devotion of his mind.

*How the Lord called him back when he
desired to cross over to Morocco*

He took to the road in preparation to cross over to Morocco. God's power, though approving, blocked his great enterprise; because it had destined him as a governor to many,
it delayed his lethal journey with a salubrious fever and com- 85
pelled him, though indignant, to return, saving him against
his will. Perforce he returned to Assisi, and he gained for
Christ's warfare as many as he could; under sure leadership,
he directed toward victory's prize all who followed his banners. But despite all this, not yet did the love of an honor- 90
able death that he had conceived grow cool. Rather, he committed himself to a ship, the ship to wind and waves, the
wind and waves to God, under whose governance Damietta
received him in her longed-for port. A great conflict raged 95
there of Christians against pagans and vice versa, and Damietta stood as the war's efficient cause and the prize of future triumph. They were able to fight neither hand to savage hand nor with drawn sword, but farther off with bow,

100 funda, balista. Plage quasi grando pluebant.
Neue suas possent conferre propinquius iras
illius intererat fluuii pars septima (cuius
uel penitus non est uel inexplorabile reddit
torrida zona caput, oculis inperuia nostris).
105 Hec excercituum mediatrix unda fluebat,
telaque suscipiens ab utraque pluentia parte,
motus aque nullos dilatabatur in orbes,
et momentorum dimensor circulus usquam
non poterat fieri quia punctus ubique fiebat.

Quomodo inermis ad paganos per Nilum transierit

110 O uirtus animosa uiri, qui flumine tanto
cimba transuectus modica, tot solus ad hostes
armatos et inermis abit per tela, per ignes
non extinguibiles, per mille pericula mortis!
Pretendit uia mille metus; plus meta minatur.
115 Set neutras timet ille minas, fluuiumque rapacem
transit et intrepidus medios effertur in hostes.
Ante tamen quam progrediens pertingere possit
ad faciem regis Persarum, cuius ad aures
in primis uerbum Domini deferre uolebat,
120 seuicias plures expertus, fuste cruento
uapulat. Exterius liuet caro, sanguis ab intus
profluit: exterior uiolas uiolencia pingit,
interiorque rosas, nec mens dolet ipsa dolore
artubus artatis quos utraque purpura uestit.
125 Hostis enim cum sit anime caro, cur ea lese
compateretur ei? Qui plus corroborat hostem

sling, and ballista. Blows rained down like hail. A seventh   100
part of the river Nile lay between to prevent them from in-
flicting their wrath nearer at hand. (That stream's source either does not exist, or else the torrid zone, which our eyes
cannot penetrate, renders it unexplorable.) This wave   105
flowed as buffer between the armies, and the water's motion, receiving the weapons that rained down from either
side, did not broaden out into rings, and the circle could nowhere become a measurement of the movement, for everywhere there was another center point.

How he crossed to the pagans unarmed through the Nile

O spirited virtue of this man! Carried across such a river in a   110
little skiff, alone and unarmed he went out to meet so many
armed enemies, through weapons, through inextinguishable
flames, though a thousand deadly perils! His path offered a
thousand terrors; his destination threatened more. But he   115
feared neither threat, crossed the devouring river, and was
fearlessly conveyed into the midst of his foe. Yet before he
could in his progress arrive before the face of the king of
the Persians, to whose ears first of all he wished to bring the
word of the Lord, he experienced more savagery, and was   120
beaten with a bloody cudgel. His flesh grew dark blue without; the blood flowed forth from within: on the outside, the
violence painted him with violets, on the inside with roses,
nor did his mind grieve over the pain when his limbs, covered with both shades of purple, were bound. For since   125
the flesh is enemy to the soul, why should the soul have
compassion on its injury? One who strengthens his foe

et sese plus debilitat. Franciscus obinde
interior nullum cupit exterioris honorem,
cuius nanscissi uult perdicione salutem,
130 pressuris apices, dampnis lucra, funere uitam,
penis delicias; animamque molestia carnis
exhilarat, gemitus confortant, lesio sanat,
probra probant, nocumenta iuuant, angustia soluit.

Quomodo Soldanus eum benigne susceperit

Sancti fama uiri quem nulla domare flagella
135 sufficiunt postquam Persarum castra repleuit,
tantos admirans animos clemencia regis
magnifice suscepit eum preciosaque dona
optulit; ille suis contentus dona refutat
regis et audiri pro summo munere poscit.

Quomodo Franciscus coram rege et populis predicarit

140 Auditurus enim rex ipse silencia turbis
indicit, totosque iubet cessare tumultus,
et famulis, "Michi philosofos accersite," dixit,
"iudicio quorum doceatne fideliter iste
constet, an intendat pocius seducere turbas."
145 Collectis igitur sapientibus, ille loquendo
philosofum sapiens probat ex quo fonte sophiam
hauserit, et totas rapit in celestia mentes
sermonesque nouos edisserit, et quasi sensum
transcendens hominis, nichil ignorare uidetur.
150 Sillogizat enim mortalibus agnita paucis
aut soli manifesta Deo primordia rerum,

weakens himself the more. The inner Francis thence desired no honor of the outer man, by destruction of which he wished to gain salvation; by its oppression, exaltation; by its 130 loss, gain; by its death, life; by its pain, delight. The affliction of his flesh gladdened his soul, his groans brought it comfort, his wounds healing, his reproaches approbation, his injuries aid, his constriction release.

How the Sultan received him with goodwill

Once the reputation of the holy man, whom no scourging sufficed to vanquish, had filled the encampment of the Per- 135 sians, the king's clemency, admiring such courage, sumptuously received him and offered precious gifts; he, content with his own goods, refused the king's gifts and requested as the greatest boon that he should be heard.

How Francis preached before the king and people

When the king in his own person was about to give ear, 140 he enjoined silence upon the crowds and bade all tumult cease. To his servants he said, "Summon my philosophers, by whose judgment we may establish whether this man teaches in good faith, or else intends to seduce the masses." And so, when the wise men had gathered, that wise man, 145 redolent of the philosopher, by his speech proved from what font he had drawn his wisdom, caught up all their minds in heavenly matters, brought forth a new discourse, and, like one who surpasses human understanding, appeared to be ignorant of nothing. For he syllogized the beginnings of the 150 world—known to few mortals, or, indeed, manifest to God

ex quibus insinuet Prime perpendia Cause,
peruersamque scolam Machometi dampnat, et unum
esse Deum, turbamque docet non esse deorum;
155 qualiter ex Uno sunt omnia; quomodo primi
sit mora principii simplex, substancia simplex,
instanti mora simplicior, substancia puncto;
quam mirabiliter essentia talis ubique
tota sit absque loco, semper sine tempore presens;
160 unde superbierit, et quomodo qui fuit olim
Lucifer est lutifer; quantoque redempcio mundi
constiterit precio, quibus incarnacio causis;
qualiter antiquus serpens dampnauerit Euam,
Eua prothoplaustum, prothoplaustus posteritatem,
165 posteritas Christum, serpentem Christus, in ipsum
a quo prodierat compulsa morte reuerti;
quomodo non solum caro glorificata, set ipsas
glorificans animas Christi caro uiuida dotes
excellens anime simul et semel undique tota
170 diuersis sit in ecclesiis, et qualiter unam
Christus in Ecclesiam sanctos confederet omnes;
quomodo baptismus sit spirituale lauacrum
emundans animas a primi labe parentis.
Articulos fidei sic docet ore diserto,
175 philosofos regemque mouet, nullusque nocere
audet ei. Preconis enim sic uoce iubetur.
Itque reditque frequens; set tot conuertere Persas
cum per se non sufficiat, desintque ministri
propositum quibus eius eget, desistere ceptis
180 cogitur et reduci fertur super equora uento.

alone—from which to then infer the consideration of the
First Cause, and he condemned Mahomet's perverse school
and taught that there is one God, and not a mob of gods;
how all things are from One; how the present moment of   155
the First Principle is simple, and its substance simple, its
present moment is simpler than an instant, its substance
than a point. He taught how such an essence is miraculously
everywhere, entirely present without location, always present outside of time; whence Lucifer grew proud, and how he   160
who was once the Light-bearer is now the Filth-bringer; at
what a price the redemption of the world was set, from what
causes proceeded the Incarnation; how the ancient serpent
condemned Eve, Eve the first-made man, he his posterity,
his posterity Christ, and Christ the serpent, when death was   165
forced to turn around against him from whom it had come;
how Christ's flesh is not only glorified, but his living flesh,
glorifying souls and excelling the soul's gifts, is entirely present at one and the same time in various churches, and how   170
Christ brings together all the saints into one Church; how
baptism affords a spiritual washing that cleanses souls from
the stain of the First Parent. So with his erudite speech he   175
taught the articles of the faith, moved the philosophers and
the king, and none dared harm him. So, indeed, the herald's
voice intoned. He passed repeatedly back and forth; but
since on his own he was not sufficient to convert so many
Persians, and the ministers that his plan required were not
at hand, he was compelled to leave off what he had begun
and passed over the deep on a returning wind.   180

Quomodo Damiata reuersus auibus
predicarit

Ad natale solum cum solo fratre reuersus,
non homines solum uerum pecuaria laudes
diuinas efferre iubet, mireque frequenter
accidit ut, quamuis racione carencia, uerbis
185 eius obedirent intelligerentque loquentem.
Dumque iuuat patrie diuersos uisere fines,
iuxta Beuanium collectas agmine denso
cernit aues uarias, quibus exspectare benignum
ipsius accessum placito ducentibus ausu
190 causam miratur, et mansuetudinis eius
unde datum sit eis archanum scire tenorem.
Quas adiens fratresque uocans, "O nobile," dixit,
"primipotentis opus! Quantas exsoluere laudes
uos illi de iure decet, qui corpora mundo
195 uestra superponens plumis amiciuit et alis,
qui uobis planas offendiculoque carentes
in celi regione uias et in aere puro
constituit, nostreque nichil grauitatis habente.
Qui quamuis uno produxerit ex elemento
200 et uos et pisces, uobis tamen altera longe
nobilitas, cicior cursus, diffusius aruum,
maior libertas et diliciosior esca.
Ergo simul laudate Deum, benedicite nomen
eius qui tanto uos insigniuit honore."

How, having returned from Damietta,
he preached to the birds

Having returned to his native soil with a single brother, he bade not only men but beasts to bring forth praise of the divine, and often it miraculously happened that, though they lacked reason, they obeyed his words and understood 185 his speech. And when it pleased him to visit his homeland's various territories, near the Bevano he saw diverse birds in thick flocks. As they led him on, he marveled what caused 190 them to await his benevolent approach with calm confidence, and how it was granted them to know the hidden disposition of his mildness. Approaching them and addressing them as brothers, "O noble work of the Almighty!" he said. "What praises it rightfully befits you to pay him, who set your bodies above the world and clothed you with feathers 195 and wings, who established clear and unimpeded highways in the region of heaven and in the pure air that has nothing of our heaviness. Though he produced both you and the fishes from a single element, your nobility is quite different, 200 your course swifter, your territory broader, your liberty greater and your food more select. Therefore together praise God, bless the name of him who marked you with such honor."

Quomodo ad eius exhortationi omnes aues concinnuerint

205 O rerum natura creans, O gloria quamuis
sensum transcendens nullis incognita rebus!
Vocibus humanis siluestria corda mouentur,
auctorisque sui gaudent mansuescere seruuo.
Unde Creatori se subicit, inde creatus
210 quisque sibi subicit. Nichil est quod obaudiat eius
uocem, qui uoci diuine semper obedit.
In uolucres humana uenit discrecio; quicquid
ille iubebat eas intellexisse putares.
Nam species quamquam diuerse, uox tamen una
215 omnibus, aut uni similis, super ethera concors
effertur, nomenque Dei modulamine laudant
quale sibi natura dedit. Concentibus aer
acclamat, colles reboant, silueque resultant.
Delectatus eis plusquam cithareque lireque
220 cantibus, et letas tollens ad sidera palmas,
per medias Franciscus aues utrobique canentes
fertur, et inmotas atrectarique ferentes
prolixe gaudet tunice contingere limbo,
et benedicit eas dulcique licenciat ore.
225 Permisse surgunt, pedibus tellure repulsa,
celsaque subportant libratis corpora pennis.

How all the birds sang together at his urging

O nature creative of all things, O glory, although surpassing sense yet recognized in everything! The hearts of forest creatures were moved by human voice, and they rejoiced to grow tame before the servant of their maker. Just as he subjected himself to the Creator, so every created thing subjected itself to him. There was nothing that disobeyed the voice of him who always obeyed the voice of God. Human discernment entered the birds; whatever he commanded them, you would think they understood. For however diverse their species, yet one voice of all (or nearly so) was raised in harmony above the ether, and with melody they praised God's name as their nature granted them. The air resounded with their singing, the hills echoed, the forests resonated. Delighted by them more than by the melodies of cithara and lyre, and raising joyful hands to the stars, Francis passed through the midst of birds singing on either side. He rejoiced greatly that, unflinchingly enduring his caress, they touched the hem of his tunic, and he blessed them and with sweet speech gave them license to depart. Dispatched, they rose, pushing off with their feet from the earth, and carried their swift bodies upward on balanced wings.

205

210

215

220

225

[Liber 9]

Nouus yrundineis ponentem frena susurris,
sistentemque uagas, leporis piscisque fauorem
scribit et in uinum conuersam celitus undam,
sanantemque uirum morbis et moribus egros.

Suspiciens miratur aues per inane uagantes
sermonis grauitate sui potuisse teneri,
et tactum uoluisse pati placidumque dedisse
carmen et attente laudes cecinisse supernas.
5   Exemplumque trahens uolucres ubicumque repertas,
ut studeant laudare Deum debere moneri
censet, easque uelut homines inuitat ut aures
inclinent uerbo Domini; blandeque uocatas
quando stare iubet stant, quando surgere surgunt,
10 quando silere silent, et quando psallere psallunt.

Quomodo yrundines eo iubente conticuerint

Gauisus fluxisse suo miracula iussu,
propositum pedes explet iter, quem meta diete
excipit Albianum, turbis ubi mane sequenti
undique collectis, sacra uult proponere uerba.
15 Set tot irundinibus circumuolitantibus auras
et tenues querulo crepitantibus ore susurros
ipse replebatur locus ut nullius ab ipsis
iuxta se positis audiri diccio posset.

[Book 9]

The ninth book records how he curbed the swallows' murmurs and stilled their wandering; the affection of hare and fish; water turned by heavenly means into wine; and how the man healed those sick through disease or in their disposition.

Beholding the birds, he marveled that the gravity of his speech could retain them as they darted through the air; that they willingly endured his touch, poured forth their placid song, and attentively sang praises of the Most High. Taking them as an example, he judged that the birds wherever he found them should be exhorted to praise God, and invited them like human beings to bend their ears to the Lord's word. Being gently summoned, they kept still, rose, fell silent, and sang as he commanded them.

How the swallows fell silent as he bade them

Joyful that these miracles took place according to his command, he pursued on foot his proposed journey, which took him as the day's goal to Alviano. There, the next morning, when crowds had gathered on all sides, he wished to expound scripture. But so many swallows filled the place, flying about through the air and warbling their soft calls from chirping beaks, that bystanders could hear no one's speech.

139

Tantis affectus garritibus ille, "Sorores,"
20 inquit, "sufficiat uos hactenus esse locutas.
Nunc et ego dicam, nunc uestras uocibus aures
inclinate meis, quod nec presumo iubendum,
set uos auctoris moueat reuerencia uestri,
cuius ego sacras populis annuncio laudes."
25 Finierat monitus; tenuere silencia cuncte
manseruntque locis nec presumpsere moueri
donec ad extremum completus sermo fuisset.
Presentes hec intuiti miracula dicunt
inter se quia "sanctus is est meritoque colendus,
30 cuius sic uox est autentica, cuius et ipsa
turba uolatilium non audet omittere iussus."

Quomodo lepus dimissus ab eo sponte
manserit apud eum

Inde petens aliud castrum cui Grecia nomen
imposuit, susceptus ibi dum forte moratur,
non cane set laqueo cursore lepusculus arte
35 captus et insidiis uiuus conceditur illi.
Quem miseratus ait, "Cur uincla, lepuscule frater,
cogeris ista pati, cum sis ita res fugitiua?
Cur non fugisti ne decipereris ab isto
uenatore rudi cuius te rete fefellit?
40 Multorum tibi debuerant exempla cauere,
deceptusque semel ne decipiare secundo
propria te reddat nunc experiencia cautum."
Talia premittens, illum uocat. Ille uocantis
confugit in gremium, factusque domesticus ultro,

Moved by such chattering, "Sisters," he proclaimed, "be 20
content with what you've said thus far. Now I too shall
speak, now incline your ears to my words. I don't presume
to command you, but let reverence for your maker move
you, whose holy praise I declare to the people." He finished 25
his exhortations. The birds all kept silent, remained in their
place, and did not presume to budge until at last his sermon had ended. Those present to behold these miracles said
among themselves, "He is a holy man and rightly to be revered, whose voice is of such authority, and whose com- 30
mands even the winged flock dares not disregard."

How a hare he had released remained
with him of its own accord

From there he sought out another town to which Greece
gave its name, and while he was received and sojourned
there, a little hare cunningly captured not by a running dog 35
but by a deceitful snare was given to him alive. Taking pity
on it he said, "Why, Brother Rabbit, are you constrained to
endure this imprisonment, when you are a thing so prone
to flee? Why didn't you flee and avoid being taken by this
churlish hunter whose nets deceived you? The examples 40
of many should have made you wary. May your own experience now render you more cautious, so that, having been
fooled once, you won't be fooled a second time." Saying such
things, he called the hare. The animal fled into the bosom of
the one who called him, and, being tamed of his own accord,
rather than going out into the field when released from his

45 quamuis libertas sibi restituatur eundi
quo uelit exemptus uinclis non exit in aruum,
set redit in latebras, seruiturusque iubenti
mauult Francisco regredi quam liber abire.

Quomodo piscis quem in aquam
reiecerat luserit coram eo

Sic et aues et quadrupedes notissima sancti
50 mansuetudo uiri sibi conmansuescere cogit.
Nec solum feruet pietate uolucribus auras
restituente, feris siluas, set piscibus undas.
Accidit inde fide maius, mirabile dictu,
cum piscatoris magnum deuocio piscem
55 presentasset ei, tanto gratancius auro
suscipiens fratremque uocans, "In sanguine, frater,
utilitas michi parua tuo consistere posset.
Absit ut ergo meos breuis oblectacio sensus
incitet ut longum uite tibi subtrahat usum.
60 Liber et indempnis ad auita reuertere tecta."
Dixit, et in medias saluandum reicit undas.
Qui libertatis quamuis dispendia passus,
exiciique metum, tamen inperterritus altas
fluminis egrediens latebras, in margine coram
65 seruatore suo ludit, nullumque recusat
accessum tactumue pati, fiducia tanta
experte pietatis inest; nec ludere cessat
donec eum tandem iubeat Franciscus abire.
Cuius preceptum non ausus omittere, corpus
70 concolor argento medio tenus ampne recondit.

bonds, although freedom was restored to him to depart 45
where he would, he retreated to his hiding place and preferred returning in service to Francis as his master rather
than departing in freedom.

How a fish that he threw back into
the water sported before him

So the holy man's renowned mildness compelled both birds 50
and beasts to grow tame toward him. He was fervent in a
mercy that not only restored birds to the air and beasts to
the forest, but fish to the water. So it happened—beyond
belief and wondrous to relate—that a fisherman's devotion
presented him with a great fish. Taking it up more joyfully 55
than so much gold, and addressing it as brother, he said,
"Brother, little profit could come to me from your blood.
Heaven forbid, then, that a brief delight should incite my
senses to deprive you of enjoying a long life. Go back to your 60
ancestral dwellings, free and unharmed." So he spoke, and
cast it back safe into the midst of the waves. Although it had
suffered the loss of its liberty and fear of death, rising nonetheless unperturbed from the depths of the river, it played 65
along the bank before its savior and willingly endured his
approach and touch, such trust it had in the mercy it had
experienced; nor did it cease until Francis at last bade it depart. It dared not disregard his command, but hid its silvery 70
body in the stream's midst.

Unde recedentem grauis infestacio morbi
Franciscum cogit decumbere, set medicinam
exhibitura suo Christi clemencia seruo
in uinum conuertit aquas, que potio gustum
75   dulciter inmutans naturalemque calorem
confortans morbi causas eliminat omnes.
Gracia nec soli Francisco summa medetur,
set per eum multis inpendit utramque salutem.
Ad quem dum terras, dum predia lustrat et urbes,
80   urbis in introitu que dicitur Esculus, egri
conueniunt et fit conflictus ut eius ab ipsis
uestimenta queant uel saltem fimbria tangi.
Nam pro relliquiis uestes ipsius habentur,
quas ita diripiunt ut uix incedat opertus,
85   et panes illi presentant quos benedicat,
quorum mica, sale fidei condita, dolores
mitigat et morbos leuat et nocumenta relegat.

*Quomodo pregnans moriens tactu
habenarum ipsius fuerit liberata*

Arecii mulier partus grauitate laborans,
sanctorum quesita diu suffragia nullis
90   inpetrans precibus, nullis adiuta uel herbis
uel gemmis uel carminibus, phisiceque scientum
sepe set incassum uarias experta medelas
iam iacet exanimis, iam desperata uidetur
presensisse manum resecantis stamina Parche.
95   Lora superponunt lecto morientis amici,
que quia contigerat equitans in partibus illis
Franciscus credunt aliquid uirtutis inesse.

When he left there, a grave attack of illness compelled Francis to take to his bed, but Christ's mercy turned water into wine in order to offer medicine to his servant. The draft, sweetly changing its taste and strengthening the natural heat of his body, drove out all the causes of disease. Grace from on high not only cured Francis, but through him restored health of body and soul to many. When he wandered through the territory, its farms and cities, the sick flocked to him at the entrance of the city called Ascoli, and a struggle began over who might touch his garments or at least their hem. For his clothing was treated like relics, which they so tore off that he could scarcely go clothed, and they presented loaves to him for his blessing, a crumb of which, seasoned with the salt of faith, alleviated pain, relieved illness, and banished injury.

How a woman dying in pregnancy was relieved by the touch of his reins

A woman was experiencing a difficult childbirth at Arezzo. None of her prayers had obtained the long-sought suffrage of the saints. No herbs, gems, or incantations had brought assistance, though she had often, but in vain, tried the various remedies of wise men's physic, and now she lay lifeless, now appeared hopelessly to sense in advance the hand of the Fates cutting her life's thread. The dying woman's friends placed on her bed reins which they believed contained some power, because Francis had touched them while

Protinus illa parit, claususque repagula fetus
soluit et egreditur obtusa cubilia uentris.

*Quomodo funis quo acingebatur
pregnantibus opem tulerit*

100 A simili funem Francisci quo quasi zona
circa principium consueuerat ordinis uti
in Castro Plebis habitans Galfridus habebat.
Quem ne sacra reum possessio redderet, egris
sepe superponens illum mulieribus, ampla
105 inpendebat eis solo solacia tactu.
Tusquelana refert, testatur Narnia, narrat
Eugubium, quod ibi puer extenuatus et eger,
hic mulier nulla discernens luce colores,
uirque paraliticus, ibi femina quam manuale
110 incuruans utriusque manus contractio neruos
inflans articulos nichil excercere sinebat,
Francisci pia pertulerint suffragia, uerbo
contactuque breui longos curancia morbos.

Quomodo fratrem a uexacione demonis liberarit

Horribilis quendam uexabat passio fratrem.
115 Sepe uolutatur spumans, alliditur, artus
discerpens et dilanians, et rictibus ora
distorquens, et nunc se contrahit in breue, nunc se
porrigit in longum, furibundaque lumina toruum
uersat et astantes terret stridore minaci.
120 Talia perpessum Francisci dextera signat
exorcismatibus Sancte Crucis et benedicit.

riding through those parts. At once she gave birth, and the trapped infant broke the barrier to come forth from the blocked chamber of her womb.

How the rope with which he was girded brought
assistance to pregnant women

Likewise, Galfridus, who dwelt in Castro, possessed the rope that Francis had used as a sash in the early days of the Order. So that possession of this holy object should not render him guilty, he often placed it upon ailing women and afforded them much comfort by its mere touch. Tuscolana reports, Narnia witnesses, Gubbio relates, that in one place a thin, sickly child, in another a woman who saw no colors with her eyes, along with a paralyzed man, and in the third a woman who could perform no manual task because of a contraction that curled the muscles of both hands and inflamed the joints—all these experienced Francis's merciful suffrage, which cured prolonged illnesses by brief word and touch.

How he freed a brother from a demon's torment

Horrible suffering tormented a certain brother. Foaming at the mouth, he often thrashed and suffered injury, tearing and lacerating his limbs, twisting his mouth contortedly. Now he curled himself up, now stretched out, wildly rolling his crazed eyes and terrifying those nearby with his menacing shriek. Francis's right hand signed with the exorcisms of the Holy Cross the man who suffered such things, and

Tam sacra tam sacri nequit exorcismata ferre,
set, uexilla uidens diuina, diabolus exit
tristis ad excussum nunquam rediturus asilum.
125 Dum sic antiqui furias eliminat hostis
sanctus et humane contraria queque saluti,
zelum concipiunt et spiritualis ab illo
milicie triginta uiri uexilla capessunt.
    Sancti deuota Gemini susceptus in urbe,
130 obnixis precibus pulsatur ab hospite cuius
uxorem miseram dudum possederat hostis,
ut sacro dignetur opem sibi ferre precatu.
Blandas ille preces exaudit iusta petentis,
tresque uocans fratres, "Nullus uacet angulus," inquit;
135 "unum quisque trium teneat, quartumque tenebo,
sitque figura quasi contradictoria, que nos
in cruce disponat, ne spiritus iste malignus
confidat se posse manus euadere nostras."
Hiis ita dispositis, "Quid," ait, "nequissime demon
140 an nescis, an dissimilas, quia corpora soli
baptizata Deo sedem prebere tenentur?
Ergo tu, cum sis inmundus spiritus, exi,
sub pena tibi precipio, nec uasa furori
usurpare tuo diuina, diabolus, aude."
145 Hiis illo flagrante minis et flagra minante,
tam subito demon abscedit tamque latenter
ut sibi Franciscus hunc illusisse, nec illam
conualuisse putet. Set res ex fine probantur,
neu dubitaretur Deus exaudisse precantem.
150 Accidit ut rursum processu non diuturni

blessed him. The demon could not endure such holy exorcisms of so holy a man, but rather departed in sadness when he saw the divine tokens, never to return to his ravaged lair. When thus the saint had driven out the ancient enemy's ravings and everything contrary to human salvation, thirty men took up under him the banners of spiritual warfare. 125

When he was received into the sacred city of San Gimignano, his host insistently entreated him that by his holy prayers he should bring aid to his poor wife, whom the Foe had long possessed. He heard the mild prayers of a rightful petitioner, and summoning three brothers, "Let no corner remain empty," he said; "each of the three of you, occupy one, and I the fourth, and let our cruciform arrangement stand in contradiction to this malignant spirit's confidence that he can escape our hands." When things were so arranged, he said, "Lo, most wicked demon, do you not know, or do you pretend not to know, that the bodies of the baptized afford a seat to God alone? Go out, then, since you are an unclean spirit, I charge you under penalty, and do not presume, devil, to lay claim to holy vessels for your rage." When Francis blazed forth with these threats and threatened a thrashing, the demon departed so suddenly and secretly that Francis supposed he was mocked, and that the woman had not recovered. But things are proven according to their outcome, lest there should be any doubt that God heard his prayer. It happened that after no long interval of 130 135 140 145 150

temporis intendens non illuc ire, set illac
forte uideret eam, que sensus et racionis
composite compos grates utriusque salutis
ignaro deuota refert, liquideque fatetur
155 quod demon et eo cogente recesserit, et non
ausus eo fuerit interdicente reuerti.

Quomodo a muliere obsessa demonem expulerit

Tunc energuminis longe lateque medentem
urbs de Castello deuote suscipit, et pro
obsessa muliere rogat stridoribus altis,
160 planctibus horrisonis, populi turbante quietem.
Ille sibi fratrem premittit qui studiose
inuestiget utrum spontanea, siue coacta
humanis soleat turbare tumultibus urbem,
siue diabolicis. Obtemperat ille iubenti,
165 et uenit ut temptet quidnam sit. Set uenientem
Franciscum non esse sciens, obsessa cachinnat
et linguam profert, et nares rugat et ore
distorto uarias intendit pingere laruas,
et digitis interposito dat pollice ficum.
170 Ille quasi confusus abit, narratque chachinnum
qualiter obsesse perpessus sit mulieris.
Agreditur Franciscus eam. Non sustinet eius
inclusus demon obsessaque femina uultum,
immo uolutatur in terram. Voce iubetur
175 ipsius mulier exsurgere libera. Demon
exturbatus abit nulloque reuertitur ausu.

time he chanced to see her again there—though he had not intended to travel to that place—and she, being in control of her senses and settled wits, thanked him devoutly for her deliverance in body and soul, of which he had known nothing: she confessed in clear terms that the demon had departed under his compulsion and had not dared return in the face of his prohibition.

How he expelled a demon from a possessed woman

The city of Castello then devoutly received that one who healed the possessed from far and wide, and entreated him on behalf of a possessed woman who troubled the population's peace with loud screams and horrid wailing. He dispatched a brother ahead of him to inquire diligently whether she disturbed the city of her own will or under compulsion, and whether with human or diabolical disruptions. He obeyed Francis's command and came to determine the circumstances. But knowing that the one who came was not Francis, the possessed woman cackled and stuck out her tongue, wrinkled her nose, made various faces with her twisted mouth, and gave him the fig with her thumb stuck between her fingers. He departed like one confounded and told how he had endured the possessed woman's mockery. Francis approached her. The possessed woman (and with her, her inner demon) did not endure his countenance, but rolled upon the earth. By his voice the women was commanded to rise up free. The routed demon departed and never dared return.

Sic exturbantis Furias, facientis in orbe
signa, dietantis egros, releuantis onustos
mos est Francisci, dum predicat, omnia certis
180 explanare modis, uno persistere uultu,
nullius faciem contempnere uel reuereri.
Verum non uno plus paupere mille potentes
extimet, aut uno plus simplice mille peritos.
Set neque iudicio refert ipsius, an uni
185 predicet an multis: operosus predicat uni
ut multis, multis inpremeditatus ut uni.
Circumspecta tamen facundia non apud omnes
est eadem, non uoce rudes informat eadem
qua monet instructos. Rudibus communia quedam
190 ad confirmandos hominum faciencia mores
et quid de uicio, quid de uirtute sequatur,
historiasque patrum, liquideque probancia sanctos
uiuere post mortem miracula, gestaque Christi
et precepta refert, et compungencia mentes
195 sanctorum tormenta quibus meruere coronam;
in quo iusticie consistant siue reatus,
et que pena reos maneat, que premia iustos.
Hiis autem quos et doctrina celebrior et mens
alcior et sensus prouexit acucior, unam
200 de mediis texit uiginti quatuor artem,
et quid uirtutes confederet indicat, et quo
ordine descendant ex primis quatuor omnes;
quis medium reperire labor, quam lubrica uite
semita, quam grauiter possint extrema caueri.

So Francis drove out the Furies, worked miracles upon the earth, treated the sick, relieved the burdened. When he preached, it was his habit to explain everything in a fixed way, to maintain a single expression, and neither to ignore nor to focus on the countenance of anyone in particular. He esteemed a thousand powerful men no more than a single pauper, or a thousand of the learned no more than one simpleton. Neither did it affect his judgment whether he preached to one or to many: he preached as carefully to one as to many, as extemporaneously to many as to one. Yet his circumspect eloquence was not the same before all, nor did he instruct the uneducated with the same words as the learned. To the uneducated he proclaimed certain commonplaces conducive to confirming men's character; what follows from vice and from virtue; the lives of the fathers; miracles clearly proving that the saints live on after death; the deeds and teachings of Christ; the saints' torments which impress themselves upon the mind, and by which they merited their crown; in what consists justice or guilt, and what punishment awaits the guilty, what rewards the just. But to those further advanced by their illustrious learning, a higher mind, and sharper understanding, he expounded an art in twenty-four divisions and explained what unites the virtues, and in what sequence they all derive from four; what labor it is to find the middle way, how slippery is the path of life, how seriously one should beware of its end.

[Liber 10]

Declarat decimus quo papam, quo sapientes
mouerit eloquio, pape presaga futuri
nuncia protulerit, multos releuarit onustos,
sit miseratus ouem miserosque reduxerit agnos.

Nomine uir celeber, uirtute celebrior omni,
tempore sanctus eo pater exstitit urbis et orbis,
culmen honestatis et honoris, Honorius, ad quem
Franciscus ueniens proponere thema iubetur.
5 Ille, licet coram tot fratribus et reuerendo
patre locuturus, non exponencia textum
uerba magistrorum, non integumenta librorum,
non propriam mentem preconsulit, immo repente
oris in excursu quod nusquam cespitat, apte
10 singula continuans exquisitissima, profert.
Retoricos eciam satagens pretendere gestus,
non solum lingua loquitur set corpore toto,
nutibus et signis extraque mouetur ut intus,
et motus artis per motos explicat artus.
15 Cuius ne propria sermo leuitate uacillans
uergat in ambages, inter sua uerba priorum
dicta quasi quosdam serit inter gramina flores,
utque coherenter propriis aliena coaptet,
alta prophetarum reserans enigmata, legis
20 et scripturarum uastas explorat abyssos,
et fidei scrupulos euuangeliique profundum,
ipsiusque Dei secreta latencia mundum.
Sermo suis adeo placet auditoribus, ut plus

[Book 10]

The tenth book declares the eloquence with which he won over the pope and the learned, uttered predictions of the future to the pope, lightened the burdens of many, took pity on the sheep, and led back home the pitiable lambs.

A man illustrious of name, and more illustrious in every virtue, was at that time the holy father of the city and of the world, acme of honor and honesty, Honorius. Francis on arrival was bidden to expound upon a theme in his presence. Though he was about to speak before so many brothers and 5 the reverend father, he did not consult the words of the masters who explain the text, nor the allegories of books, nor his own mind, but rather he brought forth immediately by oral disquisition, fitly pursuing every careful point, a 10 speech that nowhere failed. Taking care as well to offer the gestures of rhetoric, he spoke not with his tongue alone but with his whole body, made movements of head and hand as he was moved from within, and signaled the transitions in his argument by moving his limbs. Lest his speech on ac- 15 count of its facility should veer into ambiguity, among his own words he sowed like so many flowers the words of his predecessors, and in order to fit others' words coherently to his own, unlocking the prophets' deep riddles, he explored the vast depths of the Law and the scriptures, the scruples 20 of faith, the profundity of the Gospel, and the secrets of God himself that lay hidden from the world. His sermon so pleased his listeners that those who understood him better

admiretur eum qui plus intelligit. Omnes
25 querendo tacite fratres mirantur (et ipse
papa) quis in laici sic spiritus ore loquatur,
cuius in auditu deuocio clamat eorum,
ora silent, uultus figuntur, corda mouentur,
intellectus agit, sensus uacat, et racionis
30 erecta facie facies diuina uidetur.
Non tamen hostis abest qui commendanda maligne
carpat, set dominus Huguelinus, episcopus Hosti-
ensis, Francisco clipeus, cui gracia sese
celitus infudit sanctorum uota fouendi,
35 eius uirtutes attollit, dicta tuetur,
et detractores propria grauitate cohercet.

Quomodo noticiam Pape Gregorii primo fuerit assecutus

Huius noticiam patris primumque fauorem
dudum nactus erat, numerum dum forte Minorum
multiplicare uolens Francos Franciscus adiret,
40 cumque recepisset peditem Florencia fessum,
audito quod ibi legatus episcopus idem
esset, adiuit eum. Quem uultibus ille paternis
suscipiens ut erat sidus, flos, gloria, gemma—
sidus honestatis, flos morum, gloria cleri,
45 gemma sacerdotum—quesiuit quo proficisci
uellet et ad quod opus, et transalpare uolenti
persuasit reditum fratresque reuisere iussit,
seque suis precibus comendauere uicissim.
Ex tunc iunxit eos indissociabile fedus,
50 integra pax et uerus amor, talesque fuerunt
in seclo comites quales post secla futuri.

admired him more. Silently questioning, all the brothers 25
(and the pope himself) wondered what spirit spoke thus in
the mouth of a layman. While listening to him, their devotion called out, but their mouths were silent; their faces
were fixed upon him, but their hearts moved; their understanding was active, their sensuality was stilled, and the
divine countenance of reason was seen in their upturned
countenance. Nevertheless, a foe was at hand to detract 30
with ill will from what should have been commended. But
the lord Ugolino, bishop of Ostia, a shield to Francis, upon
whom heavenly grace was poured out to further the prayers
of holy men, extolled his virtues, defended his words, and by 35
his own authority warded off detractors.

How he first attracted the notice of Pope Gregory

Francis had first won this father's attention and favor when
in his desire to increase the Minors' number he was en route
to the Franks. Having arrived exhausted on foot in Florence, 40
and hearing that the bishop-legate was present, he approached him. That man, with fatherly countenance receiving him like a star, a flower, glory, a gem—the star of hon- 45
esty, the flower of good character, the glory of the clergy, the
gem of priests—asked where he was headed and why. He
persuaded him to come again (since he wished to cross the
Alps), and bade him visit the brothers once more, and each
commended the other to his prayers. From then on, they
were united by an indissoluble bond of pure peace and true 50
love, and were such comrades in this world as they will be at

Expertusque sacer sacrum, fidusque fidelem,
tanti Franciscus tutele presulis omnem
ordinis et fratrum curam commisit agendam.
55 Depositum suscepit onus nulloque fefellit
presul in articulo, quem premia quanta manerent
sepe profabatur Franciscus pontificemque
tocius mundi presaga uoce uocabat.
Iam rebus se dicta probant: qui tunc Huguelinus
60 nunc est Gregorius: qui tunc caput unius urbis
nunc caput est orbis, in quo uiget ordo Minorum.

Quomodo Dei iudicio magnates honorem ei detulerunt

Et bene summorum meruit reperire fauorem
cuius honorabat deuocio grata pusillos.
Iustus namque Deus sua cuilibet acta latenter
65 retribuit, talesque sibi reperire meretur
maiores, qualem se quisque minoribus offert.
Eius uero modum superans miseracio, postquam
omnia dispersit, nec suppetit ulla facultas
unde satisfaciat propriis affectibus, audet
70 ore uerecundo auidam confundere frontem,
mendicans a diuitibus quid donet egenis.
Nec solum sustentat eos, set honorat et omni
uoce molestari prohibet, Christique pusillos
ne quis presumat tumidis offendere uerbis,
75 fratris ab unius exemplo corripit omnes.

its end. Francis, a holy man, found him holy, and, a man of
faith, found him faithful, and he entrusted to the protection
of such a bishop the execution of all care for his order and
his brothers. The bishop assumed the burden laid upon him   55
and failed in no point; Francis often foretold what rewards
awaited him, and with prophetic voice called him pontiff of
the whole world. His utterances are now proved true by the
outcome: he who then was Ugolino now is Gregory; he who   60
then was head of a single city now is head of a world in which
the order of the Minors flourishes.

How by the judgment of God great men paid him honor

And rightly did he deserve to receive the favor of the greatest men, since his welcome devotion honored the small. For
God in his justice covertly rewards the deeds of every man,
and each deserves to find his superiors disposed to him just   65
as he presents himself to those beneath him. But once he
had distributed everything and had no further means to satisfy his own impulses, his mercy, surpassing all moderation,
dared to mingle humble entreaty with an appearance of ava-   70
rice, as he begged from the wealthy what he might give to
the poor. Not only did he support them, but honored them
and forbade with his every word that they should be troubled, and from the example of one brother he corrected all,   75
lest any should presume to offend Christ's little ones with
proud words.

Quomodo fratrem quemdam pauperi
obiurgantem correxerit

Ille uidens inopem, "Caueas, karissime," dixit,
"ne paupertatem simules." Franciscus ut audit
talia dicentem iubet ut sibi dicta remitti
nudus et ante pedes prostratus pauperis oret.
80 Hec est Francisco reuerentia pauperis, ut de
paupere dicta notet de Christo scandala dici.
Et si quem uideat lapides aut ligna ferentem
aut aliud pondus non absque labore ferendum,
supponens humeros quamquam breue robur habentes,
85 mauult ipse premi quam pauper mole prematur.
Sic inhonoratos deuotus honorat, onustos
exhonerat, quem non hominis solummodo, uerum
et bruti miseret miserum quodcumque ferentis.
       Inde per Anchonie confinia dum, comitatus
90 Paulo cui suberant fratres in partibus illis,
siluas et fluuios, saltus pertransit et agros,
in grege caprarum septam fetentibus hircis
cernit ouem, Paulumque uocans, "Dic, Paule uidesne,"
inquit, "ut hec inter capras incedit et hyrcos?
95 Sic inter scribas iuit Ihesus et Phariseos.
Hinc precor ut precium soluentes de grege fedo
educamus eam." Consentit Paulus; at ambo
quid preter uiles tunicas exponere possint
circa se non inueniunt. Set forte uiator
100 qui transibat ouis precium persoluit emende.
Introeunt urbem; miratur episcopus unde

How he corrected a certain brother
who was rebuking a pauper

That man, seeing a poor fellow, said, "Beware, best beloved, of feigning poverty." When Francis heard him say such a thing, he commanded that, naked and prostrate before the pauper's feet, he should beg forgiveness for his words. Such was Francis's reverence for the poor, that he viewed words spoken of a poor man as a scandal spoken of Christ. Even if he saw anyone carrying stones or wood or another burden that could not be carried without labor, setting to with his own shoulders, however slight of strength, he preferred himself to be weighed down, rather than that a poor man should be weighed down by that mass. Thus he devoutly honored the dishonored, unburdened the heavy-laden, taking pity not only on men, but on beasts carrying any wretched load.

When he was thence crossing forests and streams, woodland pastures and fields through the territory of Ancona, in the company of Paul, who presided over the brothers in those parts, he saw a sheep surrounded by stinking billies amid a flock of goats, and summoning Paul, he said, "Tell me, Paul, do you see how this ewe walks among the nannies and billies? So Jesus passed among the scribes and Pharisees. And so, I beg you, let us pay the price and lead her forth from this stinking herd." Paul agreed; but neither found about their persons anything to barter save their wretched tunics. But as chance would have it, a passing wayfarer paid the price of the sheep they aimed to buy. They entered the city; the bishop marveled how it happened that two men so

80

85

90

95

100

accidat ut tanquam fatui duo tam sapientes
sic unam dignentur ouem traducere secum.

Quomodo dominabus Sancti Seuerini
ouem traderit alendam

Egressos urbem domus excipit hospita Sancti
105 dicta Seuerini, dominabus ydonea sedes
corpora casta Deo mentesque dicantibus almas.
Tradit eis Franciscus ouem clementer alendam.
Lete suscipiunt et multo tempore seruant,
de cuius tunicam Francisco uellere mittunt,
110 quo secus Asisium sinodum celebrante, minister
ingrediens, "Pater, hanc habeas ex parte tuarum,"
dixit, "ouisque tue tunicam de uellere textam."
Donum Franciscus capit acceptabile, narrans
fratribus euentum. Fratres letantur in ipsa
115 simplicitate patris tantum consistere fructum.

Quomodo agniculos morti addictos
tunica sua redemerit

Nec modo Francisci pietas semel hoc ita fecit,
set quociens animal uidit miserabile cuius
uel prece uel precio posset differre dolorem.
Cuius ut exemplum referam de milibus unum,
120 fratre supradicto comitatum Marchia rursus
excipit Anchonie predicta, duosque ferenti
obuiat agniculos quorum, pendente deorsum
pondere, uincla pedes astringunt dura tenellos,
oraque soluentes miseri balancia uoce

wise should thus like two fools see fit to lead a single sheep with them.

How he handed the sheep over for feeding
to the nuns of San Severino

When they left the city, the guest quarters of a house dedi- 105
cated to San Severino received them, a dwelling fit for the
nuns who dedicated their chaste bodies and pious minds to
God. Francis mercifully handed over the sheep for them to
feed. They received it joyfully and long kept it, and they sent
Francis a tunic made from its wool. When he was celebrat- 110
ing a synod at Assisi, a servant entered and told him, "Father, take from the portion of your sisters and of your sheep
this tunic woven from its wool." Francis accepted the welcome gift, telling the story to his brothers. The brothers rejoiced that such profit came of their father's simplicity. 115

How he purchased with his own tunic
lambs consigned to slaughter

Francis's mercy did thus not just once, but as often as he saw
some pitiable animal whose suffering he could avert by entreaty or purchase. To relate a single example among thousands, the aforesaid Marche of Ancona welcomed him again, 120
along with the aforesaid brother, and he came upon a man
who carried two little lambs whose delicate feet were tied
in bonds, their weight hanging down, and with the voice

125 quam natura dedit, emittunt signa doloris.
     Inferri nocumenta piis et pessima cernens
     et peiora timens, querit Franciscus ab ipso
     qui portabat eos fieri quid debeat inde.
     Ille refert, "Intrabo forum uendamque necandos
130 carnifici." Franciscus ad hec, "Ne feceris," inquit,
     "set placidus placidis, insons insontibus esto.
     Quoque libens parcas, quantum daret ut morerentur
     ipse tibi lictor? Tantum dabo ne moriantur."
     Sic pia pro miseris deuocio supplicat agnis.
135 Neue superuacuo sermone ceciderit auras,
     exutus clamidem dat agresti, lege statuta
     et iuramentis interuenientibus, ut de
     compedibus uinctos educat et educet agnos.

[Liber 11]

Explicat undecimus res quomodo duxerit omnes
hortandas laudare Deum fratresque uocarit;
qualis homo fuerit; natalia quomodo Christi
festa celebrarit propriis recitata figuris.

Optima uirtutum pietas infusa sereno
sic animo miseris fert adiutoria rebus,
nil fieri crudele sinens set quaslibet arcens
seuicias dampnumque timens conscire cruoris.
5 Nec minus est simplex quam clemens, set quasi quoddam

nature gave them the poor things opened their bleating 125
mouths to express their pain. Seeing that the worst treat-
ment was inflicted on them, and fearing even worse, Francis asked the man who carried them what would happen
next. He replied, "I shall go to market and sell them for the
butcher to slaughter." To these words Francis replied, "Don't 130
do it, but be peaceable toward peaceable creatures, and innocent toward the innocent. To make you glad to spare
them, how much would the executioner give for them to
die? I'll give you that much that they should not." Thus his
merciful devotion interceded for the wretched lambs. Lest 135
he should assail the air with vain speech, having shed his
cloak, he gave it to the fieldworker, by stipulated contract
and exchange of oaths, that he might take the bound lambs
from their hobbles and rear them.

[Book 11]

*The eleventh book explains how he judged that all beings should be
exhorted to praise God, and how he called them his brothers; describes what sort of man he was; tells how he celebrated the feast of
Christ's birth, narrated through the appropriate images.*

Pity, that best of virtues, thus infused in his calm mind,
brought succor in distress, allowed nothing cruel to be per-
petrated, but fended off savagery of every kind and feared
to bring about bloodshed. No less simple than gentle, he 5

electrum redolet, quod conficit una duorum
mixtio, simplicitas clemens, clemencia simplex.
Hiis alis sublime uolans — sublimior astris,
inferior sese — socialiter omne creatum
10 tractat et ad ueram docet aspirare salutem.
Et socio subiecta sibi dignatus honore,
sicut Ananias, Azarias, Misael, unam-
quamque creaturam fraterno nomine censens,
dulciter affando studet ad preconia Summi
15 inuitare Boni: celos et sidera, solem
et lunam, tenebras et lucem, tempus et annos,
ymbriferas nubes et uersicoloribus yrim
distinctam radiis, tonitrus et fulgura, rores
et pluuias, uentos et brumas, frigus et estum,
20 aera qui mundi complectitur undique centrum,
usque speram sese protendens, omnia mutans
humiditate sui, mutatus ab omnibus idem,
et genus aligerum speciesque uolatilis omnis,
tellurem mare circuiens, quod luna latenter
25 incitat, et causans centri natura Caribdim,
squamiferos pisces conchisque natabile uulgus,
ponderibusque suis libratas undique terras,
quas eque distando ligat reuerencia celi,
montes et ualles, campos et prata, metalla
30 et lapides, et quas numerus non prendit harenas,
fontes et fluuios, flores et gramina, siluas
et segetes, ortos et uites, nobiliusque
omnibus hiis animal genus, innumerasque sub illo
reptilium species, animalque ualencius istis
35 quadrupedes, partim domitos partimque feroces,
et genus humanum cui cetera queque ministrant,

was like an alloy that a single mixture forms of two components—a merciful simplicity, a simple mercy. Flying high on
these wings (higher than the stars, but lower than himself)
he treated every creature as a companion, and taught it to   10
aspire to true salvation. And deigning to honor as his fellows things subject to himself, thinking like Hananiah, Azariah, and Mishael that every creature should be called by
the name of brother, he was zealous to summon them with   15
sweet speech to praise of the Highest Good: heaven and the
stars, sun and moon, darkness and light, seasons and years,
rain-bearing clouds and rainbows decked out in multicol-
ored rays, thunder and lightning, rain and dew, wind and
frost, cold and heat; the air that on every side enfolds the   20
earth as its center, extending itself everywhere as a sphere,
changing everything by its humidity, changed by all things
at the same time, and the winged race and every species of
flying thing; the ocean that encircles the earth, which the   25
moon secretly influences; the nature of the center that cre-
ates Charybdis, the scaly fishes and the race that swims in
shells, the landmasses everywhere balanced by their own
weight, which reverence for heaven constrains at due distance, mountains and valleys, fields and meadows, metals
and stones, the sands that number does not comprehend,   30
springs and rivers, flowers and grasses, forests and standing
crops, gardens and vines; and the animal kingdom nobler
than all these: at its lowest level, countless species of rep-
tiles, and animals more worthy than these, the four-footed   35
creatures, some tame and some wild, and the human race
whom all the others serve, and that noble cohort of heaven

ordinibusque nouem distinctum nobile celi
agmen—et effectus nature prouocat omnes,
laudibus ut Primam studeant attollere Causam.

Quomodo eius simplicitas scriptis honorem detulerit

40 Nec solum uenerans nature facta set artis
ficta, decus nimium scriptis ubicumque repertis
exibet, et tollens abiecta reponit honeste.
Et si scribatur quandoque superflua casu
littera, simplicitas ipsius tam reueretur
45 scripturas ut eam deleri non paciatur.

Descriptio Francisci secundum corpus

Supradicta tibi Franciscum carmina pingunt.
Neue tuus dubia teneatur ymagine sensus
quam pocius recolas, hanc corporis accipe formam.
   Stature mediocris homo, uicinior autem
50 exiguo Franciscus erat, set corde gigantem
effigians, cuius nigri mollesque capilli,
erectum spericumque caput, subuecta breuisque
auris, defossa sinuosaque timpora, leuis
paruaque frons, humiles rectique superciliorum
55 arcus, subnigre circumspecteque pupille,
paccate blandeque faces, iocunda placensque
effigies, simplex directaque linea nasi,
exhauste tenuesque gene, macra pressaque labra,
coniuncti niueique sedent ex ordine dentes,
60 raris barba pilis nigra, laxis guttura fibris
marcida, subuectis humeri ceruicibus alti,
brachia parua, manus tenues, subtilia crura,

divided into its nine orders. And so he summoned all the effects of nature to attend to the praise of their First Cause.

How his simple nature reverenced written documents

Venerating not only nature's creations but art's contrivances, he paid inordinate honor to written documents wherever he found them, and, rescuing those that had been cast away, he stored them with respect. Even if an otiose letter was at any time written by accident, his simplicity so revered writing that he would not suffer it to be destroyed.

A description of Francis according to physical appearance

The above-mentioned songs represent Francis for you. Lest your senses be hindered by an unclear image, listen to this description of his body for you to remember better.

Francis was a man of medium stature—yet closer to short—but imitating a giant in his heart. His hair was black and soft, his head upright and round, his ears flat and small, his temples sunken and ridged, his forehead smooth and small, the arcs of his eyebrows low and straight, his pupils nearly black and searching, his eyes calm and gentle, his likeness agreeable and pleasing, the line of his nose unbroken and straight, his cheeks hollow and slight, his lips thin and compressed, and his snow-white teeth sat joined in order. His beard was black with wispy hair, his throat withered with lax sinews, his shoulders high, with his neck raised above them, his arms small, his hands thin, his thighs slight,

exiguique pedes, digiti manuumque pedumque
proceri, carnemque domans asperrima uestis.

Descriptio morum eiusdem

65 Corpore perpenso, si uis perpendere mores,
mente fuit simplex et supplex, carne pudicus
et celebs, utraque nitens et purus, in astris
diues et excelsus, in terris pauper et ymus.
Discumbendo sitit et ieiunat, recubando
70 obsecrat et uigilat, bellando sudat et alget,
affectu dulcis et rectus, corde benignus
et pius, auxiliis intendens et studiosus,
sensu perspicuus et mobilis, ore disertus
et celer, ingenio feruens et acutus, ad omnes
75 clemens et lenis, ad se crudelis et asper,
ad dicenda sagax et sollers, ad facienda
prouidus et sapiens, ad discucienda morosus
et grauis, ad ueniam uelox et promtus, ad iram
frigidus et torpens, ad singula cautus et aptus.

Causa supradictarum descripcionum

80 Forte superuacuum credas depingere sancti
effigiem moresque uiri. Set oportuit ambo
describi, nam causa subest et ydoneus usus.
Talis enim completa breui descripcio uersu
qualem Franciscum recolam uel ymaginer in se
85 continet expressum mentique relinquit ydeas
partim consimiles, etsi non prorsus easdem.

his feet little, his fingers and toes long, and his very rough clothing taming his flesh.

A description of his character

Having considered his body, if you want to consider his 65 character, he was simple and suppliant in mind, chaste and celibate of flesh, shining and pure in both, wealthy and exalted in heaven, poor and abject on earth. At the table he thirsted and fasted, lying in bed he prayed and kept watch, 70 in combat he sweated and was cold, being sweet and upright in his affections, benevolent and merciful of heart, intent and zealous in giving aid, clear and swift in his understanding, eloquent and quick of speech, fervent and sharp of wit, gentle and easy toward all, cruel and harsh toward himself, 75 wise and skilled in what he said, provident and wise in action, deliberate and slow to judge, swift and ready to forgive, cool and sluggish toward anger, careful and well suited in everything.

The reason for the aforesaid descriptions

You might perhaps suppose that depicting the saint's ap- 80 pearance and character is unnecessary. But it was fitting to describe both, for a reason and suitable benefit is indeed involved. Such a description, completed in brief verse, contains within itself Francis as I recall or imagine him, and af- 85 fords the mind ideas of at least partial likeness, even if not entirely identical.

Quomodo partum Virginis representans
se et multos compunxerit

Monstris iam dudum domitis mundoque subacto,
ardua Francisci uirtus immilitat astris,
nil mortale gerens. Semper misteria Christi
90   quid meditetur habent. Hanc incarnacio Verbi,
hanc hominis stimulans assumpti Passio nunquam
inmemorem sinit esse sui, cordisque medullas
concremat et celi facit exardescere uoto.
      Hec eciam propriis representare figuris
95   deliciasque suas aliis impendere gaudet.
Porro semel celebrare uolens natalia Christi,
effingi presepe iubet. Sua pabula fenum
bos asinusque trahunt, et adest quodcumque decenter
uirginei recitare potest misteria partus.
100 Ad sacra conueniens populus sollempnia, replet
ecclesiam, dat cera faces, thus spirat odorem.
Post matutinas misse celebrantur ad illud
festum spectantes, Euuangeliumque canoro
Franciscus dulcore legit, tacitoque sedenti
105 sermonem populo facit, indurataque corda
mollit et ex duris producit flumina saxis;
mixtaque leticie resilit conpunccio, plausus
desiccat lacrimas, humectat lacrima plausum,
totaque nox instansque dies in cantica festi
110 exit et in laudes pueri de uirgine nati.
Acceptans celebrata sibi misteria Christus
premia retribuit, fenique superstitis esu
bruta relaxantur quocumque tumencia morbo.
Eiusdem tactu pregnantes et diuturna

How by representing the Virgin's childbearing
he moved himself and many others

Having long tamed monsters and subdued the world, Francis's lofty virtue exercised itself among the stars, undertaking nothing mortal. Christ's mysteries always contained something for him to meditate upon. The incarnation of the Word, the Passion of his assumed humanity, goaded his virtue never to forget itself, enflamed the marrow of his heart, and caused it to blaze with desire for heaven.   90

He also rejoiced to portray these matters according to their own imagery and to share his pleasure with others. So, wishing on one occasion to celebrate Christ's birthday, he ordered the construction of a manger. Ox and ass received straw as their fodder, and everything was present that could honorably relate the mysteries of the Virgin Birth. The populace, coming to these holy solemnities, filled the church, candles gave light, incense breathed forth its fragrance. After Matins, Mass was celebrated before those who witnessed that feast, and Francis read the Gospel with a tuneful sweetness and preached a sermon before the congregation as they sat in silence: he softened their hardened hearts, and brought forth streams from hard stones. Compunction mixed with joy sprang forth, joy dried their tears, tears moistened their joy, and the whole night and following day passed in the songs of the feast and in praise of the child born of a virgin. Christ granted a reward in acceptance of the mysteries celebrated in his honor, and beasts, when they ate the leftover hay, were released from the swelling of any disease whatsoever. By touching it, pregnant women   95   100   105   110

115 mole laborantes facili soluuntur hyatu,
obtuseque patent pueris nascentibus alui.
Presepisque locus nunc est in honore beati
cellula Francisci populo gaudente dicata.

[Liber 12]

Certa duodecimus predicit tempora mortis.
Apparet cherubin crucifixus. Passio Christi
afficiens animam perhibetur in artubus extra.
Triste dolens oculos medicum uix curat adire.

Non cessans a miliciis quibus alta premuntur
colla superborum, cohibendo nociua, domando
monstra, tribus lustris totidem subiunxerat annos.
Dumque semel Fuligineum fuligine purgans
5 peccati, uerbique Dei fulgore serenans,
pernoctaret ibi fratri pulcherimus uni
presbiter apparet respersus timpora canis.
Viso frater eo miratur, at ille, "Fer," inquid,
"nuncia Francisco: sit premunitus ad horam.
10 Parcha stat ante fores, annis pulsura duobus.
Istud habet spacii, nec tempora plura supersunt."
Francisco perpensa refert prenostica frater.
Qui, sibi perpendens instare nouissima uite
tempora, desertum secrecior introhit hospes,
15 ut, si quis pedibus terrenus puluis adhesit,

who labored under their long burden were released into an 115
easy childbirth, and blocked-up wombs opened for the children being born. The place of that manger is now a chapel
dedicated, to the joy of the people, in honor of the blessed
Francis.

[Book 12]

The twelfth book predicts the sure time of his death. The angel ap-
pears crucified. The Passion of Christ as it affects his soul is re-
vealed externally in his limbs. Grievously pained in his eyes, he
scarcely takes trouble to find a physician.

Unstinting in the combat that presses down the necks of
the proud, he passed eighteen years constraining and subdu-
ing noxious monsters. When once he was cleansing Foligno
of the tarnish of sin and making it bright with the splendor 5
of God's word, as he passed the night there, a handsome
priest with white hair scattered at his temples appeared to
one of the brothers. The brother marveled at the sight of
him, but the priest said in answer, "Take this message to
Francis: let him be fortified in advance against the hour. Fate 10
stands at the doors and will knock in two years. He has that
much time, but no further seasons remain." When the
brother had considered these prophetic words, he reported
them to Francis. Considering that the last period of his life 15
was at hand, Francis entered the desert in more clandestine

excuciat, mentemque meram non distrahat ullis
Martha ministeriis, set contemplacio totam
occupet et reliquos superis indulgeat annos.
Dumque moram faciens ibi contemplatur et orat,
20 nil preter Christum uel corde uel ore reuoluens,
inspirante Deo coreptus amore sciendi
quid sibi fatorum series prouiderit, et quo
tramite de terris sit migraturus ad astra,
anxius inuigilat: humana quod quia non est
25 arte requirendum, diuina sorte requirit.
Porro superponens altari grande uolumen
ex euuangeliis contextum, pronus adorat
et petit hoc ut ei Dominus manifestet aperti
prima parte libri, libroque patenter aperto
30 in primis offert Domini se passio Ihesu
Christi. Neu casu sic euenisse putaret,
rursus idem cernens in libro rursus aperto
multociens miratur idem contingere, uel si
non eaedem uoces, eadem sententia semper.
35 Ex quo, sicut erat uir prudens, coniicit ante
mortem se grauibus subici debere flagellis.

Quomodo uiderit seraphin crucifixum

Quoque probabilior ea coniectura uideri
possit et ambigui tenebras abstergere cordis,
succedens ad idem facit altera uisio, cuius
40 indicio seraphyn sex alas cernit habentem,

visitation, so that if any earthly dust still clung to his feet, he might shake it off, and so that Martha might not distract his pure mind with any duties, but that contemplation should occupy it entirely, and lavish his remaining years on things above. And while he tarried there in contemplation and prayer, attending with heart or speech to nothing but Christ alone, and seized by God's inspiration with a passion for knowing what the sequence of fate foresaw for him, and the path by which he would pass on to heaven, he kept anxious vigil: because this must not be sought out by human endeavor, he sought it out according to divine lot. At once placing on the altar a great volume composed of the Gospels, he prostrated himself in prayer and entreated the Lord to manifest this to him by the first passage of the book to open; and when the book was opened, the Passion of the Lord Jesus clearly and immediately presented itself to him. Seeing the same passage when the book was opened again, lest he should suppose this had happened by chance, he marveled that the same thing occurred so many times, if not in the same words, then at least always according to the same content. As a result, wise man that he was, he surmised that before his death he must be subjected to grave afflictions.

How he saw the seraph in crucified form

That his surmise might seem more likely, and that all the murkiness of a doubtful heart might be wiped away, another vision followed signifying the same as the first. According to its message, he saw a seraph with six wings, with feet

coniunctis pedibus, extensis in cruce palmis,
alarumque duas supra caput eius in altum
ire, duas corpus amicire, duasque uolare,
aut in procinctu uidet apparere uolandi.
45 Heret in aspectu, conciuem namque futurum
exultare iubet tanti presencia ciuis.
Hoc autem dubitat contristaturque studendo
quale sibi talis pretendat uisio mirum,
cur ita res simplex inpassibilisque uideri
50 suppliciis addicta uelit, multumque laborat
scire, set in sese reperit quod querit in illo.
Passio namque Ihesu sic permanet insita cordi
eius, sic anime totis inpressa medullis,
ut minus abscondi queat exteriusque redundet,
55 annexamque sui consignet ymagine carnem,
et ueluti per diaphonos transpareat artus.
Quinque Redemptoris in eo quasi uulnera certis
apparent inpressa locis. Vix lancea possit
non credi fodisse latus, manibusque uideres
60 et pedibus clauos ex ipsa carne subortos,
et signata suis referuntur ydonea signis.
Mortis enim Domini caro conplantata figure
imperiis anime penitus subiecta laborans,
et non manducans, triturans ore ligato,
65 saucia ciliciis, attrita laboribus, esa
uermiculis, constricta gelu, resoluta calore,
extenuata fame, post tot certamina tandem
tot defecta malis uarios insurgere morbos
sentit et exhaustas non posse resistere uires.
70 Frontis et insignes geminas animeque fenestras
obturant nubes, perturbant nubila, neruum

joined and hands extended on a cross, and he saw that two
of the wings rose on high over his head, two covered his
body, and two flew, or looked to be preparing for flight. He   45
stopped short at the sight, for the presence of such a citizen of heaven bade his future comrade to rejoice. But he
hesitated and grew sad in preoccupation over what sort of
marvel such a vision might portend to him, why a being so
simple and impassible should wish to be seen consigned to   50
torment, and he labored greatly to understand, but found
within himself what he sought in the angel. For the Passion
of Jesus remained so ingrown in his heart, so impressed on
all the marrow of his soul, that it could scarcely be hidden
and overflowed so as to be seen externally, marked his flesh,   55
which was conjoined to it, with its image, and shone through
as though his limbs were transparent. The Redeemer's five
wounds appeared as though imprinted in their sure places.
The lance might scarcely be believed not to have pierced his
side, and you might have seen the nails protruding from the   60
very flesh of his hands and feet, and these signs suitably recalled what they signified. His flesh—implanted with the
image of the Lord's death, laboring in complete servitude to
the commands of his soul, eating nothing (like an ox threshing while muzzled), wounded by hair shirts, worn down by   65
labor, eaten with maggots, frozen with cold, melted by heat,
weakened by hunger, finally undone after so many struggles
and by so many ills—perceived that various diseases were at-
tacking, and that its exhausted resources could not resist.
A cloudiness blocked and murkiness troubled the two no-   70
ble windows of his face and soul; that is, an intolerable pain

scilicet opticum dolor intollerabilis angit.
Cachochimis pupilla rubet densataque uisum
palpebra deformat aciesque molestia torquet.
75 Inuitat dolor ipse manus, digitique medelam
dum prebent, adimunt. Est namque uenenifer ille
tactus et intendens eciam nocumenta iuuando.
Hoc etenim uirtus uisiua remittitur, ex quo
incipit esse frequens, palpebrarumque medulla
80 prurit, et inficitur tunice septemplicis humor.
Ille dolens ultra quam posset credere quisquis
non sentiret idem, pacienter sustinet omnem
corporis accidiam, diuinaque ne uideatur
nolle flagella pati, medicos adhibere recusat.
85 Cuiusdam fratrum tanto compassa dolori
persuadet pietas consulcius ut medicinam
corporis acceptet, concludens per Salomonem
quod propter mortale genus, ne nulla dolorum
in terris fomenta forent, Altissimus artem
90 ipse salutiferam medicasque creauerit herbas.

Quomodo propter quendam medicum donantem
occulos Reatum perrexit

Franciscus fratris motus pietate diserta
permittit medicos accedere, qui nichil omnes
proficiunt, ualidisque malum radicibus herens
non solum nequeunt emplastra repellere, uerum
95 obiectu quocunque furit sensuque resultat
oppositi, ceu flamma latens in calce recenti,
sentit ut infusos latices, uehemencius ardens
exilit et subito perturbat lumina fumo.

afflicted the optic nerve. His pupils grew red with malignant chyme, his thickened eyelids skewed his sight, and pain deflected his focus. The pain summoned his hands, and his fingers deprived him of relief even as they offered it. For his very touch was noxious, and brought injury even as it gave aid. The power of sight was reduced when this began to occur frequently; the inner part of the eyelids itched, and the humor of the sevenfold sheathing was infected. In pain unimaginable to any who did not experience it, he patiently endured all bodily grief, and, in order not to seem unwilling to suffer divinely sent punishment, he refused to call in doctors. But the pity of one of the brothers, in compassion for such pain, persuaded him that he should more wisely accept medicine for his body, concluding from Solomon that on account of our mortality, the Most High himself created the healing art and medicinal herbs, lest there should be no alleviation of pain on earth.

How he went to Rieti on account of a certain doctor who restored eyesight

Moved by the eloquent pity of his brother, Francis allowed the doctors to come to him, none of whom availed. Not only were their poultices unable to ward off the tenaciously rooted illness, but whatever was applied, it raged all the more and reacted in the opposite direction, just as a flame concealed in newly cut limestone, when it perceives water being poured on, leaps forth to burn more vehemently and assaults the eyes with sudden smoke. Seeing that no

Nulla uidens emplastra sibi prodesse, set ipsis
100 deterior curis effectus, adire Reatum
cogitur a sociis, ubi dicebatur haberi
phisicus excellens, ad quem proficiscitur, eger
sanari cupiens qui tot sanauerat egros.

[Liber 13]

Tercius a decimo medicis nichil artibus illum
profecisse refert, et quomodo uectus in urbem
Assisii mortis non formidauerit horam,
exequiasque suas cantauerit instar oloris.

Urbis in ingressu uenientem curia pape
existentis ibi sollempniter excipit. Omnes
occurrunt celeres, sua nullus agenda procurat,
et iuris quecumque sui dispendia passis
5 Franciscum uidisse sat est. Non altera cuiquam
appetitur merces: hec sufficit omnibus una.
Cum sit enim magnum Chirona uidere bimembrem,
aut subuertentem taurum Mynoys Athenas,
aut lynces Bachi penetrantes omnia uisu,
10 aut Fenica breui reparantem morte iuuentam,
immissumue ferum Calidonibus aut elephantem
Cesaris aut onagros, quorum caua naris ut arcus
hostica Meotidas emittit in ora palludes,
aut longo quecumque maris secreta recessu

plasters did him any good, but, being made worse by the 100
cure itself, he was compelled by his companions to go to Ri-
eti, where an excellent physician was said to dwell. He who
himself had healed so many of the sick set out to seek him,
in hope of having his sickness healed.

[Book 13]

*The thirteenth book reports that he profited nothing from the heal-
ing arts, and how, being carried back to the city of Assisi, he did not
fear the hour of his death, and like a swan sang his own exequies.*

The curia of the pope, who was sojourning there, solemnly
received him. Everyone ran swiftly to meet him upon his
entrance into the city. None was concerned with his own
business, and for all those who had suffered any diminu-
tion of their legal rights, it was enough just to behold Fran- 5
cis. No one sought any other reward; this single boon was
enough for all. For though it might be a great event to behold two-formed Chiron, or Minos's bull destroying Athens,
or Bacchus's lynxes piercing everything with their gaze, or 10
the Phoenix recovering its youth after a brief demise; or the
beast set loose upon the Calidonians, or Caesar's elephant,
or the beasts whose nasal cavities like a bow shoot the water
of Scythian marshes into the face of the enemy; or whatever other secrets, far sequestered by the recesses of the sea,

15 climatibus nostris non assueuere uideri—
quanto maius erat mirabiliusque uidere
hic hominem, qui non erat hic set in ethere sursum
totus, et in terris celestem cernere ciuem.
Ipse licet mundi curas distractus in omnes
20 papa libens admittit eum, cuntique benigne
suscipiunt fratres, cuntisque benignius Hugo,
sub quo florebat tunc temporis Hostia felix,
cuius erat proprius qui toti sufficit orbi
presul, et humani generis moderatur habenam.

Quomodo mox alium medicum querens Senam adierit

25 Cumque supradictus non posset ferre medelam
phisicus, experto quicquid prodesse putabat,
alterius medici defertur fama per urbem,
qui lesis solitus occulis succurrere prudens,
urbanusque senex habitabat in urbi Senensi.
30 Hunc iterum Franciscus adit, nulleque dolorem
alleuiant cure, set totum passio corpus
occupat et quedam parit accessoria mortis.
Marcet epar, turget stomachus, uicioque duorum
nature sedes alimentaque mitia sanguis
35 euomitur, ruptis intra precordia uenis.
Tantis fama malis postquam specialis alumpni
et quem Franciscus multis prefecerat aures
perculit, accelerat dilectum uisere patrem.
Viso Franciscus ita confortatur alumpno,
40 nil animum cohibere potest quin gaudeat, et cor
gaudia dilatant, et dilatacio cordis

are usually unseen in our regions—how much greater and 15
more wonderful it was to behold here a man who existed not
here on earth but was set entirely in heaven above, and to
witness on earth a citizen of heaven. Though distracted by
all the cares of the world, the pope admitted him freely, and 20
all the brothers benevolently received him, but Ugo more
benevolently than all, under whom Ostia then happily flourished, which then possessed as its local bishop the man who
now suffices for the whole world, and holds the reins of the
human race.

How, seeking another doctor, he soon went to Siena

And when the aforesaid physician, having tried everything 25
he thought would help, was unable to offer a cure, report of
another doctor came through the city who was wont to offer wise succor to ailing eyes, and dwelt in his old age in the
city of Siena. Francis sought out this man as well, and no 30
cure lessened his pain, but suffering claimed his whole body
and engendered certain signs that accompany death. His
liver wasted, his stomach swelled, and through the defect of
both, when the veins ruptured within his breast, he vomited 35
out blood, which is the foundation and mild nourishment of
nature. When report of so many ills had reached the ears of
the special foster son whom Francis had promoted above
many, he hastened to visit his beloved father. At the sight of
his foster son, Francis was so strengthened that nothing 40
could restrain the joy of his mind. His joy opened his heart,

egressum dat spiritibus, morbumque repellens
copia spirituum facit ut natura resultet.
Inde quasi sospes Cortonam sustinet ire,
45 sed subiti cum sint animarum gaudia motus,
nec possint anime subitoque diuque moueri,
gaudia Franciscus paulatim dicta remitti
sentit et effectum causa perimente perempta.
Postquam spirituum cessat uehemencia, surgit
50 morbus et insultus patitur natura priores.
Gressum crura negant, marcentibus undique neruis,
et stomachi iam debilitas alimenta refutat,
nullaque defectos immutat passio gustus.

Quomodo moriens Assisium est reuersus

Sic ubi, prenimios anima tolerante dolores,
55 mortis in extremo Franciscus agone laborans
arboris appositam radicibus esse securim
sentit et aduentum pulsantis ad hostia Christi,
tranferri petit Assisium, non propter amorem
natalis patrie, recto set ut ordine terras
60 inde relinquat ubi terrena reliquit, et inde
ad Christum migret ubi Christo primitus hesit.
Vectus eo—nec enim propria uirtute moueri
iam poterat—tenui pendentem stamine uitam,
quam saluare nequit pro tempore, saluat in euum.

the opening of the heart gave the spirits a passage out, and the abundance of spirits, repelling the disease, allowed nature to recover. He found the strength as though in good health to go from there to Cortona, but since joy is a sudden movement of the soul, and the spirits could not be moved both suddenly and long, Francis felt those said joys gradually subside, along with their effect—for destruction of the cause destroyed effect in turn. After the force of his spirits failed, the disease arose again, and nature once more suffered its previous assaults. His legs refused their service, all his muscles wasted; his stomach in its weakness now rejected food, and no feeling overcame his failing sense of taste.

How the dying man returned to Assisi

Thus, his soul enduring extreme pain, Francis labored in the final agony of death. When he felt the ax laid to the root of the tree and the approach of Christ knocking at the door, he asked to be moved to Assisi, not out of love for his native land, but that in due order he might relinquish the earth where he had relinquished earthly things, and might pass on to Christ where he had first clung to Christ. Having been carried there—for he could not move under his own strength—he saved for eternity the life that he could not save in this world as it hung by a slender thread.

Quomodo moriens supra cilicium conuocatis
fratribus benedixit

65 O ualide certans et inexpugnabilis heros,
quem neque Fata domant! Ex ipsa namque uigorem
debilitate trahit et eum facit hoc animosum
quod facit exanimem. Nam prelia que studiose
in uita gessit in morte uirilius explet.
70 Aspersus cinere suprapositusque meloto
et quamuis extrema uidens emergere fata,
nulla timet, quia nulla cupit mortalia; spernit
tristiciam mortis quia spreuit gaudia uite,
et quos participes gaudebat habere laboris
75 participes eciam summe mercedis habere
obsecrat, utque prius benedicat quam moriatur
eius eis anima, circa se conuocat omnes,
et per presentes absentibus omnia mandit
que mandanda placent et utrosque ualere precatur.

Quomodo fratres mortem suam plangentes fuerit consolatus

80 Interea mesto patris accedente recessu,
exit in exequias dolor, emollitaque corda
stringit et in facies riuos deducit aquarum.
Ille suis nolens existere causa doloris,
"Propter me quid fletis," ait, "qui flere tenerer
85 propter uos pocius? Ego namque repatrio, set uos
exilium retinet. Ego post tormenta quiesco,
uos sudatis; ego sum ciuis, uos peregrini.
In refrigerium per aquam traducor et ignem,
discrimenque uie compensat gloria mete.

How, while dying upon his hair shirt,
he blessed the assembled brothers

O mighty combatant and unconquerable hero, whom not   65
even the Fates subdued! Indeed, he drew strength from his
very weakness, and the very thing that made him faint made
him courageous. For the battles that he had zealously waged
in life he even more manfully concluded in death. Sprinkled   70
with ash and laid upon a hair shirt, he feared nothing, even
though he saw his final fate approaching, since he desired
nothing mortal; he scorned the sadness of death because he
scorned the joys of life, and he prayed to have as sharers   75
in his final reward those same men with whom he had rejoiced to share his labor. That his soul might bless them
before he died, he summoned them all around him, and,
through those present, gave to those absent such directions
as it pleased him to issue, bidding farewell to them all.

How he consoled the brothers when they wept for his death

While their father's sad passing approached, grief turned   80
to lamentation, constrained their softened hearts, and drew
streams of water from their faces. Not wishing to be the
cause of their grief, he said, "Why do you weep on my account, when rather I should weep for you? For I am going   85
home, while exile still detains you. I rest after my torments,
while you labor; I am a citizen while you are foreigners.
Through water and fire I am led to refreshment, and the
glory of my goal compensates the danger of the journey.

90 Quid nisi mors mea uita fuit, uel quid nisi uita
mors erit? Hanc animam pro Christo perdere duxi,
pro nobis perdente suam, reddetque benignus
pro dampno lucrum, pro perditione salutem.
Iam qui certaui suspirauique frequenter
95 et ieiunaui, post tot certamina tandem
uado triumphatum, post tot suspiria uado
gauisum, post tot ieiunia uado comestum.
Quid uos uerborum multiplicitate tenerem?
Hic miser, hic mestus, hic infimus, hic moribundus,
100 hic ego fessus eram; set nunc ad regna uocatus
migro beata miser, ad gaudia mestus, ad astra
infimus, ad uitam moribundus, ad ocia fessus.
Inde peto ne quis michi compaciatur amicus;
immo coexultet michi congaudere uocato
105 de penis ad delicias, de carcere mundi
ad libertatem celi; Christoque labores
dignanti finire meos exsoluite letum
carmen et ympnidicas pro me depromite laudes."
Dixerat. Incipiunt astantes psallere fratres.
110 Iamque licet moriens canit ille, canentibus illis,
et psalmum qua uoce potest erumpit in illum,
"Voce mea ad Dominum clamaui." Mox sibi poscit
hec euuangelii recitetur leccio: "Certus
ante diem Pasche Ihesus quia uenerit hora
115 eius ut ad regnum Patris de carcere mundi
transeat," et reliqua—quo precipiente minister
fert apperitque librum tantique uoluminis inter
tot uarias eadem se leccio primitus offert.

What has my life been but death, or what will my death 90
be but life? I saw fit to lose my life for Christ's sake who lost
his own for ours, and he will benevolently grant reward
for my loss, salvation for my destruction. Now I who frequently struggled, sighed, and fasted pass at last, after so 95
many struggles, to triumph, after so many sighs to rejoice,
after so many fasts to feast. Why should I detain you with
so many words? Here I was wretched, sad, lowly, beset by
death, exhausted; but now, at this summons, a wretch, I pass 100
to a blessed kingdom; sad, to joy; lowly, to the stars; beset by
death, to life; exhausted, to my ease. And so I ask that no
friend of mine should pity me, but rather be glad to rejoice
with me as I am called from punishment to delight, from 105
the prison of the world to the liberty of heaven. And so to
Christ, who deigns to end my labors, sing a joyful song and
offer hymns of praise on my behalf." So he spoke. The brothers who stood nearby began to sing. And now he, though dy- 110
ing, himself broke forth amid their song, with such voice as
he was able, into the psalm, "With my voice have I cried to
the Lord." Next he asked that this Gospel reading should be
recited: "Before the day of Passover, Jesus, certain that his
hour had come that he should pass from the prison of the 115
world to the kingdom of his Father," etc. At his command,
the lector brought forth and opened the book, and among
so many various passages in such a great volume, this very
same reading at once presented itself.

[Liber 14]

Concludit quartusdecimus qua morte supremum
clauserit ille diem; que carnem signa notarint;
quam celse fuerit auctorizatus et a quo;
quomodo cum Christo uiuit per secla beatus.

Sanus ad hec egra non passus mole teneri
amplius in superas euadit spiritus auras,
nullaque preteriens Lethen obliuia gustat,
set patriam sedem comparque reuisitat astrum
5 liber et annexam rapturus in ethera carnem.

De contrario statu corporis et anime

O rerum contrarietas mirabilis! Idem
qui iacet in terris stat in astris; hic modo dormit,
semper ibi uigilat; hic mortuus est, ibi uiuus —
mortuus hic ad tempus, ibi per secula uiuus —
10 hic in re uera nec homo nec spiritus, illic
spiritus humanus, homo spiritualis: utrimque
sanctus, set proprie sacer hic, ibi dicitur almus.

Similitudo Dominice passionis carni eius impressa

Presentes Christi representancia mortem
signa notant dum quinque uident in carne beati
15 uulnera Francisci roseo respersa cruore.
Claui namque pedes et palmas, lancea dextrum
transfixisse latus, crux distendisse uidetur

[Book 14]

*The fourteenth book explains at last the death with which he con-
cluded his final day; what miracles distinguished his flesh; who
granted him his authority, and how exaltedly; and how he blessedly
lives forever with Christ.*

His healthy spirit, suffering no longer to be detained under
these circumstances, escaped into the air above and bypass-
ing Lethe, tasted no forgetfulness. In its freedom, ready to   5
draw his conjoined flesh up with him into heaven, it visited
once more his native dwelling and the stars of which he was
the equal.

On the opposed state of his body and soul

O wondrous opposition of entities! The same man who lies
prone on earth stands among the stars; here he now sleeps,
there he is forever awake; here he is dead, there he lives—
dead here for a season, there he lives forever—here in truth   10
he is neither man nor spirit, there he is a human spirit, a
spiritual man: a saint in either place; but here he is properly
called holy, there bountiful.

The likeness of the Lord's passion imprinted upon his flesh

When those present saw the five wounds in the blessed
Francis's flesh, spattered with red blood, they took note of   15
those tokens as representing Christ's death. For nails appeared to have pierced his feet and palms, the lance his side;

corpus, et in Ihesu signum quodcunque reliquit
passio, sic penitus se representat in isto.

Modus et causa predicte inpressionis

20 O nouitas miranda! Quis hoc audiuit ab euo?
Preter Franciscum quis partibus insita certis
uulnera quinque tulit morientis ymagine Christi?
Mors equidem Christi multis illata, set isti
est innata; crucem multi subiere coacti,
25 iste crucem sic mente tulit, sic pectore fouit,
sic studiis coluit ut et ipsa caractere carnis
se manifestarent animi secreta profundi.

De sepultura eius et miraculis

Conueniunt populi, concurrunt undique fratres
patris ad exequias, et in ipsa quam fabricarat
30 ecclesia Sancti Damiani corpus humatur
eius honorifice nitida de marmore tumba.
Ad sacrum cuius tumulum leprosa frequenter
mundantur, morbosa uigent, defuncta resurgunt
corpora. Paralisis tremor in plerisque residit
35 ydropisisque tumor febrisque extraneus ardor,
letargi pigra frigiditas, epilepticus horror.
Huic ceci, claudi, surdi, mutique sepulcro
accumbunt: cecis mos est ibi cernere claudos
saltantes, surdis mutos audire loquentes.

and a cross to have stretched out his body, and every sign left on Jesus by his passion thus was completely reproduced in this man.

The manner and cause of the aforesaid imprinting

O marvelous novelty! Who from the world's beginning has heard of this? Who apart from Francis bore in their various members five wounds inflicted in the image of the dying Christ? A death like Christ's was certainly inflicted on many, but it came intrinsically to this man. Many endured the cross under compulsion, but this man so bore the cross in his mind, so cherished it in his heart, so worshipped it in zeal, that the secrets of his deepest spirit displayed themselves through an imprint on his flesh.

Of his burial and miracles

The people assembled, from everywhere the brothers hastened together to their father's funeral, and in the very Church of Saint Damian which he had built, his body was honorably buried in a tomb of gleaming marble. At his holy grave, leprous bodies are frequently cleansed, the sick revive, the dead rise. The tremor of paralysis subsides in a great many, the swelling of dropsy, the exterior burning of fever, the sluggish chill of lethargy, the shudder of epilepsy. At this sepulcher, the blind, lame, deaf, and dumb lie down to sleep; the blind are wont to behold the lame leap, the deaf to hear the mute speak.

De colleccione magnatum et recitacione miraculorum

40 Hec fieri Nonus dum papa Gregorius audit,
et testes audita probant, et fama probatis
acclamat, petit Assisium cum fratribus, et sunt
undique collectis insufficiencia turbis
atria; uix ipsi capiunt tot milia campi.

45 Assunt et proceres comitesque ducesque, nec ipsa
magestas regalis abest; examine denso
abbates et pontifices et quilibet ordo
ecclesie stipant caput admirabile cleri
Gregorium uerbi celestis uina pluentem.

50 Cuius thema fuit, "Quasi matitutina nitorem
stella dat in medio nebule, quasi luna diebus
plena suis, quasi sol splendens, sic iste refulsit
in templo Domini." Completur sermo fidelis,
sermo quasi gladius penetrans, quasi flamma uirorum

55 pectora succendens, quasi mel precordia replens.
Signaque Francisci que fecit ad eius honorem
Christus et eterna uoluit clarescere fama
in commune bonum legit Octauianus aperte,
declarat dominus Reinerus apercius, ille

60 annis, hic animis maturus: in ordine fratrum
posterior sed simpliciter prelacior illo
exstitit hic, etate minor sed stemmate maior.

Of the gathering of great men and the
recitation of his miracles

When Pope Gregory IX heard that these things were hap- 40
pening, when witnesses proved what he had heard, when
reputation acclaimed what had been proved, he went to
Assisi with his brothers, and the halls were insufficient for
those who had gathered from everywhere; even the fields
could scarcely hold so many thousands. Princes, counts, and 45
dukes were present, nor was royal majesty itself absent; in
a dense throng, abbots, bishops, and every order of the
Church flanked Gregory, the clergy's admirable head, as he
rained down the wine of heaven's word. His theme was, "As 50
the morning star sheds light in the midst of a cloud, as the
moon is full of its daylight, as the sun shines forth, so this
man shone in the temple of the Lord." His faithful sermon
was completed, a sermon like a penetrating sword, like a 55
flame kindling men's hearts, like honey filling their breasts.
Octavian read aloud Francis's miracles which Christ had
worked in his honor, wishing them to shine forth with eternal fame for the good of all, and the lord Reinerus proclaimed them even more openly—the former man mature 60
in his years, the latter in his spirit: in the order of the brothers, the latter came afterward, but was clearly more advanced than the former, lesser in age but greater in nobility.

Quomodo papa canonizauerit eum

Sanctus corde pater compuncto, uoce serena,
"Ad laudem Trinitatis," ait, "Christique Marie
65 Matris, sanctorum Petri Paulique beatum
patrem Franciscum quem glorificauit in astris
Christus et in terris auctorizare tenemur."
Sic in cathalogo sanctorum solus habebat
iure pater sanctus patrem conscribere sanctum.
70 A tali tanto talem tantumque decebat
autorizari patre patrem, qui didicisset
ex eius meritis in uita quanta referri
premia deberent post mortem, qui ueneratus
esset uiuentem uenerareturque sepultum.
75   Propter nos autem pocius fecisse uidetur
istud, quam propter Franciscum, quem uenerando
dispensauit ei cultum nobisque salutem.
Estque salus pluris quam cultus. Nam sine cultu
res est magna salus, cultus nichil absque salute.
80 Iusticiaque Dei tot respiciente labores,
Franciscus fato iam non obnoxius ulli
uulnificos hostes aduersaque cuncta subegit.
    O quam sublimi mercede remunerat huius
militis acta sui Dominus fortesque triumphos!
85 Qualiter humanam transcendens gloria mentem
inmutare statum sacri dignatur alumpni!
Scilicet in partes hominis compage soluta,
terrea pars terram sortitur, celica celum.
Quas meliora manent, nec enim trahet omne per euum
90 celica naturam terre, sed terrea celi.

How the pope canonized him

His heart moved, his voice serene, the Holy Father said, "In praise of the Trinity, of Mary the Mother of Christ, of Saints Peter and Paul, we are obliged to grant authority also on earth to Father Francis, whom Christ has glorified in heaven." The Holy Father alone had the right to inscribe a holy father in the catalog of the holy in this manner. It was fitting that such and so great a father, who had honored him while living and now honored him after burial, should grant authority to one like him, who had learned from his merits while he lived what rewards ought to be accorded him after death.

But it can be seen that he did this for our sake more than for that of Francis, in veneration of whom he granted him worship, and granted us salvation. And salvation is of greater value than worship. For salvation without worship is a great thing, but worship without salvation is nothing. While God's justice looked down upon so many labors, Francis, unbeholden to any fate, subdued his dangerous foes and all adversities.

O with what a sublime reward does the Lord recompense the deeds of his soldier and his mighty triumphs! How does his glory, surpassing human understanding, deign to transform the state of his holy foster son! Now that the human amalgam has been reduced to its components, the earthly part seeks the earth, the heavenly part the heavens. Better things await them, nor will the heavenly part always retain the nature of earth, but the earthly part will receive the nature of heaven.

O felix uictor quem florida serta coronant!
Qui minor in terris est maior in ethere, qui nil
hic habuit proprium, nunc omnia possidet, et qui
tot mala sustinuit, nunc delectatur in ipso
95 fonte boni. Cuius nos ad consorcia Christus
perducat, cum quo sit Patri Spirituique
Sancto maiestas et gloria nunc et in euum.
Amen.

O happy victor crowned by plaited flowers! He who was lesser on the earth is greater in heaven, he who here possessed nothing of his own now possesses all things, he who sustained so many ills now delights in the very fount of 95 goodness. May Christ lead us into his company, with whom, to the Father and the Holy Spirit, be majesty and glory now and forever. Amen.

LIFE OF OSWALD

In noua fert animus antiquas uertere prosas
carmina, que numero, mensura, pondere firmet
inmutabilibus librata proporcio causis:
perpetuare uolens mundum Deus in tribus istis
5 a primo stabiliuit eum, causamque manendi
contulit una trium cunctis precisio rebus.
Quantum diuine permittitur artis honorem
ars humana sequi, tantum pro posse sequetur
hunc in presentis operis mea Musa tenore,
10 que tamen istius nichil artis adinuenit. Immo
sic apud antiquos erat assuetudo uirorum
scribere uirtutes et perpetuare triumphos
ut memorata magis uirtus imitabilis esset;
quoque superstitibus animos exempla priorum
15 uiuendi post fata darent, aliquando poete
intertexebant aliquid de stamine falsi,
augendo titulos et fictis facta iuuando.
Alciden yperbolice commendat Homerus,
Galterus pingit toruo Philippida uultu,
20 Cesareasque minus laudes Lucanus adauget.
Tres illi famam meruerunt, tresque poetas
auctores habuere suos; multo magis autem
Osuualdi regis debent insignia scribi.
Quis fuit Alcides? Quis Cesar Iulius? Aut quis

My intention is to turn old prose into new song, grounded in balanced proportion by immutable causes through number, measure, and weight: God, wishing to ensure the world's continuance, made it stable from the start in these three aspects, and a single determination of all three imparted to all things the cause of their permanence. To such extent as human art is allowed to emulate the honor of divine art, so far (according to my abilities) will my Muse pursue it in the sequence of this present work—though she innovates nothing of this art. Rather, it was customary among the ancients to write of men's virtues and to perpetuate their triumphs, in order that virtue, being commemorated, might be more subject to imitation. And so that the models of how to live given by those who went before might after their death impart courage to the living, poets sometimes wove in a little something of the weft of falsehood, augmenting praise and helping the facts along with fiction. Homer hyperbolically commended Hercules, Walter depicted the son of Philip with fierce countenance, and Lucan to a lesser extent augmented the praise of Caesar. Those three deserved their fame and had three poets as their own authors; but far more should the signal deeds of King Oswald be recorded. Who was Hercules? Who was Julius Caesar? Or who was

25 magnus Alexander? Alcides se superasse
    fertur, Alexander mundum, set Iulius hostem;
    se simul Osuualdus et mundum uicit et hostem.
    Tres igitur reges quot de se magna poetis
    deseruere tribus magno dicenda paratu,
30 suscepi subito dicenda tot unus ab uno;
    nec minor est moles que nanum sarcinat unum
    quam fuit hec sub qua tres sudauere gigantes.
    Inde laborandum michi sollicitudine summa est,
    ne nimia pressus oneris grauitate uacillem,
35 regis enim tanti merus historiographus alto
    hunc teneor memorare stilo meteque petende
    liber inoffenso spacium percurrere gressu.

Inuocacio ad Sanctum Osuualdum regem et martyrem

    Neue sibi tantum mea mens usurpet honorem
    regis ego uictoris opem suus inuoco uates:
40 ipse michi queso dignetur adesse, meisque
    immarcessibilem ceptis apponere dextram.

Inuocacio ad abbatem de Burgo

    Tu quoque digneris precor aspirare labori,
    flos cleri Martine, meo, qui talis es inter
    abbates qualis patronus tuus et inter
45 pontifices: hic est primas, tu primus eorum;
    istorum tu concilio collatus haberis
    sol, illud stelle; flos, illud gramina; phenix,
    illud aues; laurus, illud dumeta; Lieum,
    illud ceruisie; topacius, illud harene—
50 talis enim uiget inter eos tua gloria, qualis

Alexander the Great? Hercules is reported to have con- 25
quered himself, Alexander the world, and Julius the foe; Oswald at one and the same time conquered self and world and
foe. As many great deeds, therefore, as three kings deserved
to have told, with much artifice, by three poets, I have all at 30
once and on my own undertaken to say of one man; nor is
the weight that burdens a single dwarf less than this under
which three giants labored. And so I must work with the
greatest solicitude, not to stumble when pressed by the
enormous weight of my burden, for as the simple annalist 35
of such a king I am obliged to commemorate him in high
style and to run freely and with unimpeded step through the
course toward the finish line for which I aim.

Invocation to Saint Oswald, king and martyr

And so, lest my mind should claim so much honor for itself,
I invoke as his poet the help of the victor king: I pray he may 40
deign to attend me and to lay his incorruptible right hand
upon my enterprise.

Invocation to the Abbot of Peterborough

And you, too, deign, I pray, to inspire my work, Martin,
flower of the clergy, who are among abbots as your patron is
also among bishops: he is primate, you are first among them; 45
compared to their council one might take you for the sun,
the others for the stars; you for the flower, them for the
grass; you for the phoenix, them for mere birds; you for the
laurel, them for thorn bushes; you for wine, them for ales;
you for a topaz, them for sands—for so your glory thrives 50

sol inter stellas, flos inter gramina, phenix
inter aues, laurus inter dumeta, Lieum
inter ceruisias, topacius inter harenas.
　　Sol igitur splendendo michi, flos fructificando,
55　phenix durando, laurus redolendo, Lieum
exhilarando uelis, topacius esse uigendo.
　　Utque facis, semper Osuualdi gesta gerende
exemplar uirtutis habe. Nam quid sit agendum
nullus sanctorum perhibet manifestius isto
60　cuius dextra docet post fata quid egerit ante.
Nullo uerme perit, nulla putredine tabet;
dextra uiri nullo constringi frigore, nullo
dissolui feruore potest. Set semper eodem
immutata statu non ens est: mortua uiuit.
65　Hoc per Aidanum sua munificencia munus
illi promeruit, seseque quibuslibet idem
redderet effectus eadem si causa subesset.
In te causa subest, quo munificencior alter
non conuersatur sub sole; set hoc quia multis
70　iudicibus constat precor ut me iudice constet.

Inuocacio ad priorem

Uirque benigne, prior primis et prime priorum,
qui cleri, Rogere, *ro*sam *ger*is, annue uati.
(Forsitan hoc nomen usurpo, meque moderni
philosophi reputant indignum nomine uatis;
75　set quantum ueteres me precessere poete,
tantum philosophi ueteres uicere modernos —

among them as the sun among stars, as a flower amid the grass, as the phoenix among birds, as the laurel among thorn bushes, as wine among ales, as a topaz amid sands.

And so may you desire to be my sun in your radiance, my flower in bearing fruit, my phoenix in perdurance, my laurel in your fragrance, my wine in gladdening, my topaz in strength. 55

Hold ever fast (as indeed you do!) to Oswald's example in performing deeds of virtue. For none of the saints declares more clearly what should be done than he whose right hand 60 teaches after his death what he accomplished before death. It perishes by no worm, withers through no decay; that man's right hand can be frozen by no cold, decomposed by no heat. Yet it is no unchanging entity perpetually in the same state: in death it lives. His generosity merited this gift 65 from Aidan—and the same effect would be revealed in anyone if the same cause were present. That cause is present in you, than whom lives none more generous under the sun; but since this is evident by the judgment of many, I beg that 70 it may be evident by my judgment.

Invocation to the Prior

And, goodhearted man, Prior among the first-rate and first among priors, O Roger, you who bear the rose of the clergy, give assent to your bard. (Perhaps I usurp this designation, and modern philosophers think me unworthy of the name of bard; yet as much as ancient poets surpassed me, 75 so much did ancient philosophers conquer the moderns—

set tu cui soli patet utrorumque facultas,
da michi te placidum, dederisque in carmina uires.)

Inuocacio ad sacristam

Tuque sacrista sacris instans, qui iure uocaris
80 Simon, id est humilis, quo nemo benignius implet
abbatis precepta sui, uelocius audit,
tardius obloquitur; qui tot mea carmina seruas
scripta uoluminibus, nec plura requirere cessas,
preteritos laudas, presentes dilige uersus.
85   O rerum mutabilitas subitanea! Nuper
tu michi Typhis eras in humo, Palinurus in undis.
Nunc alter Typhis, alter Palinurus habetur:
hic est Galterus. Quis tu? Quis hic? Ut tibi dicam,
tu Dauid, hic Salomon; Helyas, hic Heliseus;
90 Moyses, hic Iosue; tibi successisse uidetur
qualiter aut Salomon Dauid, aut Helyseus Helye,
aut Iosue Moysi (quod scilicet est quasi prudens
prudenti, sanctus sancto, fidusque fideli).
Ambo fauete michi, queso, quia si michi uester
95 fauerit applausus Phebum dederitis in illo.

Inuocacio ad conuentum

Uos etiam domini quibus hunc ostendo libellum,
quorum conuentus alios supereminet omnes,
deprecor ut uestro clemencia uestra poete
arridere uelit, nec enim me posse putarem

but you, to whom alone the faculty of either is an open book, dispose yourself favorably to me, and give me strength for my songs.)

Invocation to the Sacristan

And you, Sacristan, who dwell on sacred things, who rightly are called Simon, that is, "humble": no one fulfills with bet- 80 ter will than you the precepts of his abbot, hears him more swiftly, or is slower to disobey. You who conserve my songs written in so many volumes and do not cease to ask for more, and who praise my earlier verses: bestow your love upon these present lines.

O sudden mutability of things! Recently you were a 85 Typhis to me on dry land, a Palinurus amid the waves. Now there is another Typhis, another Palinurus: that is, Walter. Who are you? Who is he? If you will permit me, you are David, he Solomon; you Elijah, he Elisha; you Moses, he 90 Joshua; he appears to have succeeded you as Solomon succeeded David, or Elisha Elijah, or Joshua Moses (which is to say, as one prudent man, one holy man, one faithful man, succeeds another). Both of you, favor me, I implore you, because if your applause favors me, by that you grant me the 95 light of the sun.

Invocation to the convent

You also, my lords, to whom I show this little book, whose convent surpasses all others, I beg your clemency see fit to smile upon your poet, for I would not suppose that I could

100 aduersos tolerare michi uos unicus omnes.
Tanta meis humeris imponere pondera nullo
impellente labo; quanto magis ergo labarem
si me uestra manus digito quocumque moueret.
Corruit impulsu facili quem propria moles
105 stare uetat, set dedecus est impellere tales
quos proprium labefactat onus. Prosternere nullus
dignatur uictor uictum uel honestus onustum.
    Ergo sonante metro sensus precludite uestros
plausibus alternis: liuoris namque maligni
110 detractiua lues odiique uenifica pestis
uult inferre nephas, uult inspirare uenenum,
ut suspensiuos immurmuret egra susurros.
Hiis super articulis obstate uiriliter hosti
antiquo, uatique nouo prebete fauorem.

EXPLICIT PROLOGUS. INCIPIT
PRINCIPALE OPUS.

De Sancto Osuualdo, rege et martire, cuius caput apud
Dunelmum habetur, brachium apud Burgum

115 Tempore quo nuper Iuti, Saxones, et Angli
ultima contulerant miseris alimenta Britannis,
dux Germanorum ex antiquissimis Yda
Bernicie Deyreque fuit lustrisque duobus
et totidem regnauit ibi feliciter annis.
120 Tantaque prosperitas ne successore careret,
sex habuit pueros de sponsa, sex aliunde,
et primogenitus fratrum fuit Edda suorum.
Cum Fortuna tamen nichil inuariabile prestet,

212

bear alone all of you set against me. I stumble in placing 100
such a weight upon my shoulders even if no one gives me a
shove; how much more, then, would I stumble if even one
finger of your hand should move against me. One whose
own load does not allow him to stand falls if pushed even 105
lightly, but it's shameful to push such men, who totter under
their own burdens. No victor should deign to lay the conquered low, nor an honorable man to topple one under onus.

Therefore, while the meter resounds, bar your senses
from other enthusiasms: for the derogatory plague of ill- 110
willed envy and the poisonous pestilence of hatred desire
to inflict wickedness, desire to inject their poison, that in
their sickness they may murmur their halting whispers. On
these points manfully oppose the ancient enemy, and to a
new poet offer your favor.

HERE ENDS THE PROLOGUE. THE PRINCIPAL
WORK BEGINS.

Of Saint Oswald, king and martyr, whose head is
kept at Durham, his arm at Peterborough

In the time when of late the Jutes, Saxons, and Angles had 115
conferred their last banquet upon the wretched Britons,
Ida, descended from the oldest of the Germans, was leader
of Bernicia and Deira and for twelve years reigned there in
felicity. In order that such prosperity should not lack a suc- 120
cessor, he begat six sons of his wife and six from elsewhere,
and Edda was firstborn among his brothers. But since Fortune never offers anything unchanging, it was necessary to

regna bipertiri morientis oportuit Yde.
125 Uni namque simul duo successere: uir Elle
sceptra tulit consanguinei, puer Edda parentis,
Eddaque Berniciis, Deyris est preditus Elle,
recte succedens hic, collateraliter ille.
    Rex sacer Oswaldus de quo tractatus habetur
130 ambobus mediantibus hiis descendit ab Yda.
Nobilitas cuius quo sit magis agnita, regum
quos naturalis successio subdidit Yde,
Edda fuit primus, alter Glapa, tercius Hussa,
Fridwolfus quartus, Tidericus quintus, Ethricus
135 sextus: sex isti sibi successere, nec omnes
regnauere nisi triginta quattuor annis.
    Hiis pater Oswaldi successit rex Ethelfridus,
qui natam regis Elles sanctique sororem
Edwini cunctis redimitam dotibus, Accam,
140 duxit in uxorem, trux blandam, turpis honestam,
barbarus egregiam, coniugalique ligantur
federe quos pocius soluit discordia morum.
Non bene conueniunt hic impius, illa benigna,
hic ferus, illa placens, hic perfidus, illa fidelis!
145 Hunc et eam iungens, feritatem simplicitati,
perfidiam fidei, nigrum confederat albo
copula, congeries, fedus, set copula longe
dissona, congeries incongrua, fedus iniquum.
Lex annectit eos, amor et concordia lecti;
150 set lex qualis? Amor qualis? Concordia qualis?
Lex exlex, amor odibilis, concordia discors.
Fecundata tamen hec illi sponsa marito
est pueros enixa duos patrisque figuram
ille representat, hic matris ymagine fulget,

divide the kingdom in two upon the death of Ida, for two si- 125
multaneously succeeded him: Aelle wielded the scepter of
his cousin, and Edda that of his father, Edda being given to
the Bernicians and Aelle to the Deirans, the one succeeding
in direct line, the other from a collateral branch.

The holy King Oswald of whom we speak descended 130
from Ida through both of these men. That his nobility may
be better known, Edda was the first of the kings whom natural succession placed after Ida, Glapa the next, Hussa the
third, Fridwolfus the fourth, Tidericus the fifth, Ethricus 135
the sixth: these six succeeded one another, nor did all of
them reign more than thirty-four years.

King Aethelfrith, the father of Oswald, succeeded these
men. He took as wife Acca, the daughter of King Aelle
and sister of Saint Edwin, acquiring her with all bride gifts: a 140
savage, shameful, barbarous man marrying a gentle, honorable, and excellent woman, and by marital compact those
two were joined whom their differing characters more
forcefully put asunder. This impious, fierce, and faithless 145
man and good-hearted, pleasant, and faithful woman were
hardly compatible. The bond, union, and compact that
joined them associated fierceness with simplicity, perfidy
with faith, and black with white, but the bond was quite dis-
sonant, the union incongruous, the compact unequal. Law,
love, and concord in bed joined them, but a law, love, and 150
concord of what sort? A lawless law, a hateful love, a discor-
dant concord. Yet, having become pregnant, the wife bore
her husband two sons, and the one reproduced the likeness
of his father, the other shone with the image of his mother,

155 Ainfridus natu prior Oswaldusque secundus.
Oswaldus sensu matris sexum patris ornat,
et regit Ainfridus, sexu sensuque patrissat.
   O quanta grauitate sui latet omnia Prime
cognicio Cause! Fratres sunt hii duo; neuter
160 uel penam meruit mortis uel premia uite;
protulit hos ambos hec una parentibus hiisdem.
Quis sciat hanc causam, quis disserat hanc racionem?
Cur execretur hunc et cur diligat illum,
et cur presciat hunc et cur predestinet illum?
165 Seu Cloto similis, seu constellacio compar,
siue planetarum motus non affuit idem,
non subsistit in hiis illius causa. Priusquam
esset Cloto, priusquam constellacio uel quam
ipse planetarum motus, prouidit utrumque
170 eius mens infallibilis; non ergo per illa
euenit hoc, nec enim presentis causa futura
esse potest, nec erunt cause postrema priorum.
O quam dissimiles pueros, quam dispare rerum
euentu, quam dissimiles genuere parentes!
175 Nec minus, hoc eciam geniti patre, matribus autem
diuersis, fratres istorum quinque fuerunt,
Oswius, Oslacus, Oswaldus, Osaphus, et Offa.
Forsitan Oswaldo dissentit mens aliquorum
stulta, uidetur enim quod deroget eius honori
180 uel pater infandus uel frater apostata, set nec
patris seuicia nec fratris fraude meretur
detrimenta pati uenerabilis eius honestas.

Eanfrith being the elder and Oswald second by birth. Os- 155
wald adorned his father's sex with his mother's understanding, while Eanfrith ruled and took after his father as to both
sex and attitude.

O, with what grave import is the knowledge of the First
Cause concealed from all things! These two were brothers;
neither of them merited either the penalty of death or the 160
rewards of life; this single cause brought them forth to these
same parents. Who may know this cause, who may expound
this reason? Why should it revile the one and love the other,
why foreknow the one and predestine the other? Neither 165
similar Fate, nor equal stars, nor the same motion of the
planets attended them: the cause of the former did not sub-
sist in the latter. Before there was Fate, the order of the
stars, or the movement of planets, an infallible mind fore- 170
saw them both; the result did not therefore come about
through those things, for the future cause is not able to be
that of the present, nor will later things be the causes of
things earlier. O, what dissimilar parents brought forth such
dissimilar sons, and how disparate the matter in outcome!
What is more, they had five brothers begotten of this father 175
by different mothers: Oswy, Oslac, Oswald, Osaph, and
Offa. Perhaps the mind of some fools might be alienated
from Oswald because either his wicked father or his apos- 180
tate brother would seem to detract from his honor; but his
venerable respectability deserves to suffer no detriment because of either his father's savagery or his brother's deceit.

Ipse methaforico meruit cognomine dici
fons fidei, seu gemma uirum, seu mel pietatis,
185 seu flos milicie. Set eis contraria ponunt
limum, siue lutum, seu ceram, seu saliuncam;
est autem certum quia si fons associetur
limo, gemma luto, mel cere, flos saliunce,
nil fons humoris ideo, nil gemma uigoris,
190 nil mel dulcoris, nil flos amittit odoris.
Ergo collatus hic eis quamcumque propinqua
ipsorum nullam trahit ex habitudine labem.
Assistens auro cuprum non derogat, immo
admotum cupro nitet excellencius aurum.
195 Elles interea Deyrorum sceptra tenentis
adiecit regnum sex lustris quatuor annos;
regnantem uero post Ellen rex Ethelfridus
expulit Edwinum, licet ille sororius eius
esset et adicerent fedus commune nepotes.
200 In tantum facinus tantum prorumpere regem
compulit ambicio, uicium quod nec pietatem
attendit, nec iura tenet, nec federa seruat.
Federis impietas uehemencius obice feruet,
blanda nec effecit mediatrix Acca duorum
205 seuus ut innocuo sponsus mitescere fratri
uellet: auaricia partes racionis agente
fraus nichil exorret, stimulata cupidine lucri.

Comparacio

Utque uirescentis ridens lasciuia prati
aspera quando mouet ualidos in bella iuuencos,
210 iunior et cuius nondum palearia pendent,

He deserves by metaphorical designation to be named the wellspring of faith, a gem among men, the honey of piety, the flower of soldiery. But mire, mud, wax, and odorous nard offer their contrary qualities to these things; now it is certain that if a wellspring is set next to mire, a gemstone next to mud, honey next to wax, a flower next to nard, the wellspring loses for all that nothing of its moisture, the gem nothing of its brightness, the honey nothing of its sweetness, the flower nothing of its scent. By analogy with these, then, he incurs no flaw from an association with them, however close. Juxtaposition with copper does not detract from gold, but rather gold shines all the more excellently when set next to copper. Meanwhile, the reign of Aelle who held the scepter of Deira amassed thirty-four years; but after Aelle's reign King Aethelfrith expelled Edwin, even though he was his brother-in-law and their grandparents offered a common bond. Ambition drove so great a king to break out into such wickedness—a vice that neither attends to piety, observes the law, nor keeps its treaties. Impiety seethes all the more vehemently when fealty opposes it, nor did the gentle Acca, acting as mediator between the two, succeed in making her savage spouse show mildness to her innocent brother: deceit, goaded on by the greed for wealth, abhors nothing when avarice takes the place of reason.

Simile

And just as, when the smiling pleasure of a green meadow sometimes moves strong bullocks to fierce battle, the younger—whose wattles don't yet hang down, nor the blood fill

non uenas implet sanguis, non ossa medulle,
non nerui pectus armant, non cornua frontem,
postquam perpendit se uiribus inferiorem,
discedit profugus ignotaque pabula carpit
215 dum ualidum robur totos solidauerit armos —
mox redit et pugnat et taurum uincit eundem
a quo uictus erat et pabula prima resumit —
sic ubi se uim ui non posse repellere nouit
Edwinus quocunque fugam compulsus inire
220 exul apud regem Radwaltum tempore multo
diuertit, cum quo sibi suffragante reuersus
strauit Ethelfridum gemmataque sceptra resumpsit
que tribus optinuit lustris annisque duobus.
Sic forti leso prestatur causa nocendi;
225 predo facit diues raptorem de spoliato.
Territa morte uiri puerorum sedula custos
a facie fratris ad Scotos Acca profugit
cum pueris et ibi latuit dum frater obiret.
Ante diu sacra mater eis ostenderat omnes
230 articulos fidei set nullo teste probatos.
    Mox ubi Scottorum fuit acclamante senatu
hec illis manifesta fides, baptisma salutis
insiliere simul, set non simul insiliere,
ut fratres set non ut fratres insiliere
235 omnino penetrans set non omnino penetrans;
sicque simul loti, simul apparere fideles
in primis poterant, set in hiis examina fallunt,
euentus mutant (a fine sciencia pendet),

up his veins, or marrow his bones, whose muscles do not yet
fortify his breast, nor horns his forehead—departs in flight
when he realizes that he's inferior in strength. He grazes
on unknown fodder until oaken strength fully solidifies his
shoulders; soon he returns, fights, conquers that same bull
by whom he had been conquered, and claims again his original grazing places: just so, when Edwin knew that he could
not ward off force with force and was compelled to flee
somewhere, he sojourned in long exile at the court of King
Raedwald. Returning with his support, he laid Aethelfrith
low and took up again his gem-studded scepter, which he
wielded for seventeen years. Thus a reason for doing harm is
afforded a strong man in his injury; a wealthy robber makes
the one he despoils into a plunderer. Terrorized by her husband's death and zealously guarding her sons, Acca fled from
her brother's presence to the Irish, and hid there with her
sons until her brother's death. Their holy mother had long
since revealed to them all the articles of the faith—but without the proof of witnesses.

Soon, when this faith was revealed among them by the
acclamation of the Irish nobles, they entered together the
baptism of salvation, yet did not enter it together; entered
as brothers, but not as brothers, a baptism that pervaded
everything and yet did not pervade everything; and so, being
washed together, at first they were able to seem together
faithful, but in these matters the evidence was deceptive
and the outcomes changed (knowledge depends on the

diuinamque pari uultu set dispare cultu
240 suscepere fidem; uiteque nepotibus una
causa fuit patrui mors expectata tot annis,
quem simul auxilio Pende Cadwallo peremit.
    Berniciam repetens cum natis Acca duobus
est ibi cum magno procerum suscepta fauore,
245 cuius honorando fratri duo regna tenenti,
scilicet Edwino, duo successere tiranni,
e quibus hic Deyris (hoc est Osricus) et ille
Berniciis (hoc est Ainfridus) prefuit, ambo
sacrilegi quos iusta Dei sentencia damnans
250 uix tulit ut possent unum regnare per annum.
Baptizatus enim Christumque professus uterque
postquam suscepit patrui moderamina regni,
ingratus Christo uite regnique datori
suscepte fidei proiecit apostata cultum,
255 factoremque suum nullo dignatus honore
pronus adorauit manuum figmenta suarum.
(Sic ingratorum mos est: pro culmine lapsum,
pro merito culpam, pro dono reddere damnum.)
Tantis equa malis referente stipendia Christo,
260 fastus iniquorum primo prosternitur anno
utque malos alterna sui contencio perdat
morte repentina Cadwallo preoccupat ambos.
    Terribilem nullus euadit apostata finem:
non impune potest fidei constancia ledi.
265 Hanc ubi uindictam diuina subintulit ira,
rex cuius reges premit excellencia, cuius
presens eterno liber attitulatur honori,
Oswaldus, regi patruo successit, eorum

endpoint), and they received the holy faith with the same 240
countenance, but with disparate reverence; and to the neph-
ews the uncle's death, awaited for so many years, was the
sole cause of life, when with Penda's help Cadwallon destroyed him.

Acca, setting out once again for Bernicia with her two
sons, was there received with great favor by the nobility.
Two usurpers succeeded her honorable brother Edwin, who 245
had held two kingdoms. One, that is Osric, held sway over
the Deirans, and the other, that is Eanfrith, over the Bernicians, both of them blasphemers whom God's just sentence
of condemnation barely allowed to reign for a single year. 250
For though both had been baptized and had professed
Christ, becoming apostates ungrateful to Christ, the be-
stower of life and realm, they cast aside reverence for the
faith they had received, once they had taken up the governance of their uncle's kingdom. Having judged their maker 255
worthy of no honor, they bowed in adoration to the work of
their own hands. (Such is the custom of ingrates: they repay
exaltation with a fall, merit with guilt, a gift with destruction.) When Christ returned a fair reward for such evils, the 260
pride of those unjust men was laid low in their first year, and
in order that mutual contention might destroy them in their
wickedness, Cadwallon overtook both with sudden death.

No apostate avoids a terrible end: constancy in faith
cannot be violated with impunity. When divine wrath had 265
inflicted this vengeance, Oswald, that king whose excellence surpassed kings, whose book in this present world
was inscribed with eternal honor, succeeded to his uncle's

iure tenens utrumque locum. Sic namque decebat
270 heredem consanguineum rex religiosus
ut regni pariter et religionis haberet.
Et placuit cunctis regum numerantibus annos
neuter ut illorum quos supradiximus inter
catholicos reges deberet apostata scribi,
275 set regno regis Oswaldi cederet annus
in quo suscepte fidei fregere tenorem,
ut decus Oswaldi regni sibi tempus adeptet
quo se fecerunt indignos. Crimine, fraude,
fastu, seuicia, luxu, sordebat eorum
280 fama; set illius effulsit uita fidesque,
maiestas, uirtus, et prosperitas: sine luxu
prosperitas, sine seuicia uirtus, sine fastu
maiestas, sine fraude fides, sine crimine uita.
Cuius ymago decens, uirtus, et cetera dotum
285 copia talis apud ueteres describitur Anglos:
statura rectus et celsus erat quasi cedrus,
cesarie flauus et crispus, fronte serenus
et uiuens, naso precisus et equus, ocellis
ridens et glaucus, facie tener et rubicundus,
290 ore decens et conspicuus, mento spaciosus
et biuius, uultu speciosus et orbicularis,
renibus et uentre gracilis quasi uirgo, lacertis
et digitis longus, humeris et pectore latus,
ossibus et neruis rigidus, uirtutibus et ui
295 compropagatus, animis et corpore quadrus,
moribus et studiis simplex, sensu et racione
prospicuus, titulis et origine clarus, honore
et dicione grauis, uerbis et corde benignus.
Quid refero? Natura parens affuderat uni

kingdom, rightfully obtaining the place of them both. For it
was indeed fitting that a religious king should have an heir
of his own kin in both realm and religion. And it pleased
all those who tallied the years of kings that neither of
the aforesaid apostates should be recorded among catholic
kings, but that the year in which they broke the constancy
of the faith which they had received should be conceded to
King Oswald's reign, that to the honor of Oswald's reign
might accrue the time in which they had made themselves
dishonorable. Their reputation was sullied by crime, guile,
pride, savagery, and indulgence; but the life, faith, majesty,
strength, and prosperity of that man shone forth: a prosperity without indulgence, a strength without savagery, a
majesty without pride, a faith without guile, a life without
crime. His seemly image, virtue, and the further abundance
of his endowments was thus described among the English of
old: he was upright and tall of stature like the cedar, with
curling blond hair, calm and lively of brow, with a straight,
even nose, smiling gray eyes, tender and ruddy of face,
seemly and comely of mouth, with a wide, cleft chin, an attractive, round visage, with slim loins and belly like a girl's,
long of arm and finger, broad of shoulder and chest, solid in
bone and muscle, advanced of strength and vigor, solid of
courage and body, simple of character and zeal, foresightful
in his senses and his reason, illustrious of title and birth,
grave of honor and authority, benevolent of word and disposition. What more is there to tell? Mother Nature poured

270

275

280

285

290

295

300 omnia que pocius uel perfectiua fuerunt
roboris humani uel adornatiua decoris.
Huic eciam Fortuna fauens dictante Sophia
illius imperiis arrisit, eaque iubente
Berniciis Deyros, Pictos, Scotosque subegit.

305 Iamque Britannorum seuire tirannica pestis
ceperat ulterius, nondum contenta cruore
martiris Edwini sceleratorumque duorum
quos regis feritas iniusti iure peremit.
Eius enim feruebat adhuc insania, nulli

310 parcere proponens de successoribus Yde
militibusque suis nil posse resistere iactans.
Nam proprie proprium Cedwelle nil nisi cedem
uelle fuit, nec habere uias nisi sanguine fuso.
Innumeris quorum uix milibus ampla ferendis

315 sufficiebat humus; calcabat regna, Deoque
nec par esse ualebat, nec minor esse uolebat.
Miles ab auerso suplex Oswaldus, et armis
plus fidei fidens quam ferri, ferre triumphum
presumit non de sociorum uiribus, immo

320 de uirtute Dei, cuius suffragia sperans
hostes contemnit, excercituique superbo
omnia milicie tot milibus arua prementi
audet dux humilis socios opponere paucos,
nec tamen in pugnam subito prorumpere cursu

325 cum quadam feritate placet, set supplice dextra
exaltat lignum sancte Crucis ut mediante
exaltetur eo, Christumque profusus adorat
ut uelit indomite fastum prosternere gentis
prosperiusque suis donare fidelibus omen.

out on one man everything that could more powerfully ei-   300
ther perfect human strength, or adorn human beauty. Fortune, also favoring this man according to Wisdom's dictates,
smiled upon his reign, and by her command he subdued Bernicians, Deirans, Picts, and Irish.

And now the Britons' pestilence of tyranny began to rage   305
still further, not yet content with the gore of the martyr Edwin and of those two wastrels whom the savagery of an unjust king rightfully killed. For indeed his madness seethed
still, with the intention of sparing none of Ida's successors,   310
and boasting that nothing could resist his soldiers. For it
was Cadwallon's own nature to desire nothing except slaughter and to tread no path save one of bloodshed. The ample
earth barely sufficed to support his innumerable soldiers;   315
he trampled kingdoms, and neither was he able to equal
God nor did he wish to be beneath him. Opposing him, the
suppliant soldier Oswald, trusting more in the arms of faith
than in those made of iron, presumed to bear away the triumph not through his fellows' strength, but through God's   320
power. Trusting in God's help, he despised the foe, and that
humble commander dared to set his few companions against
the proud army that pressed all the fields with so many
thousands of its troops. And yet it did not suit him to burst
forth into battle amid the savagery of some precipitous
course, but with suppliant right hand he raised the wood of   325
the holy Cross—that by his assistance it might be raised—
and prostrate he beseeched Christ to lay low the haughti-
ness of an unconquered race and grant his faithful a more

330 Finitis precibus, facta cruce rursus et alte
inposita fouee manibusque duabus ab ipso
undique suffulta, foueam tellure sodales
firmiter inpressa glebisque uirentibus implent:
sicque triumphali uexillo castra fidelis
335 premunita ducis replet inspirata superni
gratia consilii, prosternendisque pauorem
hostibus inmittit Crucis admirabile signum.
  Consiliumque fuit quod promulgasse beatus
dicitur Oswaldus, ut uoto supplice flexis
340 ante crucem genibus colleccio tota precetur
eternum uerumque Deum, qui dimicat eque
in paucis sicut in multis quatinus in se
sperantes seuo dignetur ab hoste tueri.
  Imperio regis exercitus omnis obedit;
345 hostibus inde suis congressus ab incipiente
diluculo iuxta fidei monimenta triumphat,
parte Britannorum iaculo pereunte timoris,
parte superuacuum bellis adhibente laborem.
Iamque parum prosunt galee ceruicibus: ensis
350 fulminat in galeas et sanguis inebriat ensem.
Inde ferus sonipes laxis spaciatur habenis;
inde pedes, hinc crura iacent, hinc brachia nuper
corporibus diuulsa suis, cruor undique manat
concoloresque rosis facit herbas. Namque suorum
355 Cedwallam cedes uallant quem regius ensis
cedit et ulterius cedendum mittit Auerno.
  Iure quidem cecidit unus ne cederet omnes.
Quale scelus, talis infligitur ulcio; mortem

prosperous omen. When his prayers were finished, when 330
he had fashioned the Cross anew and had set it deep in a
pit, supported on either side by his two hands, his comrades
filled the pit with earth pressed down firmly and with green
sods: and so the inspired grace of heavenly counsel filled the 335
faithful commander's encampment, which now was fortified with that triumphal banner, and the wondrous sign of
the Cross struck fear into the enemies he would lay low.

The blessed Oswald is said to have admonished them
that, in humble prayer on bended knee before the Cross, 340
the whole assembly should beseech the true and eternal
God, who fights equally on the side of small forces as of
great, that he should deign to protect from the fierce foe
those who hoped in him.

The entire army obeyed their king's command; thereaf- 345
ter, from the day's first dawning, those who had gathered
near the faith's monuments triumphed over their foe, with
some of the Britons perishing by the shaft of fear, while others added pointless exertion to their battles. Too little now
did their helmets avail their necks: the sword flashed against
their helmets and grew drunk on their blood. There the 350
fierce steed ambled with loosened reins; there feet, here legs
and arms lay sundered from bodies; gore flowed everywhere
and turned the grass the color of roses. For the slaughter of 355
his men hedged in Cadwallon, whom the king's sword slew
and dispatched to further slaughter in the Underworld.

Rightfully did one fall that all might not fall. Such vengeance was inflicted as suited his crime; he who thirsted for

qui sitit alterius, propriam gustare meretur.
360 Sic pereunt hostes nulloque superstite de tot
milibus, ad nichilum tam pauca gente redactis.
Oswaldus, gaudens habito pro uelle tropheo,
se uirtute Crucis hoc obtinuisse fatetur.

O Crux bellipotens, O formidabile signum
365 hostibus, in cuius sic nomine uincitur hostis!
O uere lignum super omnia ligna, uirescens
fronde, nitens flore, speciosum germine! Dulce
lignum, quam dulces clauos, quam dulcia gestans
pondera perpetuo miseros a compede soluit.

370 Nec mirum, si Crux mortalem conterat hostem
cuius ad effigiem nec spiritualis adesse
audet—ab antiquo uictus fuit ille per illam.
Summo namque Patri talem de iure decebat
reddi, qualis Adam fuerat, de uirgine terra

375 quem Deus efficeret natura non mediante,
peccati qui labe carens, uirtutis honore
primitus excellens, deitatis ymagine fulgens,
morte scelus lueret pro quo mors strauerat Adam;
sicque Patri talem prestante per omnia Christo,

380 ex quo per lignum serpens seduxerat Euam,
ex ligno decuit talem constare stateram
qua trucinaretur perpendiculariter, utrum
pena redemptoris grauior foret an scelus Ade.
In qua dum Christus ex una parte pependit,

385 humanum genus ex alia, Christus moriendo,
humanumque genus peccando, Passio Christi,
humani generis grauior quocumque reatu,
mole sua fecit aliam descendere lancem.
Set quantum pressit hanc, tantum sustulit illam:

the death of another deserved to taste his own. So the foe 360
perished with no survivors among so many thousands, reduced to nothing by so small a force. Oswald, rejoicing in
triumph according to his desire, declared that he had obtained it by the power of the Cross.

O Cross mighty in battle, O token fearsome to the foe, in 365
whose name the foe is thus subdued! O tree truly surpassing
all trees, green of leaf, white of flower, lovely of shoot! This
sweet tree, bearing such sweet nails, so sweet a burden, released the wretched from eternal shackles. Nor is it a won- 370
der if the Cross grinds down a mortal foe, for in the presence of its image neither does the spiritual foe dare to linger,
since of old he was conquered by it. For according to the
Law it was fitting that such a one should be rendered to the
Father on high as Adam had been, whom God fashioned of 375
virgin earth without nature's mediation: one who, free of
sin's stain, outstanding at the beginning in the honor of his
virtue, shining with the image of the Godhead, might by his
death expiate the crime by which death laid Adam waste.
And so, when Christ offered the Father such a one in all respects, since by a tree the serpent had seduced Eve, it was 380
fitting that of a tree should be made such a balance on which
might hang straight down the determination as to whether
the Redeemer's penalty or Adam's sin should have more
weight. When Christ hung upon it on one side, the human 385
race on the other, Christ in his death, and the human race in
its sin, the Passion of Christ, being heavier than any guilt of
the human race, made one arm descend of its own weight.
But as much as it pressed this side down, so much it raised

390 hec igitur Christum detrusit ad infima mundi,
     hec genus humanum tulit ad fastigia celi;
     cumque teneretur magni perhibere duelli
     finis an humanum genus eternalibus esset
     suppliciis dignum subcumbere, ius quasi censor,
395 Crux quasi campus erat, serpens et Adam quasi partes,
      mors et uita quasi pugiles—O nobile bellum,
     O felix campus, ubi mors et uita duello
     conflixere pari naturalique trihumpho
     mors superata fuit! Vel enim pulsata recurrit
400 uel constans natura manet cuiuslibet entis.
     In Crucis hoc igitur bello (quia contigit ille
     motus et illa quiaes), uite natura recurrit
     et mortis natura manet; se uita resumpsit,
     se mors conseruat, et permanet utraque secum.
405 Post Ade lapsum, de iure decebat ut aut mors
     uiueret, aut uita moreretur, et in Cruce uita
     mortua, ne sineret in nobis uiuere mortem,
     mortem uiuentem uita moriente peremit.
     In Cruce prostrauit mors uitam uitaque mortem:
410 mors uitam uita priuauit uitaque mortem
     morte trucidauit; set uita uita carere
     non longum potuit; mortem mors semper habebit.
     Nempe prothoplausti crimen, mors, uita parentis—
     crimen preteritum, mors presens, uita futura—
415 exegere sibi Crucis hec misteria: crimen
     causa fuit mortis, et mors priuacio uite.
     Hoc in conflictu Crux in se iura redegit

up the other: and so the one side dragged Christ down to   390
the world's lowest depths, the other raised the human race
to the heights of heaven; and when, in order to demonstrate
whether the human race would fittingly fall under eternal
punishment, inquiry was made into the outcome of the
great contest, the Law was like the judge, the Cross like the   395
field of contest, the Serpent and Adam like plaintiff and de-
fendant, death and life like their champions—O noble warfare, O happy field, where death and life in equal contest
strove, and death was overcome by a triumph in accordance
with nature! For the nature of any being either reacts when
struck, or else remains in stasis. In this battle of the Cross,   400
therefore (since such motion and such stasis were both in
evidence), life's nature revived, while the nature of death remained in stasis; life resumed, death preserved itself, and
each remained as it was. After Adam's fall, it was fitting ac-   405
cording to the Law that either death should live, or life
should die, and on the Cross life, by dying, destroyed living death, lest a dead life should allow death to live in us. On
the Cross death subdued life, and life death: death deprived   410
life of life, and life slew death with death; but life could not
long remain lifeless; death will always remain dead. Indeed,
the crime, death, and life of our first-made parent—past
crime, present death, future life—required for themselves   415
these mysteries of the Cross: crime was the cause of death,
and death the privation of life. In this conflict, the Cross
enacted within itself the rules of crime, and death, and life,

criminis et mortis et uite, facta lauacrum
criminis, excidium mortis, reparacio uite.

420 Inde pauere Crucem didicere Diabolus et Mors;
miraque diuine dat dispensacio dextre
ut cum non possit apud omnes esse fideles
Crux eadem Christi, nec enim se tam breue corpus
in tot sufficeret mundi diffundere partes,

425 forma recompenset defectum materiei,
et crux que non est Crux lignum sufficit ut sit
Crux signum; non Crux ea, set Crucis eius ymago.
Cumque sit hec eius sic complantata figure,
deriuatiue speciei ducit ab illa

430 nomen et effectum, persone nomen, honoris
effectum; nomen crucis, effectumque triumphi.
Illa quidem uite mortem pessumdedit; ista
pignoribus uite subiecit pignora mortis,
scilicet Oswaldo Cedwellam, catholicisque

435 ydolatras, placidisque truces, sacrisque prophanos.
Permissusque locus tantum conscire triumphum
tunc primo sciuit causam cur nomen haberet
"Heuenefeld," hoc est celestis campus: id illi
nomen ab antiquo dedit appellacio gentis

440 preterite, tanquam belli presaga futuri,
nominis et causam mox assignauit ibidem
celitus expugnans celestis turba scelestam
et sacra sacrilegam, simplexque supersticiosam.
Neue senectutis ignauia possit honorem

445 tam celebris delere loci tantique triumphi,
ecclesie fratres Augustaldensis adesse
deuoti missasque solent celebrare quot annis,
quoque loci persistat honos in honore beati

being made the purification of crime, the demise of death, the restoration of life. Thence the Devil and Death learned to fear the Cross; and the wondrous dispensation of God's right hand granted that, since that same Cross of Christ could not be present to all the faithful, nor its limited material suffice for distribution through all the world, its form might compensate for its insufficient matter, and a cross that was not the Cross as to its wood might still signify the Cross; being not the Cross as such, but the image of the Cross. And since it was imprinted as to its form, it took from it the name and effect of derivative appearance: the name of its personage, the effect of honor; the name of the Cross, the effect of triumph. The true Cross indeed overcame the death of life; this cross laid low the children of death before the children of life—that is, cast down Cadwallon before Oswald, idolaters before catholics, the savage before the peaceable, the profane before the sacred. And the site that was permitted to experience so great a triumph then for the first time knew why it had the name Heavenfield (that is [in Latin] the celestial plain): the nomenclature of a bygone race so named it of old as a presage of the war to come, and soon the celestial, holy and guileless company there assigned the cause for its name, by routing with the help of heaven a wicked, sacrilegious, and superstitious force. Lest listless antiquity should be able to blot out the honor of so illustrious a site and so great a triumph, the brothers of the church of Hexham kept the custom every year of devoutly celebrating masses there, and, in order that the honor due the place should continue, they built there a

Oswaldi regis ibi construxere capellam.
450 Fama, decus, nomen illic illius habetur:
perpes fama, manens decus, indelibile nomen.
Predicte crucis indigene decidere quasdam
particulas laticique solent immittere puro,
quo si potetur aut aspergatur hanelum
455 aut languorosus pecus aut homo, protinus aut hoc
aut hic abesse sibi gaudet quod inesse dolebat.
Constat idem multis, supradicteque Botelmus
ecclesie frater hec in se mira probauit.
Nocte, pruinali presso caligine celo,
460 non oculo sibi set baculo prestante ducatum,
ibat et incautum festinantemque fefellit
lubrica sub pedibus glacies, fregitque lacertum;
cumque semel quidam fratrum proponeret ire
Heuenefeld propter quedam facienda, Botelmus
465 obsecrauit eum crucis ut sibi quando rediret
curaret dare particulam quamcumque minutam.
Ille reuersus ei de musco prebuit illo
unde superficies sacri fuit obsita ligni.
Cumque sedens inter socios discumberet eger
470 ad mensam, nec haberet ibi pro tempore quicquam
oblatum sibi munus ubi componere posset,
inmisit sinui; cum deinde recumbere uellet
oblitus dimisit ibi cessitque sopori.
Nocte quasi media somni torpore solutus,
475 nescio quid gelidum circa precordia sensit
admotaque manu cepit palpare quid esset,
et subito stupuit ita conualuisse lacertum
ac si nulla prius in eo lesura fuisset.

chapel in honor of the blessed King Oswald. His reputation,   450
seemliness, and name were there observed: an endless reputation, a lasting seemliness, an unerasable name.

The locals had the habit of shaving splinters of the aforesaid cross and putting them into pure water, with the result
that if a weak beast or sick man should drink or be asperged   455
with it, they at once would rejoice in the disappearance of
their ailment. Many witnessed this, and Bothelm, a brother
of the aforesaid church, made proof of these wonders in his
own person. One night, when the sky was oppressed with a
frosty darkness, he walked under guidance not of his eye but   460
only a staff. The slippery ice under his feet deceived him in
his carelessness and haste, and he broke his arm. When one
of the brothers proposed to go to Heavenfield to accomplish some business, Bothelm entreated him to bring him   465
on his return a little piece of the cross, however small. Coming back, he offered him a little of the moss with which the
surface of that holy wood was covered. When the sick man
was sitting among his fellows at table and had nowhere to   470
set aside for the moment the gift he had been offered, he
tucked it into his bosom; when he then wanted to turn in, he
forgetfully left it there as he succumbed to slumber. Around
midnight, relaxed in the torpor of sleep, he felt something   475
cold near his heart and raised his hand to begin searching for
the cause; suddenly he was dumbfounded that his shoulder
was as healed as if it had suffered no previous injury.

Inde Crucis debemus opem sperare fideles.
480 Spe directa fides operatur Cruxque salutem
exequitur, sicut patuit perhibente Botelmo.
Quoque Crucis tanto sit gracior ille fauori,
Crux memor illius fuit et Crucis immemor ille.
Hoste triumphato Crucis inpetrata fauore,
485 Oswaldi predicta fidem uictoria firmat.
Imperio cuius quantum superesse uidetur
ut qui corporeas contriuit spirituales
conterat insidias et utrosque coherceat hostes,
exturbare suis affectat finibus hostem
490 rex nouus antiquum desiderioque benigno
feruet ab omnimodo subiectos hoste tueri.
Plus cumulum pensans oneris quam culmen honoris,
plus uerbo prodesse uolens quam uerbere preesse,
quos a morte breui debet defendere morte
495 eterna dolet esse reos, optatque prophanis
in commune bonum fidei deducere lucem.
Hanc igitur cupiens toto diffundere regno
exul apud Scottos quia sacramenta salutis
sumpserat, a Scottis et poscit et optinet una
500 ut sibi mittatur antistes idoneus et qui
religione sua quamcumque supersticionem
deleat, exemplo celeber uerboque disertus.
Missus ei presul qui nomen ab auxiliando
ducit: Aidanus satis auxiliatur ad eius
505 propositum Christique fidem dilatat in omnes,
nitens ydolatras, nitens absoluere sontes
errorum tenebris, Aquilonis frigore: gaudet
ydolatras in catholicos conuertere, sontes
in sanctos, tenebras in lucem, frigus in estum.

And so we ought faithfully to hope for help from the Cross. Faith, directed through hope, when joined to the Cross works salvation, as was evident from Bothelm's story. And that he might be more grateful for such favor of the Cross, the Cross was mindful of him even when he was forgetful of the Cross.

The aforesaid victory, obtained by the favor of the Cross when the enemy were defeated, confirmed Oswald's faith. Insofar as it seemed to remain in his power that one who had defeated physical ambush should also defeat spiritual attacks and should constrain foes both physical and spiritual, the new king undertook to drive the ancient Foe from his territory, and was zealous in his benevolent desire to protect his subjects from enemies of every sort. Thinking more of the mass of his burdens than the height of his honor, wishing more to be of assistance through his words than to maintain control through force, he grieved that those he was obliged to defend from momentary death should be liable to eternal death, and he desired for the common good to bring the light of faith to the profane. Desiring, therefore, to disseminate this faith to the whole kingdom, since as an exile among the Irish he had received the sacraments of salvation, he requested and obtained from the Irish that they should send him a suitable bishop, whose religion might blot out all superstition, one illustrious in his example and skilled of speech. And so was sent to him a prelate who took his name from giving aid: Aidan quite assisted his intention and spread the faith of Christ to all, striving to free idolaters and the guilty from the darkness of error and the cold of the North: he rejoiced to turn idolaters into catholics, the guilty into saints, darkness into light, cold into warmth.

480

485

490

495

500

505

510 Eius episcopio fit Lindisfarnia sedes
deuotique studet ibi munificencia regis
grande monasterium grandi componere sumptu.
Illic iocundum uisu, mirabile dictu,
sepe solet fieri, populis antistite legem
515 insinuante Dei, documenta uidelicet huius
Scotti doctoris animo cuiuslibet Angli
auditoris erant nullum generancia sensum;
set rex Oswaldus idiomata nouerat ambo,
spargentique uiro diuini semina uerbi
520 assistens interpres erat: studet iste quid, ille
quomodo dicendum; saciande fercula mentis
hic facit, ille parat; hic decoquit, ille decorat;
hic mouet, ille locat; hic suggerit, ille ministrat.
O rex sollicitus, O regia sollicitudo!
525 Corpora rex, animas debet curare sacerdos;
Oswaldus, seruans animas et corpora, curis
dum simul ambabus uacat, inde negocia regis,
inde sacerdotis gerit, omnibus omnia factus.
Que tantum regem uirtus denominet? Omnes
530 certant uirtutes, set munificencia uincit,
eternique Boni captus dulcore bonorum
qualia mundus habet non irretitur amore.
Non uult in gemmis thesaurizare uel auro,
nec uitro gemmas cuproue libencius aurum
535 confiscare cupit, set egentibus omnia donat,
regali tantum sibi maiestate retenta.
Nullus inops ab eo fertur tolerasse repulsam
set quociens inopes uite suffragia poscunt,

Lindisfarne became the seat of his bishopric, and the de- 510
vout king's munificence strove to assemble a great monastery there at great expense. Delightful to behold and wondrous to relate, there it often happened, when the bishop
was instructing the people in God's law, that the doctrine of 515
this Irish teacher begat no understanding in the mind of any
Englishman; but King Oswald knew both languages and
stood by as interpreter when that other man scattered the
seed of the divine Word. One was zealous for what to say, 520
the other for how to say it; the one created nourishment to
satisfy the mind, the other prepared it; one cooked it, the
other presented it; one brought forward and furnished what
the other set out and served. O zealous king, O kingly zeal!
A king should attend to bodies, a priest to souls; Oswald, 525
preserving both souls and bodies, in giving his attention to
both cares at once, thereby dispatched the business of both
king and priest, being made all things to all people. What
virtue may describe such a king? All virtues strove, but gen- 530
erosity prevailed, and, being captured by the sweetness of
the eternal Good, he was not ensnared by love of such goods
as the world possesses. He did not wish to store up a treasure of gems or gold, nor did he desire to accumulate gems
more willingly than glass, nor gold more than copper, but 535
he gave everything to the needy, retaining for himself only
the royal majesty. No pauper is said to have endured his
rebuff, but as often as paupers asked for sustenance of life,

supplex Oswaldus hos audit et absque tumore
540 uiscera, pectus, eis oculos inclinat et aures;
nullum uisceribus preclusis, pectore duro,
auersis oculis, aut surda preterit aure.
Exiguum reputans quicquid pro nomine Christi
pauperibus donare potest, ubi prodigus alter
545 esse uideretur in eo se fingit auarum.
Poscenti poterit dare nemo superflua Christo,
Christus enim pro simplicibus dat centupla, plusque
fenoris accipiet qui plus acommodat illi.
Hanc quia donandi finalem regia causam
550 intendit pietas moderari munera nescit.
Nulla uidetur ei largicio prodiga, nullum
preter auariciam uicium putat esse datoris.
Hos yperbolice titulos ascribere sancto
ne uidear, superest ut de tot milibus unum
555 prosequar exemplum, reliquo iam corpore uerso
in cinerem quare maneat manus integra carne
et cute, constanter et semper mollis et alba.
    Rex et Aidanus festum Paschale colentes
clara resurgentis celebrabant prelia Christi,
560 et post missarum solemnia rite peracta,
omnibus impletis Paschali mentibus Agno,
altera corporibus querunt alimenta replendis;
cumque ligustrassent tabulas mensalia latas,
iam discumbebant ibi collateraliter, et iam
565 ceperat appositos presul benedicere panes.
Ecce superueniens quodam sacer impete frater,
cuius egenorum delegabatur agenda
cura ministerio, collectis undique multis
atria pauperibus ostendit tota repleri,

Oswald humbly heard them, and without pride inclined to   540
them his ear, eye, breast, and inward parts; he ignored none
by closing his inward feeling, hardening his heart, turning
his eye, or stopping his ear. Thinking it a trifle, whatever he
could give the poor in Christ's name, where another man
might think himself generous he made himself out to be a   545
miser. No one can give too much to Christ when he asks, for
Christ gives a hundredfold in return for simple gifts, and he
who bestows more upon him will receive all the more in interest. Because the king's piety attended to this final cause
of giving, he could not be moderate in his gifts. No largesse   550
seemed prodigal to him; he thought avarice was a giver's
only vice. Not to ascribe these attributes to the saint by way
of hyperbole, it remains to pursue one example among so   555
many thousands, as to why his hand remains intact in flesh
and skin, ever and continuously soft and white, though his
body has turned to dust.

   The king and Aidan, keeping the Paschal feast, were celebrating the glorious battles of the rising Christ, and when   560
they had duly conducted the solemnities of the Mass, and
the Paschal Lamb had filled the minds of all, they sought
other nourishment that might fill the body. When the table
linens had whitened the broad boards, they reclined there
side by side, and the bishop had begun to bless the loaves   565
that had been set out. Lo! The holy brother who was charged
with dispatching the ministry to the poor, coming forward
in haste, showed them that the antechambers were all filled
by the many paupers who had gathered from every quarter,

570 quos sperata iubet elemosina regis adesse.
Rex liber, rex munificus, rex laude perhenni
dignus, ad hanc uocem solita pietate mouetur
appositumque sibi confringi precipit illis
argenti multo constantem pondere discum.

575   Presul Aidanus, hoc delectatus in actu
principis, "Hec," inquit, "nunquam manus inueterascat!"
Vota uiri mouere Deum: manus integra regis
nunc quoque perdurat nullo uiolabilis euo.
    Interea regi tam largo, tam uenerando,

580 tam celebri causa prolis Kineburga creande
nubere debebat Kinegilsi filia regis,
uirgo statu gestuque decens, pietate fideque
insignis, sensu sexuque pudica, fauore
blandiciisque placens, uultu cultuque decora.

585 Nec tamen Oswaldi potuit superare uigorem
uel grauis anxietas, uel luxuriosa iuuentus,
uel mera simplicitas, uel splendida forma, uel ipse
omnia qui uincit amor, in connubia preceps
ut sibi uellet eam nuptu coniungere donec

590 ydolatre soceri posset prius esse patrinus
quam gener, et fidei sibi federe iungeret ambos.
Ille, ministerio sancti mediante Birini,
rege sacro multum suadente, renunciat hostis
fraudibus antiqui lauacrique renascitur undis.

595 Dicta renascentis Oswaldo filia nubit.
Soluitur in fructum flos uirginitatis uterque
quo propagatur generosa propago, puerque
prodit Athelwoldus Deyre quem sceptra manebant.

whom hope of the king's alms had compelled to put in an   570
appearance. That liberal and generous king, that king worthy of endless praise, was moved by this announcement according to his customary piety, and he ordered that a very
heavy silver dish, which had been placed before him, should
be broken up on their behalf.

Bishop Aidan, delighted by the prince's act, cried out,   575
"May this hand never grow old!" The man's prayers moved
God: the king's hand even now remains intact, inviolate
through every age.

Meanwhile, Cyneburg, the daughter of King Cynegils—a
virgin seemly of posture and bearing, excelling in piety and
faith, modest in disposition and as to her sex, pleasing in her
goodwill and charm, attractive of face and mien—was engaged for the sake of producing offspring to marry so gener-   580
ous, venerable, and famous a king. Yet neither grave anxiety,
nor wanton youth, nor pure naïveté, nor her shining beauty,
nor love itself that conquers all, was able to overcome Os-   585
wald's vigor, that, rushing into wedlock, he should wish to
join her in marriage before he might stand as sponsor of his   590
idolatrous father-in-law, prior to becoming his son-in-law,
and might join them both to himself in the compact of faith.
The other man, by the mediation of Saint Birinus's ministry
and the holy king's great persuasion, renounced the deceits
of the ancient Foe and was reborn in the waters of the font.
The said daughter of that man who was born again married   595
Oswald. The flower of either's virginity fell away into fruit
by which a nobly born progeny was brought forth, and they
produced a son, Aethelwold, destined for the throne of
Deira.

Sic igitur regnasse nouem sanctissimus annis
600 dicitur Osuualdus excellens laude, triumpho.
Cunctis uirtutum titulis effulsit; et ecce
laus: tria regna sibi subiecit. Et ecce triumphus.
  Hunc sexcentesimo quadragesimoque secundo
anno post ortum nati de uirgine Christi
605 Augustique die quinto, cum gente feroci
Penda superueniens longa iam pace solutum
occupat et, comitum dispersis undique turbis,
illius impetui nichil unde resistat habentem,
tantus tam raro uallatus milite uictor
610 cogitur instanter hosti uel cedere uel non
cedere. Si cedat, ad dedecus hoc sibi cedet;
et si non cedat, illi cedetur ab illo.
Quid faciat? Fugiatne timens, an supplicet hosti
ut sibi parcatur, an dilatoria querat
615 dum socii redeant, an pugnet uiribus impar?
Si fugiat pudor illud erit; si supplicet hosti
hostis non parcet; si dilatoria querat
non impetrabit; si pugnet uiribus impar
occidet. Ergo quid est illi consulcius? Omnes
620 hos odit casus, et oportet ut eligat unum.
Ardua consistunt hinc, inde pericula, spemque
excludit pudor hinc fame, dolor inde salutis.
Ipse graues casus circumspicit, ut meliorem
eligat et uitet mala que diuturnius obsunt—
625 omne malum peius quanto diuturnius, unde
cum sit mors hominum breuis et confusio longa,
iudice peior eo confusio morte uidetur.

So the most holy Oswald, excellent in praise and in triumph, is said to have reigned nine years. He shone forth 600 with all the designations of virtue. Behold his praise: he subjected three kingdoms to himself. And now behold his triumph.

In the six hundred forty-second year after the birth of Christ from a Virgin, on the fifth day of August, Penda with 605 his fierce people overtook and besieged him when his guard was let down because of long peace, and when he had no means to resist the attack, since the throngs of his companions were dispersed to all quarters. Such a victor, protected by so few soldiers, was at once compelled either to yield or 610 not to yield. If he should yield, this would accrue to his dishonor; and if he should not yield, he would incur slaughter. What should he do? Flee in fear, or beg the foe to spare him, or seek delay until his fellows might return, or fight though 615 outmatched in strength? If he should flee, it would mean shame; if he should entreat the foe, the foe would not spare him; if he should seek delay, he would not obtain it; if he should fight outmatched in strength, he would die. Therefore what was most advisable? He hated all these outcomes 620 and was obliged to choose one. Harsh circumstances loomed on one side, peril on the other; on one side, shame cut off the hope for reputation, on the other, pain cut off hope of deliverance. He scrutinized these grave outcomes in order to choose the better, and to avoid evils of more lasting harm. Every evil is the worse as it is more lasting, whence, 625 since man's death is brief but his perdition long, by that judgment perdition seemed worse than death.

Propter quod res est, hoc plus est, uitaque cum sit
propter honestatem, uitam precellit honestas.
630 Rex ideo prudens mauult amittere uitam
quam decus et cedi uictor quam cedere uictus.
Occurrunt quot militibus tot milia; uitam
unusquisque suam nequiens defendere uendit.
Set quis mille uiris ubi non subcumberet unus?
635 Quisque tamen pugnat pro posse, trucidat hic unum,
ille duos, hic tres, hic quatuor, hiccine quinque,
hic sex, hic septem, prout unicuique facultas
ex uirtute sui datur aut ex debilitate
alterius. Sic multa cadunt prostrata prophane
640 milia milicie set multo plura supersunt.
Utque duplex etas uiginti secula complens
quando Iouis raras decerpit ab arbore frondes,
non reuirescendi permittit inesse uigorem,
pars cadit in terram, iaculis percussa Ciclopum,
645 pars egro torpet senio, pars putrefit imbre,
parsque ruinoso reueretur uertice uentis,
tunc licet iratus quid obesse bipennifer illi
Ligurgus poterit, per se casura uidetur;
haut secus Osuualdi comites tot gentis inique
650 milibus oppositi, tanta uirtute trucidant
hostes, tot capita truncant, tot pectora cedunt,
quod uirtus motiua sue priuacio cause
efficitur tandem, naturalisque caloris
principium, sedes anime, custodia uite,
655 incipit exhaustus per menbra fatiscere sanguis:
pars gladiis effusa perit, pars corporis estu

That is greater for whose sake a thing exists, and since life exists for honor's sake, honor excels life. And so the prudent king preferred to lose his life rather than his honor, and to be slaughtered as a victor rather than to yield as one conquered. Just as many thousands attacked, as he had single soldiers; each of them, being unable to defend his life, sold it dearly. But who at some point would not alone succumb to a thousand men? Yet each fought as he was able: this one killed one, another two, three, four, five, six, or seven, as he was granted the capability by his own strength or the other's weakness. Thus many thousands of the profane army were laid low and fell, but many more remained.

And just as, when the doubled age of twenty centuries breaks the thinned branches off Jove's tree and does not allow it to retain the vigor to grow again, part falls on the earth, struck by the Cyclops's javelins, part fades with sick old age, part rots in the rain, and part bows down to the winds with its crown in ruins, and then, though enraged Lycurgus will be able somehow to oppose it as he wields his ax, the fall seems to come of its own accord; scarcely otherwise did Oswald's companions, against so many thousands of that wicked nation, slay their enemies with such power, hack off so many heads, pierce so many breasts, that the power of motion became at last the privation of its own cause, and the blood, the origin of natural warmth, the seat of the soul, the guardian of life, began to grow exhausted throughout their limbs: part perished being shed by swords, part dried up because of the body's close-bound heat, part

630

635

640

645

650

655

arefit annexo, pars extenuatur in auras;
et licet occumbant, nil proficit hostis in illis,
intus enim uix inueniens quid ledere possit,
660 mors ueluti sompnus insensibilisque subintrat.
    Pro sociis orans ne morti spirituali
succumbant quos corporee succumbere cernit,
occidit Osuualdus rex inclitus et morientes
insequitur quos non potuit defendere uiuos.
665 Cuius et abscisum caput abscisosque lacertos
et tribus infixos palis pendere cruentus
Penda iubet, per quod reliquis exempla relinquat
terroris manifesta sui regemque beatum
esse probet miserum; set causam fallit utramque,
670 ultor enim fratris minime timet Oswius illum,
immo timere facit; nec rex miser, immo beatus
est qui fonte boni fruitur semel et sine fine.
Quem quia glorificat paradisus, ne miseretur
mundus, apud mundum signis effulget apertis.
675   Iamque uoluminibus commensurauerat annum
sol et luna suis, lustrato sol semel orbe,
luna duodecies, cum necdum brachia palis
nec caput auelli sceleratus Penda sinebat.
    Osuualdi uero Christus non immemor, eius
680 hanc ignominiam conuertit in eius honorem,
cuius honorandis obtemperat artubus anni
integritas mundumque sequi non audet ut ante;
discordantque sibi qui iugiter esse solebant
unanimes, annus et mundus: quatuor ille
685 temporibus constat, et quatuor hic elementis.

250

evaporated into the air; and though they fell, it availed the foe nothing in regard to them, for death, scarcely finding anything within them to injure, crept upon them like an in- 660 sensible slumber.

That excellent king Oswald fell while praying for his companions that they should not succumb to spiritual death, though he saw them succumb to death of the body, and he followed in death those men whom he was unable to defend while they lived. The bloodthirsty Penda commanded that 665 his severed head and arms should be hung affixed to three stakes, in order to leave for the survivors clear examples of his terror, and to prove that the blessed king was a wretch; but Oswy, the avenger of his brother, cheated him of either 670 intention, for he feared him not at all, but rather compelled him to fear; nor is the king wretched, but rather blessed, who now enjoys the fountain of Goodness once and for all. Lest the world should pity him, through evident miracles it shines forth before the world that paradise glorifies him.

And now sun and moon in their courses had measured 675 out a year, the sun wandering through its circuit once, the moon twelve times, while the wicked Penda would not permit the arms nor head to be cut loose from the stakes.

Yet Christ did not forget Oswald, but converted this ig- 680 nominy to his honor: the integral course of the year deferred to his honorable limbs and dared not follow the world as previously. The year and the world were in disagreement, though they were accustomed always to stand in accord: the former consists of four seasons, the latter of four elements. 685

Tempora: uer, estas, autumpnus, hyems; elementa:
aer, ignis, humus, aqua. Per se dicitur ignis
feruens, unda gelans, aer humens, humus arens.
Conformare penes has formas quatuor illa
690 tempora deberent se quatuor hiis elementis,
set non est in eis horum complexio: formam
exuit autumpnus terre, uer aeris, estas
ignis, hiems laticis; minus humet uer, minus aret
autumpnus, minus alget hyems, minus estuat estas.
695 Quid loquor? Omne timet regalia ledere membra
tempus; aues auide fugiunt, et reptile sordens,
et nebule tristes, et turbo plus uiolentus,
et grando uehemens, et quicquid obesse decori
in casu quocumque potest. Color iminet idem,
700 integritas eadem, fluxus quoque sanguinis idem.
Sic sua defertur sancto reuerencia regi,
quodque putabatur ad probrum dedere cedit
ad decus et mire mala fiunt causa bonorum,
mors uite, dampnum lucri, contemptus honoris.
705 Iamque coronatum regis caput in paradiso
saluandasque manus operum mercede suorum
non sic infigi palis, non talia Christus
ulterius prebere sinit spectacula uulgo.
Osuuius, Osuualdi successor, frater, et ultor
710 impetit et superat Pendam fraternaque digno
condit honore caput et brachia. Nam caput aptat
in feretro sancti Cuthberti, brachia Banbire.
Set monachus quidam, legalis latro, fidelis
sacrilegus, facto pius et sceleratus eodem,
715 dextram furtiue subreptam transtulit inde
in claustrum Burgense Petri; tamen hoc ita factum

(The seasons: spring, summer, autumn, winter; the elements: air, fire, earth, water.) Fire is considered intrinsically hot, water cold, air moist, earth dry. Those four seasons ought to have conformed themselves to the forms of these 690 four elements, but in them there was no bonding of these elements: autumn shed the form of earth, spring that of air, summer that of fire, winter that of water; spring was less humid, autumn less dry, winter less cold, summer less hot. Why 695 go on? Each season dreaded to injure to the king's limbs; the birds fled in haste, the foul reptile, dour clouds, the whirlwind in its greater violence, strong hail, and whatever was by any chance able to impede their beauty. The same color, soundness, and flow of blood were visible in them. So the 700 elements' reverence was accorded to the holy king; anything likely to bring opprobrium made place for his dignity, and those evils miraculously became the cause of good, death the cause of life, loss the cause of gain, contempt the cause of honor.

And now Christ did not suffer that king's head, which 705 was crowned in paradise, and those hands, which would be preserved as a reward for their own works, to be fixed on stakes, nor that they should offer any further spectacles to the common people. Oswy, Oswald's successor, brother, and avenger, attacked and overcame Penda and buried his broth- 710 er's head and arms with due honor. For he placed the head in the coffin of Saint Cuthbert, the arms at Banbury. But a certain monk, a sanctioned robber, a faithful defiler, pious and guilty by one and the same deed, translated the right arm 715 thence by furtive abduction to the cloister of Peterborough;

disponente Deo sapiens aduertere debet:
ante coli uoluit ibi rex sacer, hic modo mauult,
clerus namque frequens est ille, frequencior iste
720 in psalmis; celeber locus ille, celebrior iste.
     Hec est illa manus Osuualdi quam benedixit
presul Aidanus. O quantum uota bonorum
pondus habent! Affectus in hoc, effectus in illo
extitit, affectus breuis, effectusque perhennis,
725 estque manus similis modo cese quam neque uermis
demolitur edax, nec contrahit egra senectus,
nec maculat uiciosa lues, nec lubricus aer
formis immutat quibus immutatur et ipse.
Nil equidem terit arriditas, nil inficit humor,
730 nil ibi constringit frigus, nil dissipat estus,
set species natiua manet, proprieque saluti
nulla foris nocitura timet, causamque manendi
intus habet, quam nulla potest elidere causa.
Inmarcessibilis manet eternumque uigebit
735 uenis et neruis caro procerusque lacertus,
osse medulloso maior quocunque moderno.
In latum procera manus protenditur; index,
pollex, et medius recti sunt, auricularis
et medicus proni sidunt palmeque coherent.
740 Sic manet illa manus, leuis cute, liuida uenis,
mollis carne; cutis est leuis et integra, nerui
liuentes et flexibiles, caro mollis et alba,
candens et mollis candore superficiei,
mollicie solida. Delectat candida uisum
745 et mollis tactum, quam qui deuocior eger
aut uidet aut tangit uisu tactuque iuuatur,

yet a wise man should take note that this was done by the
will of God: the king had earlier desired to be venerated
there, but now preferred this place, for the clergy of that
former place are diligent in the Psalms, but this congregation more so; that former place is illustrious, but this place   720
more illustrious.

This is the hand of Oswald that Bishop Aidan blessed. O
what weight do the prayers of good men carry! Affect was
evident in one man, effect in the other—a fleeting affect, a
permanent effect, and the hand is now like a cheese that de-   725
vouring worms do not gnaw, nor infirm old age shrivel, nor
the flaw of any stain blemish, nor the flowing air transform
with those shapes by which it is itself transformed. Dryness
does not wear away at it, nor moisture infect it, cold freeze   730
it solid, heat decompose it; but its native appearance en-
dures and knows no fear that any external force will lessen
its intrinsic well-being: it contains within itself the cause of
its permanence, which no other cause is able to compro-
mise. The flesh of the long upper arm remains incorruptible and forever strong of vein and muscle, larger than any   735
present-day bone filled with marrow. The elongated hand is
spread out in its breadth; the index finger, thumb, and middle finger lie straight; the fourth and fifth fingers rest prone
and touch the palm. So that hand remains, smooth of skin,   740
dark of vein, soft of flesh; the skin is smooth and intact, the
muscles dark and flexible, the flesh soft and white, bright
and soft in the brightness of its surface, solid in its softness.
Being bright, it is pleasing to sight, and being soft, pleasing to touch; the sick man who sees or touches it with more   745

et quicunque dolor abit in quamcunque salutem.
O sanctus qui prodigiis signisque choruscat,
conpescit nocumenta, fugat fantasmata, sedat
750 horrores, sanat languores, subiugat hostes!
    Quid moror in rebus quarum me turba fatigat?
Omnis sacra sacri iuuat intercessio regis,
cuius perducat nos ad consorcia Christus
rex regum, cum quo sit Patri Spirituique
755 Sancto, sicut erat in principio, decus et laus
et uirtus, et nunc et semper et omne per euum. Amen.

devotion is helped by the sight or touch, and every sort of complaint gives way to every sort of cure. O holy one who shines forth with prodigious miracles, constrains injuries, puts illusions to flight, stills tremors, heals ailments, sub- 750 dues foes!

Why do I delay over matters whose number exhausts me? Every holy intercession of the holy king is beneficial. To his fellowship may Christ the King of kings lead us; and with him to the Father and Holy Spirit be honor and praise and 755 might, as it was in the beginning, is now, and shall be forever. Amen.

LIFE OF BIRINUS

Prologus in uitam Sancti Birini, episcopi et confessoris

Et pudet et fateor quia turgeo, magna professus:
Wintoniensis enim prothopresulis inclita gesta
aggredior rudiore stilo, possumque uideri
fortunam Priami cantans et nobile bellum
5 ethnicus. Est equidem uir quem presumo canendum
dignior attolli quam sit Tyrintius heros
uel sit Alexander Macedo. Tyrintius hostem
uicit, Alexander mundum, Birinus utrumque,
nec solum domuit mundum Birinus et hostem
10 sed sese, bello uincens et uictus eodem.

De Sancto Birino. Inuocatio ad Birinum.

Alte parens, humilem non aspernere poetam,
set potius dignere, precor, Birine, labori
aspirare meo: nec enim fiducia Muse
certe mee mouet istud opus, set iussio Petri,
15 me quasi compellens, causaque ualentior omni,
summa tue laudis totum cantanda per orbem.

Inuocatio ad Petrum, Wintoniensem episcopum

Tu quoque proposito faueas, Petre, Vintoniensis
presul, Birini successor idonee, cima
ardua uirtutum, iubar admirabile cleri.
20 Grande patrocinium prebent tibi quatuor, unus
natalis patrie, tres pontificalis honoris:
Birinus, Suithunus, Adelwoldusque ducatum

Prologue to the Life of Saint Birinus, bishop and confessor

I both blush and confess that I am swollen with pride, having taken on a great theme: for I address the illustrious deeds of Winchester's first bishop—albeit with too coarse a style—and I may seem like a pagan who sings of Priam's 5 fortune and his noble war. The man of whom I presume to sing is indeed worthier of exaltation than either Hercules or Macedonian Alexander. Hercules vanquished the foe, Alexander the world, but Birinus both, nor did Birinus tame world and foe alone, but himself as well, both conqueror and 10 conquered in one and the same war.

On Saint Birinus. Invocation to Birinus.

Lofty father, spurn not your humble poet, but rather deign, Birinus, I entreat you, to breathe life into my labor: for confidence in my Muse has certainly not led to this work, but the command of Peter has more or less compelled me— 15 along with a cause more potent than any: the sum of your praise that must be sung throughout the world.

Invocation to Peter, bishop of Winchester

May you, too, favor my intention, Peter, bishop of Winchester, fit successor to Birinus, lofty summit of virtues, admirable splendor of the clergy. Four saints offer you a 20 great source of patronage, one belonging to your native land, three associated with your episcopal honor. Birinus, Swithun, and Aethelwold grant guidance to a pontiff of

pontifici dant Wintonie, Martinus alumpno
Turonie; quapropter ego de quatuor istis
25 proposui cantare tibi, Birinida scribens
ut quasi preludat aliis tribus. Aptior ordo
constituit leuiora prius, nam pectora lente
occupat et lente solet euanescere torpor.
Martini uero, de quo me scribere primum
30 iussisti, quodam laus est adeunda uolatu;
ergo uolare uolens prius euacuabo gradatim
segniciem: gradiar, curram, saltabo, uolabo,
ut librem—gradiens, currens, saliens—gradiendo
cursum, currendo saltum, saliendo uolatum.
35 Birinus siquidem mare metitur pedes—ecce
gressus; Suithunus Benedictum preterit—ecce
cursus; Adelwoldus de terris emicat—ecce
saltus; Martinus celum petit—ecce uolatus.
Hos ego ductores certo sequar ordine, motu
40 unumquemque suo; quorum tibi carmina postquam
scripsero, plura libens scribam cum plura iubebis.

De natiuitate Sancti Birini

Cum simulacrorum cultus exuta prophanos
Roma Deum coleret, in se gauisa recenter
catholicam florere fidem, puer inde sereno
45 nascitur auspicio Birinus, mente benignus,
ore decens, patria felix, et origine clarus,
ut quem commendet pia mens, illuminet oris
forma decens, autenticet urbs, sullimet origo.
Ecce labor uester, uestre plantatio dextre,

Winchester, Martin to a foster son of Tours. And so I have   25
proposed to sing to you of all four, writing a *Birinid* as pre-
lude to the other three. The better-suited order puts easier
matters first, for torpor creeps slowly into the breast and is
wont slowly to dissipate. But the praise of Martin, of whom
you first commanded me to write, must be approached by a   30
kind of flight. Since therefore I wish to fly, I shall first purge
my sluggishness step by step. I shall walk, run, leap, and
then fly, so that walking I may accelerate to a run, running to
a leap, and leaping to full flight. For Birinus traverses the sea   35
on foot—there's the walk; Swithun surpasses Benedict—
there's the run; Aethelwold shines out from the earth—
there's the leap; and Martin seeks out heaven—there's flight
for you. I shall follow these guides in fixed order, each in his   40
own motion; after I have written their poems for you, I shall
gladly write more when you command more.

On the birth of Saint Birinus

When Rome shed the sacrilegious cult of idols in order to
worship God, and she still newly rejoiced that the catholic faith flourished within her, thence Birinus was born, a lad   45
under fair auspices, benevolent of mind, decorous of speech,
fortunate of homeland, illustrious of parentage, one commended by his pious mind, illumined by the fitting beauty
of his speech, guaranteed by his city, raised high by his ori-
gins. Peter, prince of the church, and Paul, its teacher, behold how your labor, the planting of your own right hand,

50 quomodo fructificat, Petre princeps, Paule magister
ecclesie! Iam de fidei pinguedine uestre
hic est exortus frondentis palmes oliue.
Vos nectar, mons, lux; hic stilla, columpna, lucerna:
hec expressa sapit de uestro nectare stilla,
55 hec excisa riget de uestro monte columpna,
hec accensa micat de uestra luce lucerna,
estque sui uester dulcor dulcoris origo,
uirtus uirtutis, lux lucis, ut hiis tribus utens
utiliter, tristes quos toxicat ira, caducos
60 quos caro prosternit, cecos quos decipit error,
exhilaret dulcore, leuet uirtute, serenet
luce sui, curasque gregi tres conferat unus,
donans tristibus ex dulcedine mella, caducis
ex uirtute statum, cecis ex luce ducatum.
65 O uos sal terre, lux mundi publica, rerum
splendor, apostolici facies reuerenda senatus!
Ecce nouus uestri dominatus uernula, uestre
artis successor, uestre pietatis alumpnus,
uestre uirtutis imitator, quem neque pena
70 exilii, nec amor patrie, nec summa laborum,
nec formido necis, nec desperatio uite,
flectere sufficiat quin spiritualibus agris
celitus excultis diuini semina uerbi
spargat, et humanas leuet in celestia mentes.

De commendacione Sancti Birini

75 Indolis egregie puero Natura, Sophia,
et Fortuna suas certant impendere dotes.
Nature dono uelox facundia, liber

here bears fruit! From the richness of your faith here has 50
sprung forth a branching olive bough. You are the nectar,
the mountain, the light; this one is a droplet, a column, a
lamp: the droplet pressed from your nectar tastes sweet, the 55
column hewn from your mountain stands rigid, the lamp
kindled from your light shines forth. Your sweetness is the
origin of his sweetness, your virtue the origin of his virtue,
your light of his light, so that making practical use of all
three, he revives with sweetness those sad ones whom wrath
has poisoned, raises up with virtue those fallen ones whom 60
the flesh has laid low, and calms with his light blind men
whom error deceives. Though one, he confers triple benefit
upon his flock, giving of his sweetness honey to the sad, firm
standing to the fallen through his virtue, and guidance to
the blind through his light. O you salt of the earth, common 65
light of the world, splendor of all things, reverend visage of
the apostolic senate! Behold this new servant of your do-
minion, a successor to your skill, a foster son of your piety,
an imitator of your virtue! Neither penalty of exile, nor love 70
of native land, nor extreme labor, nor fear of death, nor despair for life would suffice to divert him from sowing the
seed of God's word in spiritual fields divinely tilled or from
raising human minds to heavenly matters.

On the commendation of Saint Birinus

Nature, Wisdom, and Fortune contended in imparting their 75
gifts to that child of outstanding promise. By nature's gift
his eloquence was swift, his perception clear, his under-

sensus, sullimis datur intellectus, acutum
ingenium, dominans ratio, pia uiscera, mite
80 pectus, conspicuum corpus, clarum genus, et (que
omnibus hiis pocius ualet) excellencia morum.
Cum puerum dotent tot naturalia, si quid
est imperfectum nature, dextra Sophie
suplet et apponit melioris acumina lime:
85 mentem rectificat studiosam, cor locupletat
ingenuum, pectus fecundat nobile, gestus
explicat illustres, mores componit honestos,
et deforme nichil incompositumue relinquit.
More licet proprio Fortuna sit in statione
90 mobilis, in motu stabilis, nulloque tenenda
fune, uolubiliter rapiat nunc alta deorsum,
infima nunc sursum, uoluatque perhenniter orbem,
est penes hunc oblita sui, quia non uariatur,
immo fauens etiam nolenti prosperat acta
95 eius, et euentus excludit dextra sinistros.
Hiis tribus instructo iuueni, de prosperitate
mundi, de fastu patrie, de laude parentum,
de fama populi minor est in pectore cura,
nec refert ex fortuitis euentibus inter
100 lenes et duros, inter dulces et amaros,
inter felices et leuos, inter alacres
et mestos, inter sollempnes et lacrimosos.
Hic est cos, dos, flos, et ros: cos relligionis,
dos fidei, flos ecclesie, ros dogmatis; hic est
105 libra, liber, lumen, limes, scola, scalaque: libra
consilii, liber eloquii, lumen rationis,
limes honestatis, scola morum, scala salutis.

standing exalted, his talent acute, his reason dominant, his
inward parts merciful, his heart gentle, his body attrac-   80
tive, his lineage illustrious, and (what avails above all these)
his character excellent. Though so many gifts of Nature endowed the lad, the right hand of Wisdom supplied Nature's
any defect, applying the sharp strokes of her better file. She   85
made straight his zealous mind, enriched his freeborn heart,
made fertile his noble breast, augmented his noble bearing,
consolidated his honorable character, and left nothing misshapen or ill-arranged. Though Fortune is by her very character mobile in her fixity, fixed in her mobility, and being held   90
by no constraint now unpredictably drags the lofty down,
now draws up the lowly, and endlessly turns the world, toward this one she forgot herself by showing no variation.
Rather, favoring him even when he was reluctant, she pros-
pered his deeds, and her right hand warded off inauspi-   95
cious outcomes. Favored in these three matters [of nature, wisdom, and fortune], the youth had little care for
worldly prosperity, for pride of native soil, for praise of
his parents, for popular reputation, nor among chance
events did he make distinction between mild and harsh, be-   100
tween sweet and bitter, between happy and unfortunate,
between joyous and sad, between solemn and tearful. He
was whetstone, dowry, flower, and dew: whetstone of religion, dowry of faith, flower of the church, dew of doctrine.
He was scale, book, illumination, path, school, and ladder: 105
scale of counsel, book of eloquence, illumination of reason,
path of honesty, school of character, ladder of salvation.

Moribus excellit, set sunt insignia morum
limitibus contenta suis, quos degenerare
110 non paciens in se uirtutum iurgia quedam
apparere sinit set non existere, castus
ut fenix, pulcher ut pauo, cautus ut anguis,
simplex ut turtur, grauis ut leo, mitis ut agnus,
pauperibus largus et mansuetus, sibi parcus
115 et grauis, ore decens et pulcher, corpore castus
et sacer, ad summa prudens et cautus, ad ima
simplex et sciolus. Senis amicitur in alis,
ut cum perfectis numeretur quem numerorum
perfectus fert primus ubi Perfectio Prima.
120 Mirantur quia sic coeant conuertibilesque
sint dotes, licet opposite, prudencia simplex,
simplicitas prudens, grauitas mansueta, grauisque
mansuetudo, pudor formosus, forma pudica,
sicque quasi quedam miscentur aromata quorum
125 temperat alterutrum, ne flamma libidinis aut ne
frigus auaricie fel subtermisceat acre,
omnimodoque malo uiget inpermixta bonorum
congeries, et ne uirtus in collaterale
degeneret uicium. Trahitur uirtute remota,
130 annexis igitur uirtutibus ardua scala
erigitur per quam Birinus in ethera scandit.
Thesaurizat enim studiose non ubi uermis
demolitur, ubi fur effodit, aut ubi tempus
extenuat, set ubi cunctis datur ultima rebus
135 integritas, ubi tuta fides, ubi uita perhennis.

He excelled in character, but the marks of his character were content within their bounds. Not suffering these to degenerate, he allowed the appearance (but not the reality!) of a sort of conflict between his virtues. He was chaste as the phoenix, beautiful as a peacock; wary as a serpent, simple as a dove; severe as a lion, gentle as a lamb; generous and affable to the poor, niggardly and severe toward himself; seemly and beautiful of face, holy and chaste of body; prudent and careful in the loftiest matters, simple and innocent of the lowest things. He was clothed in sixfold wings, that he might be numbered among the perfect: the first of perfect numbers carried him where First Perfection resides. All marveled that his endowments converged and were interchangeable, though opposite—his simple prudence, prudent simplicity, gentle gravity, grave gentleness, handsome chastity, chaste beauty. All were so mingled, like aromas that temper one another, that neither the flame of desire nor the chill of avarice mixed in its bitter gall; the mass of good qualities flourished unalloyed with any manner of evil, and no virtue degenerated into its corresponding vice. When virtue departs, the ladder is removed; when virtues are added the ladder is raised high upon which Birinus ascended to heaven. For he zealously stored up treasure not where worm consumes, where thief breaks in, or where time wears down, but where wholeness, sure faith, and eternal life are at the end granted to all.

Quomodo fuerit Sanctus Birinus contemplatiuus et actiuus

Tot uirtus crescens gradibus quot uita diebus
iam quasi fastidit latebras torporis et exit
in campos exercitii, pariterque uirentem
mente manuque uirum secum de puluere mundi
140   tollit et ethereos audet penetrare penates.
Ipse manu redolens Martham set mente Mariam,
est bonus et melior: bona scilicet accio circa
plurima, set melior est contemplatio circa
Unum quod nullo poterit per secula claudi
145   fine set eternos in tempore percipit usus.
Hec, inquam, melior: epulis celestibus, illa
esuriente, fruens; illa sudante, quiescens;
illa stante, sedens; illa pereunte, superstes.
Duxit in uxorem Birinus utramque sororem.
150   Stans et enim residet, distractus uero quiescit.
Ante Deum residet contemplans, statque ministrans,
et qui distrahitur in plura quiescit in Uno,
diuersisque uiis ad idem simul et semel idem
progrediens, est totus in hac et totus in illa.
155   Aduersus Christi pugilem tria bella gerentem
nec caro, nec mundus, nec demon proficit; immo
flagicium carnale perit, mundana cupido
effugit, hostilis exercitus exsuperatur.
Nam produxit eum diuina pharetra, sagittam
160   scilicet electam, que quemlibet eminus hostem
figat et aduersum Sathane transuerberet agmen.
Hic sexaginta de fortibus Israel unus
qui uigilant circa lectum Salomonis, habentes

How Saint Birinus led both a contemplative
and an active life

His virtue, increasing by as many degrees as his life in length
of days, now shunned the lair of sloth, as it were, and went
forth to the fields of combat. It raised up with itself from   140
the world's dust that man vigorous of mind and hand and
dared to advance upon the celestial thresholds. Resembling
Martha in the work of his hands but Mary in his mind, he
was a good man and a better one: his action in many things
was good, but even better was his contemplation concerning the One that a fixed end will never be able to terminate,   145
but which perceives the practices of eternity within time.
Such contemplation I declare is better: it enjoys heavenly
banquets while that other, the active life, goes hungry; it
rests while the other toils; it sits still while the other stands;
it survives when the other perishes. Birinus took both sisters
as wife. Standing, he sat quiet; though anxious, he rested.   150
He sat quiet before God in contemplation, yet stood in service, and he who was anxious for many things rested in the
One. Proceeding by diverse paths at one and the same time,
he was completely absorbed in both.

Against Christ's champion, who waged war on three   155
fronts, neither flesh nor world nor devil availed. Rather, sins
of the flesh perished, worldly desire fled, and the Foe's army
was vanquished. For he was drawn forth from God's quiver,
as an arrow chosen to pierce every foe from afar and transfix   160
the ranks of Satan facing him. He was one of the sixty strong
men of Israel who keep watch around the bed of Solomon,

in manibus gladios ad bella ualentibus. Ensis
165 uniuscuiusque super femur eius habetur
propter terrores nocturnos. Diximus umbram,
inuolucrum, paleam; sequitur lux, uisio, granum:
allegoria subest quid sexaginta figurent
excubie Salomon, ensis, femur. Inspiciantur
170 hii numeri, senarius et denarius: alter
primus perfectus mundane philosophie,
alter diuine, quibus in se multiplicatis
inde resultabit sexagenarius, estque
compositum redolens sua componentia. Duplex
175 ergo per hunc numerum perfectio dicitur, una
coram diuinis obtutibus, altera coram
mundanis, quod simpliciter non ista uel illa,
set conuersiue numeris intellige primis
qui conuersiue sunt in se multiplicati
180 sic serie conuertibili. Perfectio laudat
Birinum mundana Deo diuinaque mundo.
Dicitur in lecto Salomon, in corpore sensus;
carnis cura, femur; ratio, uersatilis ensis.
In lecto Salomon—hoc est in corpore sensus—
185 dormit, id est torpet, quem sexaginta potentes
circumeunt, hoc est quos perficit utraque uirtus.
Ense femur premitur—hoc est ratione uoluptas.
Miles enim fortis in bello spirituali
Birinus, sensum uigili ratione gubernans,
190 illecebras uirtute premit noctisque timores
pacat, et antiqui stimulos eliminat hostis.
Nil carnale sapit degens in carne, gradumque
excellens merito, nomen uirtute, sacerdos

holding swords in hands able in war. Each carries his blade 165
upon his thigh because of the terrors of the night. We have
spoken only shadow, shell, and husk, but here follow light,
vision, and kernel: an allegory lies beneath what is repre-
sented by the sixty guards of Solomon, the sword, the thigh.
We should look carefully at these numbers, six and ten. The 170
one is the first perfect number of natural philosophy, the
other that of sacred philosophy, and by multiplying them
together the number sixty will result, a compound number
that reflects its factors. Thus by this number a double per- 175
fection is declared, one in the sight of God, the other in the
sight of this world, which is straightforwardly neither the
one nor the other, but you should understand it reciprocally
according to its primary numbers, which are thus multiplied
reciprocally among themselves in an interchangeable series. 180
Human perfection praised Birinus to God while divine perfection praised him to the world. Solomon is said to be
in the bed, sensation in the body; the thigh represents the
care of the flesh, and the moving sword, reason. Solomon
in his bed—that is, sensation in the body—slumbers—that 185
is, grows sluggish. Sixty mighty men surround him—that is,
those whom both sorts of virtue perfect. A sword presses
upon the thigh—that is, reason represses pleasure. Birinus,
a valiant solider in spiritual combat, governing sensation by
watchful reason, through virtue repressed enticements and 190
calmed the terrors of the night, driving away the goads of
the ancient Enemy. Though dwelling in the flesh, he gave
of nothing carnal, and excelling his rank by his deserts, his
name by his virtue, he was supposed a priest long before

creditur ante diu quam sit, prius esse meretur
195 quam fieri possit, quasi quadam uaticinando
lingua uirtutum qualis quantusque futurus
pastor diuino sit preficiendus ouili.
Resque fidem sequitur consecratusque sacerdos
altaris diuina sacri misteria tractat,
200 in quibus attacta uerbi uirtute superni
uinum fit sanguis, panis caro, quatinus ista
ut duo sunt hominis in Christo, sic duo Christi
sint in eo corpusque duos confederet unum.
Hoc unire sibi Birinum federe Christus
205 dignatur, summus humilem, dominusque clientem.
Ille, gradus tanti dignum sortitus honorem,
quam miser et tenuis mundo, quam durus et asper
carni, quam ualidus et inexpugnabilis Hosti
existat, nec mens nec lingua retexere posset.
210 Nam cum uita prior uirtute refulserit omni,
excellente tamen premitur splendore sequentis.

De bona fama illius et potestate ampliata

Sancta tot ex meritis emanat opinio, cuius
suauis odor totam diffusus inebriat urbem.
Non latet urbs in monte sedens, et nemo lucernam
215 ponere sub modio, set tollere debet in altum
in candelabro, ne lumen inutile spargens
ardeat, immo domum Domini radiosa serenet;

he became one; he deserved that status before he could be ₁₉₅
made one, as though prophesying with the tongue of his virtues what sort of shepherd, and how great a one, he would
be made over the Lord's sheepfold. Substance followed ex-
pectation, and once ordained as priest he conducted the divine mysteries of the holy altar, in which by application of ₂₀₀
the power of God's word wine becomes blood and bread becomes flesh: thus just as these two aspects of man are present in Christ, so these two aspects of Christ are present in
man, and one body joins the two together. By this pact
Christ deigned to unite Birinus to himself, the lowly to the ₂₀₅
highest, the servant to the master. Neither mind nor tongue
might express how wretched and meager Birinus was in the
world's eyes, how hard and harsh he was toward the flesh,
how vigorous and invincible toward the Foe, once he had at-
tained the worthy honor of such a rank. For although his ₂₁₀
previous life shone with every virtue, nevertheless it was
surpassed by the splendid excellence of what follows.

On his good reputation and his increased power

From so many merits, a holy reputation flowed forth whose
pleasant fragrance intoxicated the whole city as it spread. A ₂₁₅
city set on a hill does not lie hidden, and no one should place
a lamp under a bushel but rather raise it aloft on a stand, lest
it should burn uselessly as it scatters its light, when instead
its radiance should gladden the Lord's house. So report of

famaque Birini uelut urbs in monte, lucerna
in candelabro, longe lateque choruscat.
220 Sedis apostolice presul uenerabilis, immo
nobilitatis apex et honoris, Honorius, omni
relligione sacer, omni pietate benignus,
magna stupet letus celebris preconia fame;
set que magna stupet meritis probat esse minora.
225 Summa uidens igitur sancte fastigia uite
mandat ut Asterius, Genuensis episcopus, illi
impositis manibus exaltet cornua iusti
culmine pontificis et honore coronet honestum.
Postquam Birino tria sunt collata—potestas
230 uberior, gradus ulterior, reuerentia maior—
hoc honus ei honor: papa dictante ferendum
suscipit ut fido ferat imperterritus ore
catholice fidei flauis documenta Britannis.

Sanctus in patriam peregrinat

Sanctus apostolico presul reuerenter obedit,
235 blandaque postponens note solatia gentis
et dulcis patrie consanguineique senatus,
exulat et patriam fugiendo repatriat idem;
Christus namque, pater et patria, cognitus illi
et cognatus, adest quocumque tetenderit, a quo
240 omne bonum, sine quo nullum. Non exulat ergo
cui patris et patrie presentia semper inheret.
Iam sibi prouiso ductore, uiatica sumit
aggrediturque uiam longinquam, nec modo septem
destituit montes urbis, sed climata quinque
245 orbis, eo tendens quo nullus peruenit Austri

Birinus gleamed out far and wide like a city on a hill, like a lamp on its stand. The venerable bishop of the apostolic see—Honorius, pinnacle of nobility and honor, saintly in all religious observance, benevolent in all piety—joyfully wondered at the great tidings of his widespread fame; but those great tidings at which he wondered he proved were less than his merits. Therefore, seeing the high course of his holy life, he commanded Asterius, bishop of Genoa, to exalt the horns of the just to the loftiness of the episcopate by laying on of hands, crowning the honorable with honor. When these three gifts—wider power, higher rank, greater reverence—had been conferred upon Birinus, this was both his onus and his honor: by command of the pope he took up the burden of bearing unafraid to the yellow-haired Britons the faithfully reported teachings of the catholic faith.

The saint sojourns as an exile into his native land

The holy bishop reverently obeyed the pope, and setting aside the pleasant comforts of his own race, his sweet country, and his senatorial kin, he went into exile, at once fleeing his native land and returning to it. For Christ, himself both father and fatherland, both known to him and kin, from whom comes every good, without whom is no good, was with him wherever he proceeded. And so he was no exile to whom father and fatherland remained ever present. With his guide now secured, he took provisions for his journey and set out on the long road, deserting not only the city's seven hills but the earth's five climes, proceeding where no

flatus, sed glacie tellus constricta perhenni.
Cum nec parturiat bachas nec proferat uuas,
Tetidis et Cereris celebrat connubia uulgus.
Inter se choisse deas Hymeneus abhorret;
250 pronuba Thesiphone thalamis ululauit in illis,
et cecinit dirum bubo mortalibus omen.
Connubii prolem tam detestabilis—immo
nescio quod Stigie monstrum conforme paludi—
"ceruisiam" plerique uocant. Nil spissius illa
255 dum bibitur, nil clarius est dum mingitur, unde
constat quod multas feces in uentre relinquit.
Non tamen ille timet monstri nocumenta maligni,
nec remorantur eum quecumque pericula, potus
letalis, cibus inficiens, aer grauis, equor
260 monstriferum, tellus sterilis, gens perfida, lingua
barbara; nec reuocant horum contraria, uinum
dulce, cibus sapidus, aer placabilis, equor
nullum, terra ferax, gens credula, lingua Latina.
Mille metus premit unus amor, nescitque uel ensi
265 cedere uel cedem dilectio uera uereri.

Qualiter ingressus nauem palle cum corpore Christi oblitus sit

Decursis igitur multo conamine multis
terrarum spaciis, iam flaua Britannia solo
prospicitur diuisa mari, nauisque parata
expectat fluctus refluos quibus unda redundet.
270 Tum sacer antistes iter aggressurus aquarum
sacrosancta prius celebrat mysteria Christi,
quo mediante Dei Patris impetrare fauorem

278

breath of the south wind reached, but the earth was frozen with perennial ice. Since it brought forth neither wine nor grapes, the population celebrated a marriage of Thetis and Ceres. Hymen shuddered at this congress between the goddesses. Tisiphone as bridesmaid wailed in those wedding   250 chambers, and the owl chanted an omen dire to mortals. The offspring of so hateful a union—or rather an unknown monster fit for the Stygian marsh—many call "beer." Nothing is cloudier when it's drunk, nothing clearer when it's   255 pissed out: thus it's clear that its many dregs linger in the belly. And yet he did not fear the injuries of that malevolent monster, nor did any dangers detain him: the lethal drink, foul food, heavy air, a sea full of portents, the sterile earth,   260 its treacherous race, a barbarous language. Nor did the contraries of these summon him back: sweet wine, savory food, agreeable air, no sea at all, a fertile land, a people of faith, and the Latin language. One love overcame a thousand fears, and true love knew neither how to yield to the sword   265 nor to fear slaughter.

How on entering the ship he forgot the pall
along with the body of Christ

And so having traversed the length of many lands with much effort, now he spied yellow-haired Britain, sundered by the sea alone, and the ready ship awaited the incoming tide on which the swell would surge once more. Then the saintly bishop, about to embark upon that watery journey, first cel-   270 ebrated Christ's most holy mysteries in order to obtain by his mediation the favor of God the Father, and to rejoice in

possit et emensi precio gaudere laboris.
Interea refluens operit sua litora pontus,
275   et grauis appenso diuellitur anchora fune.
Ille, sacri compos, nulla celestis omissa
parte ministerii, nauem properantior intrat.
Nec mora: conuerso puppim preit ordine prora.
Erigitur malus, firmantque sedilia funem.
280   Pendent uela, quibus felice tumentibus aura
deseritur litus; naute rapiuntur in altum.
O quotiens nocuit mala festinatio, qua sic
precipitatur opus ut non deliberet actor!
Magna feret nocumenta more qui parua recusat:
285   sanctus in exemplo Birinus, qui celebratis
rite mynisteriis ad nauem dum properaret
curas postposuit reliquas pallamque reliquit
quam discessuro donarat Honorius ille,
in qua corpus habens Christi consueuit amictum
290   circumferre sinu, sine quo non uinceret Hostem.

Recordatus rei oblite quid fecerit

Tam grauis oblitum thesauri se reminiscens
intercisa trahit mesto suspiria corde.
Poscit opem, promittit opes; suffragia naute
implorata negant. Quid tandem restat agendum?
295   Nescit an expediat procedere siue reuerti:
nam si procedat perdet post terga relictum
pignus et incurret irrestaurabile dampnum;
si redeat per diluuium sine naue redibit,
eius enim uoto communia uota repugnant.

the reward for his completed labor. Meanwhile the rising
sea covered its shores, and the heavy anchor was weighed on   275
the hauled-up rope. Having completed his sacred duty, having omitted no part of that heavenly service, he entered the
ship too hastily. The prow at once preceded the stern as the
ship turned about. The mast was raised, and the seats stead-
ied the rope. The sails hung: when they swelled in the favor-   280
able wind, shore was left behind; the seafarers were carried
off into the deep. How often does ill haste prove harmful,
when a task is so hastened forward that the one who performs it fails in his consideration! One who refuses the small   285
disadvantages of a delay will incur great ones. Take Saint
Birinus as an example, who, having duly performed his ser-
vices, in hastening to the ship neglected his remaining concerns and abandoned the pall which Honorius had given
him as he was about to depart—even though he was wont to   290
carry about in his bosom, wrapped in it, the body of Christ,
without which he might not conquer the Foe.

What he did when he remembered the forgotten object

Recalling that he had forgotten a treasure of such consequence, he drew forth choked sighs from his sad heart. He
pleaded for help, promised money, but the sailors denied
him the boon he begged. What in the end was left to do? He   295
had no idea whether it was better to go forward or turn
back; for if he went forward he would lose the relic he'd left
behind and sustain irreparable loss; if he went back through
the flood he would do so without the ship, for the will of all

300 Vult duo, uult neutrum; pauor est utrobique molestus.
Set subito litus magis elongatur et unda
altius intratur dum se sibi consulit ipsi,
et breuiore iuuans studium prolixius usu
deficit, hoc ipso quod sit, moriturque morando,
305 consiliumque minus dat consultatio maior;
mensque licet, raro dubios experta tumultus,
ex grauitate sui soleat consistere firma,
instar habet summo pendentis in aere nubis
quam flatus eque fortes Aquilonis et Austri
310 concutiunt, donec in componentia molis
prima liquefacte uapor eliciatur et humor.
Haut aliter sacrum pectus, rationibus eque
fortibus innitens, amor et timor ad dubitandum
impellunt (amor ex Austro, timor ex Aquilone),
315 donec ad extremum uapor exit amoris et humor
exprimitur fidei; qua proscribente timorem
ingreditur pro naue fidem comitesque relinquit
presul, et intrepidus tumidas maris insilit undas.
      O Christi regnum dominans, dominacio regnans,
320 lex pia, legitima pietas, tutela fidelis,
tuta fides, dignus dulcor, dignacio dulcis!
Per mare uir gradiens in naue timebat, in undis
non timet; equor enim non audet uiribus uti
in christum Domini patiturque natabile gressum.
325 Sic naturalis rerum preuertitur ordo,
et, licet inferior certis elementa gubernet
legibus et totum natura coherceat orbem,
dum noua perpendit dubio spectacula uisu,

rejected his will. He wanted both and wanted neither, and   300
trepidation assailed him on either side. But suddenly the
shore was further off, and they entered deeper water while
he deliberated, and a zeal more drawn out, dying in the delay, failed where its briefer use would have been more help-
ful. Further deliberation lessened good counsel, and though   305
his mind rarely experienced the tumults of doubt and was
wont to stand firm in its accustomed gravity, it now re-
sembled a cloud hanging high in the air, buffeted by equally
strong blasts of north and south wind, until its vapor and   310
moisture are rendered into the prime components of the
liquefied mass. Not otherwise did love and fear (love from
the south, fear from the north) drive toward doubt that holy
breast, which leaned toward equally valid arguments, until   315
at last the vapor of love and moisture of faith were pressed
out. When faith shut out fear, the bishop boarded faith in
place of a ship and left his companions behind, fearlessly
leaping into the sea's swelling waves.

O mighty reign of Christ, and reigning might! Pious law   320
and lawful piety, faithful safeguard and safe faith, worthy
sweetness and sweet worthiness! Passing through the sea in
a ship the man had felt fear, but amid the waves felt none.
For the deep dared not deploy its strength against the Lord's
anointed, but endured that swimming progress. Thus the   325
natural order of things was overturned. Although here below Nature governs the elements by sure laws and constrains
the whole world, when she considered these new sights with

hesitat et tenui querit stupefacta susurro
330 quenam prestigii sit causa, quid inferat illi
hoc preiudicium; nec enim Prudencia nouit
nec Fortuna potest eius preuertere leges.
Attamen imperii nec habet Natura rigorem
nec motus elementa suos, mirandaque prebet
335 gressibus humanis uiridis uestigia gurges
humida, terribilis, uaga, lubrica. Thecios unda
immemor ipsa sui dat eis iter, humida siccum,
terribilis tutum, uaga certum, lubrica firmum.
O res mira! Leui non subsidit graue, denso
340 non patefit rarum, solido non cedit inane.
Intus causa latet: quid in undis querimus? Unde
istud proueniat uia non habet, immo uiator;
qui cum succensus diuino flagret amore,
exterioris aque uires intrinsecus ignis
345 uincit et annexam supportat in equore molem—
scilicet ex anima constans et carne mouetur
motibus oppositis uir sanctus, set quia carnem
imperiis anime subiecit, motus in illo
forcior est anime quam carnis, et hac racione
350 plus anima tendit sursum quam carne deorsum.
    O petra Petre super quam stat stabitque per euum
ecclesie fundata fides! Si dicere fas est,
pace tua dicam, tuus iste uicarius audet
per mare de titulo fidei contendere tecum.
355 In quo precellis omnes cessisse uideris
huic uni, dum te sequitur super equor euntem.
Nauis utrique fides, set tempestate timoris

doubtful gaze, she wavered, dumbstruck, and asked in a   330
faint whisper what caused this portent, what inflicted this
prejudice against her. For neither did Providence know how,
nor was Fortune able, to overturn her laws. Yet neither did
Nature retain the force of her sway, nor the elements their
motions, and the viridian abyss—watery, terrible, agitated,   335
and flowing—afforded a wondrous path to human steps.
Thetis's wave forgot itself and granted those footsteps a
passage dry despite its waters, safe despite its terror, sure
despite its agitation, and firm despite its fluidity. O wondrous event! What was heavy did not sink below what was
light, the rarified did not open itself to the dense, the void   340
did not yield to the solid. The cause lay hidden within; why
do we seek it in the waves? The outcome was implicit in the
wayfarer, not his road. Since he burned with the flame of divine love, the fire within overcame the external power of   345
water and buoyed up on the main the mass bound to it—
which is to say, the holy man, who consisted of spirit and
flesh, was swayed in opposite directions. But since he had
subjected his flesh to the commands of the spirit, the movement of the soul was stronger in him than that of the flesh,
and for this reason he moved upward because of his soul   350
more than he moved downward because of the flesh.

O Peter, rock upon whose foundation the faith of the
church stands and will stand forever! If I may be permitted
to speak, entreating your pardon, this your vicar dared to vie
with you in the sea for the title of faith. In a matter in which   355
you excel all, you seemed to yield to this one man, when he
followed you moving upon the deep. Faith was a ship to each
of you, but when the tempest of fear swamped your boat,

absorbente tuam te cepit mergere fluctus;
hunc autem mare non potuit demergere, cuius
360 firma fides omni manet inconcussa timore.
Sic igitur litus adiens pallamque reportans
ad nauem reduci fertur super equora gressu;
interea nautis mirantibus, heret in alto
puppis et expectat immobilis et, licet omni
365 freta fauore freti uentoque potita secundo
nauiget et iuuenum ualidis discussa lacertis,
non tamen inde potest tantum diuulsa moueri
quantum funda iacit tortum Balearia plumbum.
Insistunt remis iuuenes, nauemque mouere
370 nitentes dubitant an fixa sit an rapiatur
impete monstrorum pelagi—si fixa sit, utrum
tractu sistatur adamantis an obice cautis,
cum mille lateant ibi syrtes; si rapiatur
impete monstrorum maris ingluuieque Caribdis,
375 an canibus Cille Sciculiue uoragine monstri—
incutiuntque metus diuersa pericula uanos.
Dum trepidant Birinus adest nauemque redintrat,
nulliusque notant stille uestigia uestem.
Mirari nautas obliuiscique timoris
380 cogit inauditi presens inspectio casus.
Alter in alterius iactant sua lumina; uultus
gestibus alternis iuuat inuitare stuporem.
Compuncti licet ydolatre nouitate stupenda,
se quasi certatim prouoluunt poplite flexo
385 Sancti Birini pedibus, uerumque fatentur
illius esse Deum, cui sic natura reliquit
posse suum, cui sic uehemens obtemperat equor;
iamque recognoscunt quam sint simulacra deorum

the wave began to overtake you. But the sea could not submerge this man, whose sure faith remained unshaken by any 360
fear. So, then, approaching the shore and retrieving the pall,
he was borne again across the deep to the ship with returning step. All this while, to the amazement of the crew, the
stern stuck amid the deep and attended unmoving, and
though it sailed with reliance on every favor of the strait be- 365
hind a favoring wind, and driven on by the strong shoulders of young men, still it could not be wrenched from that
spot so far as a Balearic sling casts its spinning shot. Youths
leaned to the oars, and striving to propel the ship were 370
doubtful whether it was stuck or seized by the strength of
sea monsters—if stuck, whether it was held by the pull of
adamant or on the obstacle of a rock, since a thousand reefs
lay hidden there. If it was seized by sea monsters and the
maw of Charybdis, they were unsure whether by the dogs of 375
Scylla or the whirlpool of the Sicilian monster: various perils
instilled in them vain fears. Amid their trepidations Birinus
arrived and came back on board, and the traces of not one
droplet marked his clothing. Direct sight of this unheard-of
happening compelled the sailors to wonder and forget their 380
fear. They cast their eyes toward one another, and their expressions fostered one another's amazement. Even amid
their idolatry they felt the goad of this astonishing novelty,
and with bent knee they cast themselves, as though vying
with one another, before the feet of Saint Birinus, con- 385
fessing that his was the true God, before whom Nature had
thus relinquished her power and whom the raging main thus
obeyed. Now they acknowledged how despised before the

a facie deiecta Dei quos artubus arte
390 effictis humana deos mentitur ymago.
Iam placet a cultu resilire supersticioso
diisque suis preferre Deum, queruntque quis ille
sit, quid precipiat, et qua ueniatur ad ipsum.
    Conniciens uir sanctus eis diuinitus esse
395 hoc inspiratum, uoto sicientibus uno
ad fontem properare Boni de pectore profert,
ut de thesauro, que mortis origo, quis actor,
que fuerit uite reparatio, quis reparator,
in quo premisse legis denarius, in quo
400 catholice fidei consistat tale talentum,
eterni quo possit emi medicina doloris.
Protinus ydolatris baptisma petentibus ipse
exorzizat aquam, cuius uirtute renati
uincla diabolice gaudent dirumpere fraudis.
405 Dum tamen exhorrent quod adhuc quasi fixa tenetur
nauis et innumeris non prodest uiribus uti,
tota repentino sopitur turba sopore
et quasi letargo, nulloque superstite preter
sanctum pontificem, uigili directa ducatu
410 eius in optato consistit litore puppis.

Quomodo ad litus ueniens predicauerit

Appulsus complet triduum Birinus ibidem,
indigenasque docens quis cuncta creauerit, ad quid,
quantus in excelsis, quantum reuerendus in orbe,
talibus explanat fidei primordia dictis:

face of God were the effigies of their gods, whose human   390
image feigned their godhead, their limbs fashioned by art.
Now it pleased them to retreat from their superstitious
worship and to choose God over their own deities, and they
asked who he was, what he commanded, and how one might
come to him.

The holy man surmised that God had inspired them in   395
this, and from his breast, as from a treasury, to those who
unanimously thirsted to hasten to the source of Good he expounded the origin of death; who brought it about; how life
is restored and who restores it; what constitutes the penny
of the preceding Law, and what the talent of the catholic   400
faith, with which the remedy for eternal pain may be bought.
Straightway he purified water for those idolaters seeking
baptism, and they rejoiced, once reborn through its power,
to break the chains of the devil's deceit. Yet while they still   405
shuddered in terror that the ship was held fast and no
strength availed to move it, a sudden slumber overtook as
with lethargy the whole crew, nor was any left awake save
the holy bishop, until the stern, governed by his watchful   410
steerage, stood fast upon the longed-for shore.

How, arriving on the shore, he preached

Once landed, Birinus passed three days there. Teaching the
natives who created all things, to what end, how great he is
on high, how much to be revered here on earth, he set forth
the rudiments of the faith in these words:

415   "Solus ab eterno Deus est, perfectio cuius
    nec crementa cupit nec detrimenta ueretur,
    cuius maiestas in se sibi tota, nec eius
    gloria maior erit post tempora quam fuit ante.
    Sed Deitas, liuore carens summeque benigna,
420   ne dessent quos participes bonitatis haberet,
    esse creaturas uoluit que carpere possent
    delicias numquam minuendas et fruerentur
    inmensa bonitate sua: uoluit potuitque
    et sciuit. Nichil ergo fuit quod posset obesse:
425   nulla uoluntati diuine causa resistit.
    Nam uirtus summa potuit, sapientia summa
    sciuit, amor summus uoluit; fuit ergo necesse
    ut fieret mundus, uerboque paterna uoluntas,
    componens ylen et ydeam, fecit usyam.
430   "Omnipotens opifex quando pro uelle creauit
    cuncta, creaturas Trinus subsistere iussit
    tantum tres: has corporeas, has spirituales,
    has ex corporeis et spiritualibus. Inter
    pure corporeas et pure spirituales
435   est medium sortitus homo, qui mixtus utrisque
    inter utrasque uiget, cuius perfectio maior
    mundana, minor angelica. Set ab arce superna
    angelus expelli meruit, lapsusque timore
    inuidia traxit hominem, maloque fefellit
440   (heu!) male fellito. Lapsi sunt ambo, sed ille
    corruit, hic cecidit: Zabulum sine fine ruina
    inferius pressit, hominem pro tempore casus.

"God alone is from eternity, whose perfection neither 415
wants increase nor fears loss; whose majesty is entire unto
itself, nor will his glory be greater after the end of time than
it was before. But Godhead, free of envy and supremely benevolent, lest there be a lack of those with whom to share 420
his goodness, willed creatures into existence who could receive never-to-be-diminished delights and enjoy his mea-
sureless goodness. This he willed, and had power and knowledge to do. And so nothing could oppose him: no cause 425
resists the divine will. For supreme power was capable, supreme wisdom had knowledge, supreme love willed it. So it
was necessary that the world should be made, and the Father's will, combining matter and form by his word, made its
being.

"When the almighty craftsman created everything ac- 430
cording to his will, being threefold himself he ordained the
existence of precisely three sorts of creatures: some corporeal, some spiritual, some corporeal and spiritual at once.
Mankind took the middle ground between the purely cor- 435
poreal and purely spiritual, for mingled of the two he flourishes between the two, his perfection greater than that of
the world, but less than that of the angels. But an angel
earned expulsion from the citadel of heaven, and once fallen
in fear and envy he drew down man, deceiving him, alas, 440
with an apple steeped wickedly in gall. Both took a fall, but
one absolutely, the other not so: the lapse pressed down Satan in endless ruin, but man only for a time.

"Pignora lapsus homo nobis miseranda reliquit,
exilii penas et ineuitabile fatum,
445 morsque superstitibus innascitur ex prothoplausti
delicto. Nam sic in nobis omnibus eius
crimen, ut in ramis uicium radicis, inheret;
et quia contrahimus ex carnis origine mortem,
uiuere si uolumus meliore tenebimur ortu,
450 scilicet irriguo baptismatis amne renasci.
Rursum, si uolumus ad uitam spiritualem
baptismi nobis lauachrum prodesse, tenemur
credere personas unius tres Deitatis
esse coequales omnino, coompnipotentes,
455 atque coeternas. Unum quod principiauit
omnia de nichilo (nichil est quin tendat ad illud)
Alpha uocatur et O, quia principium, quia finis.
Cur Alpha? Quia principium. Cur O? Quia finis —
principium sine principio, finis sine fine.
460 Sic igitur tres sunt persone, res tamen una.
Nam Pater et Natus et Sanctus Spiritus, hii tres
unum, non unus; hoc unum non tria, set tres.
Cum re sint unum, personali sibi distant
proprietate: Pater generat, Verbum generatur,
465 Flamen procedit. Sic ergo Pater sine patre,
Filius a solo Patre, Spiritus est ab utroque.
Sic tres nature personas astruit uni
hunc penes articulum fidei sententia nostre.
    "Nec profitenda minus est Incarnatio Verbi,
470 a quo pendebat nostre reparatio uite.
Patris enim summi Verbo si Lucifer olim
non inuidisset similis regnare uolendo,
staret; si staret, bonus esset; si bonus esset,

"That man in his fall bequeathed his pitiable legacy to us, the pains of exile and inexorable fate, and death is born in his survivors from the sin of the first-made man. For his crime inheres within us all, just as the flaw of the root inheres in the branches, and because we contract death from the origin of our flesh, if we wish to live we shall be obliged to be reborn by a better birth, namely in baptism's flowing stream. Again, if we wish the washing of baptism to be of benefit toward the spiritual life, we are required to believe that three persons of a single Godhead are entirely equal, coomnipotent, and coeternal. The One who initiated all things from nothing (for there is nothing that does not tend toward that One) is called Alpha and O, because he is the beginning and the end. Why Alpha? Because he is the beginning. Why O? Because he is the end—beginning without beginning, and end without end. So, therefore, there are three persons, but one substance. For these three, the Father, Son, and Holy Spirit, are one thing, not one person; this one thing is not three things, but three persons. Though they are one in substance, they differ from one another in the property of personhood: the Father begets, the Son is begotten, the Spirit proceeds. So, then, the Father is without father, the Son is from the Father alone, the Spirit is from both. Thus according to this article the doctrine of our faith ascribes three persons to one nature.

"Nor must we any less confess the Incarnation of the Word, upon which hangs the restoration of our life. For if Lucifer had not once envied the Word of the supreme Father and wished to reign like him, he would have stood secure; if he stood, he would be good; if he were good,

non fallax; si non fallax, homo non moreretur.
475 A primis ergo sequitur, si Lucifer olim
non inuidisset Verbo, nec homo moreretur.
Filius ergo Dei pius, immo fons pietatis,
qui longinqua fuit casus occasio nostri,
esse propinqua uolens et nostre causa salutis,
480 ut genus humanum repararet missus in orbem
a Patre, conceptus de Sacro Flamine, carnem
omnibus exemptam uiciis assumit in aluo
uirginis, et capitur utero quem non capit orbis
fitque creatura, nec desinit esse Creator.
485 O Natura stupens! Ratio rudis! O reuerendi
grande puerperii decus! O generatio mira
quam non precessit corruptio! Que nisi uirgo
digna fuit lactare Deum? Vel quis nisi Christus
dignus erat nasci de uirgine? Dignus uterque,
490 uirgine matre Deus, divaque propagine uirgo.
    "At quoniam debeat Ade transgressio plecti
morte Redemptoris, qua non erat ultio maior,
exquisita crucis tormenta subire secundum
assumptam carnem uoluit pro sontibus insons,
495 pro seruis dominus, pro transgressoribus ultor.
Lignum causa fuit mortis lignoque pependit
Saluator moriens, ut uita resurgeret unde
mors oriebatur. Sic expirauit, et ex quo
mortua uita fuit, mors quomodo non moreretur?
500 Sic ubi propter oues cesus fuit agnus ab hedis
quid potuit patuit: anima descendit ad ima,
carne resurrexit, in celum scandit utroque
qui dum pro nobis incurrit perditionem

he would not deceive; if he did not deceive, mankind would
not perish. And so it follows from first principles, if Lucifer 475
had not once envied the Word, neither would mankind perish. Therefore the merciful Son of God, indeed the very
source of mercy, who was the distant occasion of our fall,
wished to be also the proximate cause of our salvation. Sent 480
into the world by the Father so that, conceived of the Holy
Spirit, he might restore the human race, he took flesh free
of all sin in the womb of a virgin, in that womb was enclosed
although the whole world does not enclose him, and became
a creature, yet did not cease being the Creator. O dumb- 485
struck Nature! O crude Reason! O great honor of that venerable birth! O wondrous generation that no corruption has
preceded! Who but a virgin was worthy to suckle God? Or
who but Christ was worthy to be born of a virgin? Both were 490
worthy: God of his virgin mother, the virgin of her divine
progeny.

"But since Adam's transgression must be punished by the
Redeemer's death—than which there was no greater retri-
bution—he desired to undergo the cross's excruciating torments according to the flesh he had assumed, innocent on 495
behalf of the guilty, a master on behalf of slaves, an avenger
on behalf of transgressors. A tree was the cause of death and
on a tree the dying Savior hung, that life might rise up
whence death sprang forth. Thus he died, and since Life was
dead, how might Death not die? So when a lamb was slain 500
by the goats for the sheep's sake, what was possible was
revealed: his soul descended to hell, he rose in his flesh;

et recipit uitam. Sua nos a perditione
505 perditio saluat, ad uitam uita reducit.
Hic est humane reparator originis, hic est
mundi Saluator, hic est Deus; hunc ueneretur,
hunc colat, hunc celebret nostri deuotio cultus.
"Iam uos peniteat peccasse deosque scelestos
510 preposuisse Deo celesti factaque uestra
factori uestro. Nec enim simulacra beatum
esse dabunt, cum non habeant. Cur ergo coluntur?
Cur facies illis hominum simulantur in ere?
Cur pes, cur oculus, cur os, cur auris? Inane
515 unumquodque: pedis et luminis, oris et auris
nullus inest usus. Pes non est claudus eorum,
nec graditur; lumen non cecum, nec uidet; os non
mutum nec loquitur; auris non surda, nec audit.
Dii tales, non numine dii, set nomine tantum,
520 facti nil faciunt, lesi nil ledere possunt,
set nec concipiunt iram nec gaudia, nec sunt
egri nec sani, nec uiuunt nec moriuntur.
Sunt similes illis tam qui faciunt ea quam qui
confidunt in eis. Deus autem glorificetur
525 summus et excutiat uestri uelamina cordis."
Quale sopor fessis, qualis sudantibus umbra,
talis Birini sermo gentilibus. Aures
allicit et mira reficit dulcedine mentes.

De miraculis sermonem confirmantibus

Neue relinquatur populi noua uerba stupentis
530 indiscussa fides et adhuc dubitabile uerum,
uoce quod astruxit ratione probabiliori

he mounted to heaven in both, incurring destruction and
receiving life for our sake. His destruction saves us from de-   505
struction, his life leads us again to life. He is restorer of humanity's origin, he is Savior of the world, he is God. May the
devotion of our worship venerate, revere, and celebrate him.

"Now repent that you have sinned and have set shame-   510
ful gods before the God of heaven, things made by your
own hand before your Maker. For idols cannot bestow blessedness, since they themselves do not possess it. Why then
are they worshiped? Why are human faces counterfeited for
them in bronze? Or feet, eyes, mouths, and ears? Each is   515
empty, with no use of foot or eye, of mouth or ear. Their
foot neither is lame nor walks, their eye neither blind nor
sees, their mouth neither mute nor speaks, their ear neither
deaf nor hears. Such gods—gods not in divine power, but in
name only—being themselves made, make nothing. When   520
injured they are incapable of injuring, but neither do they
conceive wrath nor joy, are neither ill nor well, neither live
nor die. They are like both those who make them and those
who trust in them. But may God on high be glorified and   525
may he shake off the concealments of your heart."

Like sleep to the weary, like shade to those who sweat,
was this sermon of Birinus to the pagans. He enticed their
ears and refreshed their minds with wondrous sweetness.

On the miracles that confirm his sermon

Lest the faith of a people agape at these new words remain
unproven and the truth still remain doubtful, the holy man   530
showed by a more palpable argument what he had explained

297

uir sacer ostendit, oculusque fidelior aure
argumenta capit sperande certa salutis,
confirmatque manu Dominus quod predicat ore
535 seruus, et exprimitur diuina potentia signis,
ut credant operi qui nolunt credere uerbo.

     Haut procul inde uetus duplicis muliercula morbi
peste premebatur. Nam, sensibus orba duobus,
nec nutu nec uoce potest aduertere quicquam
540 exterius. Quicquid uel dicit uel facit alter
est sibi secretum: que fiunt non habet unde
aspiciat; si quid narratur non habet unde
audiat. Interiit oculi sic sensus et auris
ut nichil aspiciat oculo, nichil audiat aure.

545   Nocte quiescenti per uisum spirituali
uoce reuelatur ut sanctum curet adire
pontificem, qui curet eam sensusque cupitos
reddat et adiciat quod deficit in ratione.

     Surgit anus, pueroque sibi prestante ducatum
550 aggreditur medicum; uoto succensa fideli
optati desiderio fiducia crescit.
Certat anus puerum precedere, ceca uidentem—
articulus compellit anum trottare—nec etas
sistere sera potest quos currere cogit egestas.

555 Perueniens ubi sanctus erat, sibi poscit ademptos
restitui sensus, set non moderante loquelam
auditu: nescit quo proferat impete uocem
quam profert, animoque rogat, set uoce minatur.
Sic fundente preces misera muliere, beatus

by spoken word, and the eye, more reliable than the ear, took in sure arguments of the salvation for which they hoped; the Lord confirmed with his hand what the servant proclaimed through his mouth, and divine power was expressed through signs, that those unwilling to believe the word might believe the deed. 535

Not far hence, a little old woman was vexed with the affliction of a double illness. Deprived of two of her senses, she could indicate nothing outside herself by gesture or speech. Whatever another said or did was obscure to her, since she had no means to see anything that happened or to hear anything she was told. Sensation of eye and ear had grown so moribund that she could see nothing with her eye, hear nothing with her ear. 540

In the still of the night, in a vision, by a spiritual voice, it was revealed to her that she should take pains to seek out the holy bishop, that he might cure her, restore her desired senses, and make up whatever was lacking in her reason. 545

The old woman rose and sought the physician with a boy to guide her. Her trust was kindled by her faithful desire and was increased by her longing for the object of her hope. The old woman strove to get ahead of the lad, the blind one ahead of the one who saw—necessity makes an old woman trot—nor could old age keep those still whom need compelled to run. Arriving where the saint tarried, she begged the restitution of her lost senses, but without her own hearing to gauge her speech. She didn't know the force with which she uttered the sounds she uttered, and though she intended to entreat, her shout sounded like a threat. As the unhappy woman thus poured forth her prayers, the blessed 550 555

560 presul blandicias animi, non iurgia lingue,
attendit, signumque crucis cui noxia cedunt
auribus opponens oculisque medetur utrisque,
expellitque duos uno medicamine morbos.
Presentes hec intuiti miracula laudant
565 glorificantque Deum; confringunt precipitantque
ydola; cognoscunt amplectunturque salutem.

Cinigilsus rex predicatione Sancti Birini
conuersus ad Dominum baptizatur.

Expletis sacro tribus in sermone diebus,
ut plures faciat profectus, inde profectus
Geuuissos Birinus adit, quos plurimus error
570 excecat. Nam ficta colunt simulacra, Deumque
non qui fecit eos set quem fecere precantur.
Sceptra tenet Cinigilsus ibi rex, immo tyrannus,
immo leo, quem sacrilegi uesania cultus
inflat et in cunctos facit insanire fideles.
575   Sed pugil intrepidus Christi nichilominus illum
aggreditur uerbi gladio pugnatque sacerdos
aduersus regem. Ne rex uincatur ab Hoste
pugnat, et ecce quidem genus admirabile belli:
qui nocet inde iuuat, qui percutit inde medetur;
580 qui cadit inde uiget, qui uincitur inde triumphat.
Exterius pugnat Birinus cum Cinigilso,
interius Christus cum demone; uincitur autem
demon, et eripitur Cinigilsus ab illius ungue.
Vir sanctus baptizat eum, casuque secundo
585 Northanimbrorum regem contingit adesse
Oswaldum, qui de baptismate suscipit illum.

bishop attended to the pleas of her spirit, not the harangues 560
of her tongue. Setting upon her ears and eyes the sign of the
cross, from which all evils flee, he healed both and cast out
two diseases with a single remedy. Those present to see the
miracle praised and glorified God. They smashed the idols 565
and hurled them down; they acknowledged and embraced
their salvation.

> *King Cynegils is converted to the Lord by*
> *Saint Birinus's preaching and is baptized.*

At the end of three days filled with holy speech, having set
out thence to earn further profit, Birinus progressed toward the West Saxons, whom many an error blinded. They
venerated manufactured idols and prayed not to the God
who made them but to one they had made. Cynegils there 570
wielded the scepter as king, or rather as tyrant, rather as a
lion. The mad fury of a blasphemous cult puffed him up and
made him rage against all the faithful.

Yet Christ's fearless champion accosted him nonetheless 575
with the sword of the Word, and a priest fought against a
king. He fought lest that king be conquered by the Foe; and
behold, here was a wondrous sort of war: the one who did
injury thereby assisted, the one who hurt thereby healed.
He who fell, thrived; he who was conquered triumphed. Ex- 580
ternally, Birinus vied with Cynegils, but internally, Christ
with a demon; the demon furthermore was vanquished, and
Cynegils was snatched from his talons. The holy man baptized him, and by happy circumstance King Oswald of 585
Northumbria chanced to be at hand and received him from

Ille renatus aqua diuinum concipit ignem
intus et efficitur de transgressore fidelis,
de tumido simplex, de peruasore patronus.
590 Non solus rex ad Dominum conuertitur; immo
tota sui sequitur regio uestigia regis,
tota uetustatis errores, tota malignos
exuitur ritus, sacrisque renascitur undis.
O subitum quod agit Deus! O mutacio dextre
595 excelsi! Non unus homo, set tota repente
patria quod semper odiuit amat, quod amauit
odit, quod spreuit ueneratur, quod uenerata
est spernit, quasi facta sibi contraria. Christum
et sanctos spreuit, set Christum nunc ueneratur
600 et sanctos celebrat; statuas et phana colebat,
sed nunc destituit statuas et phana prophanat.

Quomodo abiectis ydolatris ecclesie fabricantur,
constitutes ydoneis prelatis

Sic ubi diuersis populos erroribus actos
uir sanctus fidei titulo collegit in uno,
a supradictis donatur regibus illi
605 Dorchecestrensis urbs, in qua pontificalem
constituit sedem, spaciumque diocesis amplum
annectens phanis destructis templa colenda
edificat, loliis auulsis lilia plantat,
ordinibusque sacris personas dotat honestas
610 et circumspectas quas possit habere suorum
participes operum, disciplinaque salubri
ornet, et optantes paradisi gaudia uerbo
exemploque sui doceat contempnere mundum.

the font. Reborn of water, he caught divine fire within, and
having been a prideful, plundering sinner he became a faithful and humble benefactor. Not only was the king converted   590
to the Lord, but the whole territory followed in the king's
footsteps, shed the errors of old with their malevolent ritu-
als, and was reborn in the holy waters.

O sudden act of God! O transformation by God's right
hand! Not one man alone but all at once an entire country   595
loved what it had always hated, hated what it had loved,
honored what it had scorned, scorned what it had honored,
as though made contrary to itself. It scorned Christ and his
saints but now honored Christ and celebrated his saints; it   600
had been wont to worship statues and temples, but now it
forsook the former and desecrated the latter.

How, with idolatry put aside, churches are
constructed and suitable bishops established

When the holy man had in this way gathered under a single charter of faith peoples constrained by various errors,
the city of Dorchester was granted him by the aforesaid   605
kings. There he established his episcopal see, joining to it an
ample expanse as his diocese. Razing the temples, he built
venerable churches; uprooting the tares, he planted lilies,
and invested worshipful and cautious personages with holy   610
orders whom he could count on to share in his task, whom
he could enhance with healthful discipline and by his word
and example teach in their longing for paradise to despise

Neue magis presit quam prosit, preest sine fastu
615 et prodest sine desidia, docet et dominator
et prefertur eis quasi discipulus, quasi seruus,
et quasi subiectus, nec enim doctrina rigorem
nec dominatus habet, nec prelatura: magister
instruitur, dominus seruit, prelatus obedit.
620 Sic quo relligio sit conseruanda tenore
ore manuque docet, set plus manus efficit ore:
os aliquando silet, manus exemplaria semper
dogmata pretendit operum, quibus ipse choruscans
iocundum reputat tristari, triste iocari.
625 Et ne spiritui caro predominetur, abhorret
omne bonum carnale; sitis potare, sitire
est illi potus, pasci ieiunia, pastus
ieiunare, quies sudare, quiescere sudor.
    Nunc igitur suplex uenerare, Britannia, patrem,
630 qui sic de tenebris errorum te reuocauit
ad lumen uere fidei. Tenebreque fuisti,
nunc autem lux in Domino. Que gratia maior
uel melior? Cuius maioris uel melioris?
De penis ad delicias, de perditione
635 ad uitam, de suppliciis ad gaudia transis;
ergo quod euadis laqueos, quod libera, gaudes.
Istud habes ab eo—gratesque referre teneris.
    Conuersis igitur multo sudore Britannis,
Sanctus Birinus, nature debita soluens,
640 labitur ut surgat, moritur ne uiuere cesset,
pontificique suo celestia regna recludit
Christus, et eterna mercede remunerat ipsum,
restituens illi post pugnam premia, post spem
rem, post exilium patriam, post funera uitam.

the world. But lest he should govern more than bring bene- 615
fit, he governed without arrogance and worked benefit
without stinting. He taught and was promoted as a master
over them as though he were a disciple, a servant, a subject.
For his teaching, governance, and prelacy were without ri-
gidity: though a master, he received instruction, though a
lord, he served, though a prelate, he obeyed. Thus he taught 620
by mouth and hand in what fashion religion was to be con-
served, but the hand accomplished more than the mouth:
the latter was sometimes silent, but his hand offered continuously the exemplary teachings of his works, gleaming
forth amid which he deemed it pleasant to be sad and sad to
make pleasantries. And lest the flesh should dominate the 625
spirit, he shunned every boon of the flesh. For him, to drink
was thirst, to thirst was drink; to fast was a feast, and food a
fast; rest was labor, and labor rest.

And so now, O Britain, do homage to your father who 630
thus recalled you from the darkness of your errors to the
light of true faith. You were darkness and are now a light
in the Lord. What grace is greater or better, or belongs to
one greater or better? You pass from punishment to delight,
from perdition to life, from torment to joy. And so you re- 635
joice that you are free, that you escape those snares. This
you have from him, and are bound to return thanks.

At long last, having converted the Britons with much labor, Saint Birinus paid nature's debt, falling in order to rise 640
and dying that he might not cease to live. Christ opened to
his bishop the kingdom of heaven and rewarded him with
an eternal recompense, rendering to him, after his combat,
a prize, after his hope, the substance, after exile, his fatherland, after death, life.

645 Quintus Birini successor episcopus, Hedda,
     eius honorandum Wentanam corpus in urbem
     magnifice transfert et collocat in cathedrali
     ecclesia, tumuloque diu requieuit in illo,
     donec Adelwoldus, qui mox successit eidem
650 uigesimus sextus, fuluo leuat illud in auro,
     relliquiisque nouis altare refulgurat altum.
        In quo crebra loco rutilant miracula Sancti
     Birini precibus, fugiunt fantasmata, cedunt
     langores, ceci claudos ibi cernere possunt
655 currentes, surdi mutos audire loquentes.
     Quid loquor? Omne mali genus euanescit in auras:
     militis ista sui meritis dat premia Christus,
     rex regum, cum quo sit Patri Spirituique
     Sancto maiestas et gloria, nunc et in euum. Amen.

        EXPLICIT UITA SANCTI BIRINI.

Hedda, Birinus's fifth successor, splendidly translated his 645
venerable body to the city of Winchester and placed it in
the cathedral church, and long it rested in that tomb, until Aethelwold, who soon succeeded him as twenty-sixth, 650
raised it in shining gold, and the high altar glittered with
new relics.

In this place gleam forth frequent miracles by virtue of
Saint Birinus's prayers. Illusions flee, illnesses give way;
there the blind can see the lame run, the deaf can hear the 655
mute speak. Why should I speak? Every sort of evil vanishes
into thin air: Christ grants these rewards to his soldier for
his merits—Christ who is King of kings, to whom with the
Father and the Holy Spirit be all majesty and glory, now and
forever. Amen.

HERE ENDS THE LIFE OF SAINT BIRINUS.

Note on the Texts

The seven texts as printed in the present volumes reflect as closely as possible their state as Matthew Paris collected them in A. In the case of the *Life of Francis* and the *Life of Oswald*, the texts consequently diverge significantly from existing critical editions of those works. The critical edition of the *Life of Francis* takes as its base the text of Assisi MS 338 (referenced in the notes to the text as F); that of the *Life of Oswald* prints the significantly expanded version extant in Bodley 40. A's text of the *Life of Francis,* as noted above, appears to record later revisions to the text, which we have no reason to believe were not authorial. A's version of the *Life of Oswald,* however, probably reflects a text closer to the original presentation copy at Peterborough Abbey. The reader interested in the specifics can consult the full record in the apparatus of the critical editions. Divergences between the two extant manuscripts of the *Life of Birinus* are less noticeable. The notation of variants in other manuscripts in the textual notes of this edition is negative: only departures from the reading of A in favor of an alternative drawn from another manuscript are here recorded. For the lives of Guthlac, Edmund, Fremund, and Thomas in the second volume, we are in any case dependent solely on the text of A.

Fidelity to the manuscript version extends to the preservation of a number of medieval orthographical conventions that diverge from the classicizing norms adopted in many volumes of the present series. *The reader unused to these medievalisms in the presentation of Latin texts is advised to expect them here.* Among these, the most ubiquitous and most notable are the following:

First and foremost, the consonantal use of *u* is not rendered as *v:* e.g., *uereor,* not *vereor.* Scribal use of *w* has been normalized to *uu;* but intermittent scribal use of *v,* either as consonant or as vowel, has been allowed to stand.

Collapsed diphthongs (*ae* and *oe*) are written (and were pronounced) as *e:* e.g., *femine* for *feminae.*

Palatalization of *-ti-* to *-ci-:* e.g., *preciosus* for *pretiosus.*

Aspiration of medial *h* to *ch:* e.g., *michi* and *nichil* for *mihi* and *nihil.*

Doubling of the vowel in forms of *hic:* e.g., *hii* and *hiis.*

Substitution of *t* for *d,* particularly in *set* for *sed.*

Addition of medial *-p-* between *-m-* and *-n-:* e.g., *alumpnus* for *alumnus, sompnium* for *somnium,* and, perhaps most unnervingly, *ompnipotentis* for *omnipotentis.*

Occasional omission (or addition) of initial *h* before a vowel: e.g., *ora* for *hora,* or the reverse.

Occasional interchange of *y* and *i:* thus *cima* for *cyma* and *yrundines* for *hirundines.*

Occasional substitution of *c* for *sc* or *sch* before *i:* e.g., *cismaticos* for *schismaticos, ceptrum* for *sceptrum.*

Notes to the Texts

1.51   moneta *ed.*: monetam *A*
1.54   mersam *F*: mendam *A*
1.205   laboraret *F*: laborat *A*
1.133   res *F*: non *A*
2.8   haras *ed.*: aras *A*
2.29   affines *F*: affinens *A*
2.31   Cachinnus *ed.*: cachinnum *AF*
2.40   incendens *F*: intendens *A*
2.54   concire *F*: conscire *A*
3.56   facias *F*: faciat *A*
3.96   limina *F*: lumina *A*
3.98   uitrice *F*: uictrice *A*
4.64   Terra *F*: *om. A*
4.70   residit: *viz.* recedit
4.76   durior *F*: dirior *A*
4.155   parua *F*: praua *A*
4.159   ut *F*: et *A*
4.161   recedere *F*: procedere *A*
5.26   in plerisque *F*: implerisque *A*
5.40   sustinet et *F*: sustinetque *A*
5.45   lumbos *F*: renes *A*
5.136   uerbisque *F*: urbisque *A*
5.203   compositi *F*: composito *A*
6.9   trahentis *F*: trahentes *A*
6.28   numerum *F*: *om. A*

6.31	finem *F*: funem *A*
6.50	apostolico *F*: *om. A*
6.54	reges *F*: *om. A*
6.68	pararent *F*: parerent *A*
6.69	agendis *ed.*: agnendis A
6.111	iussio *ed.*: uisio *AF*
6.122	considunt *F*: concidunt *A*
6.126	quia *F*: que A
6.134	extenso *F*: exterso *A*
6.141	Paterinorum *F*: patererorum *A*
6.166	hic *F*: hoc *A*
7.5	debens *F*: debent *A*
7.88	coadstantum *F*: coastandum *A*
7.120	tolerare *F*: toleraret *A*
8.3	parantem *F*: parentem *A*
8.28	funes *ed.*: fines *A*
8.126	ei *F*: ibi *A*
8.198	nostreque *F*: nostre *A*
8.209	creatus *ed.*: creata *A*
9.4	attente *F*: attende *A*
9.23	auctoris *F*: actoris *A*
9.31	omittere *F*: emittere *A*
9.85	benedicat *F*: benedicit *A*
9.91	scientum *F*: sciendum *A*
9.92	sepe *F*: spe *A*
9.94	stamina *F*: gramina *A*
9.98	fetus *F*: fenis *A*
9.108	discernens *F*: decernens *A*
9.171	perpessus sit *F*: perpesse fit *A*
10.116	Nec *F*: Hec *A*
11.30	prendit *F*: prendat *A*
11.67	utraque *ed.*: utroque *A*
11.87	*(in rubric before line)* compunxerit *ed.*: compugerit *A*
12.25	sorte *F*: forte *A*
12.72	opticum *ed.*: obticum *A*
13.1	Urbis *F*: Orbis *A*

13.32	parit *F*: parat *A*
	accessoria *ed.*: acccessoria *A*
13.54	Sic *F*: Hic *A*
13.68	exanimem *ed.*: exanimen *A*
13.112	poscit *F*: possit *A*
14.21	insita *F*: incita *A*
14.36	epilepticus *F*: epilencius *A*
14.92	Qui *ed.*: Quo *A*

LIFE OF OSWALD

13	imitabilis *ed.*: mutabilis *A*
38	tantum *B*: tantam *A*
44	patronus tuus et *ed.*: est patronus tuus *A*
67	effectus *B*: affectus *A*
90	successisse *B*: successore *A*
92	est *B*: ut *A*
105	stare uetat *B*: ferre nequit *A*
108	metro *B*: metus *A*
117	ex antiquissimis *B*: antiquissim *A*
123	inuariabile *B*: inuanabile *A*
124	bipertiri *B*: bipertim *A*
131	sit *B*: fit *A*
137	successit *B*: succedens *A*
158	latet *B*: lateat *A*
176	fratres *B*: fratris *A*
185	eis *ed.*: eos *A*
193	derogat *B*: deroget *A*
195	interea *B*: interia *A*
208	uirescentis *B*: in recesitis *A*
209	iuuencos *B*: uiuentos *A*
241	patrui *B*: partim *A*
247	Osricus *B*: asricus *A*
251	uterque *B*: utrique *A*
252	patrui *B*: patrii *A*
289	facie *B*: stacie *A*

291 speciosus *ed.*: spaciosus *A*

297 prospicuus *ed.*: prospicuis *A*

303 eaque *ed.*: eoque *A*

305 seuire *B*: seruire *A*

312 proprie *B*: propere *A*

   nil *B*: non *A*

341 dimicat *B*: dimittat *A*

354 concoloresque *B*: concolorisque *A*

386 peccando *B*: sperando *A*

389 tantum *B*: tantam *A*

428 Cumque *B*: Cum *A*

447 missasque *B*: miseramque *A*

452 decidere *B*: discedere *A*

491 tueri *ed.*: tuendi *A*

497 cupiens *B*: cupitus *A*

522 decorat *B*: decorit *A*

534 cuproue *B*: curroue *A*

576 nunquam *B*: non quam *A*

582 decens *B*: docens *A*

598 quem *B*: quam *A*

654 custodia *B*: custodie *A*

666 palis *B*: palus *A*

681 honorandis *B*: honorandos *A*

682 ut *B*: et *A*

688 humens *B*: humidus *A*

693 laticis *B*: lacitis *A*

696 fugiunt *B*: *om. A*

723 illo *B*: illa *A*

744 Delectat *B*: delectant *A*

   uisum *B*: uisis *A*

LIFE OF BIRINUS

5 canendum *B*: canendo *A*

32 segniciem *B*: segnicem *A*

63 donans *B*: donec *A*

85   rectificat *B*: reficiat *A*
86   ingenuum *B*: ingenium *A*
88   incompositumue *ed.*: incompositum ne *AB*
112   pauo *B*: uirgo *A*
133   demolitur *B*: demoliter *A*
138   exercitii *ed.*: exercii *A*: excercii *B*
143   circa *B*: cura *A*
161   transuerberet *B*: transuerberat *A*
209   posset *B*: potest *A*
239   quocumque tetenderit *B*: quodcumque retenderit *A*
289   amictum *ed.*: amicum *AB*
325   preuertitur *B*: peruertitur *A*
332   nec *B*: aut *A*
359   demergere *B*: demerge *A*
360   timore *B*: timori *A*
411   appulsus *B*: appulsis *A*
430   quando *B*: postquam *A*
431   Trinus *B*: trinas *A*
456   quin *B*: quod *A*
521   nec *B*: non *A*
523   sunt *ed.*: sint *AB*
542   aspiciat si quid narratur *B*: aeruat que uero dicuntur *A*
637   teneris *B*: tenetis *A*

Notes to the Translations

Henry of Avranches's *Life of Guthlac, Life of Fremund,* and *Life of Edmund,* referenced below, appear in volume 2 (DOML 31).

LIFE OF FRANCIS

Prol. 14   *Nor did Francis conquer only the world:* a favorite topos of Henry's in praise of his subject. Compare the openings of the *Life of Oswald,* the *Life of Birinus,* and the *Life of Guthlac.* It is reminiscent of the *De moribus* falsely attributed to Seneca, 81–82: "He is stronger who conquers desire than he who subdues a foe. Conquering oneself is the most difficult thing."

Prol. 18   *when dying bore them openly:* a reference to Francis receiving the stigmata of Christ's passion in Book 12 below.

Prol. 22   *the measure of your name:* Henry plays on "Gregorius" and the Latin "pro peccato gregis orans" (praying for the sin of your flock) and "gregis horis" (the borders around the flock).

1.1   The four verses of summary that precede each book of the *Life of Francis* recall the verse summaries that precede the respective books of Walter of Châtillon's *Alexandreis,* as well as those in many medieval manuscripts of classical epics.

1.11   *excused by hyperbaton:* that is, by invoking the rhetorical device of devising an eccentric word order.

1.69   *heat from without:* Henry here and elsewhere shows a marked fondness for digressions into contemporary medical theory.

1.179   *now added oil:* wine and then oil were poured on wounds, as in Luke 10:34.

1.193   *but rather the soft productions sent by Flanders and yellow-haired Brit-*

> *ain's unwarlike artifacts:* that is, the cloth and tapestries in which Francis was accustomed to trade.

2.93   *Venus/venom:* the translation preserves only this one of several plays on the homophony of words with contrasting meanings in these lines.

2.148   *a hypocrite according to antiphrasis:* that is, wishing to be the opposite of hypocritical.

2.208   *the Python:* see Ovid, *Metamorphoses* 1.438–72.

2.209   *Pallas/Arachne:* see Ovid, *Metamorphoses* 6.1–145.

3.14   *blind himself, ordered a man who could see:* Matthew 15:14.

3.50–51   *blessed is the man:* Psalm 39:5 (Vulgate numbering); Jeremiah 17:7.

3.106   *lest I be troubled:* Psalm 15:8 (Vulgate numbering).

3.120–21   *he made us, and not we ourselves:* Psalm 99:3 (Vulgate numbering).

3.126   *will not be confounded:* Romans 10:11.

3.131   *he must carry his soul in his hands:* compare Judges 12:3.

3.150   *from the love of God:* Romans 8:35–39.

3.200   *face to face:* 1 Corinthians 13:12.

4.112   *Paul/Peter:* Acts 14 and 12, respectively.

4.146   *A lone man sufficient for all:* 1 Corinthians 9:19–23.

4.172   *Antaeus:* Drawing his strength from the earth, Antaeus was all the more powerful in combat against Hercules when thrown to the ground. He was at last defeated only by being held aloft.

5.56   *Parnassus:* the mountain sacred to the Muses, goddesses of the arts and sciences.

5.104   *the vessel of the common ventricle:* Henry here expounds Francis's state in terms of contemporary medical theory: the "fumes and rising vapors" are food and drink digested as "spirits" that then ascend to the front ventricle of the brain, the seat of all the senses in common *(sensus communis)*.

5.139   *their successors:* that is, the successive vices that grow from initial intrapsychic impulses.

5.218   *the body's five ministers:* that is, the senses.

6.13   *to attend a mother's funeral (matris ad exequias):* this oddly unprepared and cryptic detail reflects neither the biblical precedent

in Luke 10 nor the prose sourse by Thomas of Celano, which
reads instead, "who gathers together the dispersed of Israel."

6.52   *by antiphrasis:* that is, Pope Innocent, since "innocens" in Latin
literally means "not harmful."

6.70   *Giovanni di San Paolo:* Cardinal Bishop of Sabina from 1204.

7.48   *when at the antipodes the sun . . . contracts its shadows:* that is, at high
noon on the other side of the world.

7.62–63   *predestined/foreknew:* the orthodox explanation (if not intellec-
tual sleight of hand) that while God graciously predestines the
saved, he does not actively predestine the reprobate, but simply
sees in advance their disobedience.

7.148   *the territory of the Parthians:* Francis has no intention of going
anywhere near Persia, but here, as widely in medieval Western
sources, names of various Eastern peoples are employed inter-
changeably without regard for ethnographic accuracy.

7.149   *the house of the Church:* the digression expands on a general sense
that contemporary Italy is rife with heresies and so requires
Francis's energies closer to home.

7.163   *Augustus:* that is, the Holy Roman Emperor, widely opposed by
the civic communes of Tuscany and northern Italy.

8.103   *unexplorable:* the source of the Nile was unknown to Europeans
until the nineteenth century.

8.107   *the water's motion:* Henry's abstruse conceit labors the idea that
ripples go out from every point at which an arrow strikes the
surface of the water but that the circles cannot spread because
they interrupt one another.

8.210   *nothing that disobeyed the voice:* normally the verb *obaudiat* would
mean "obey," not "disobey," but this is the sense required, as par-
alleled by Alan of Lille, *Anticlaudianus,* 6.2.22.

9.32   *to which Greece gave its name:* that is., Greccio.

9.103   *possession:* that is, possessing even this relic violates the Franciscan injunction against private ownership of anything.

9.151–52   *he chanced to see her again there:* that is, on a subsequent visit.

9.169   *gave him the fig:* the medieval Italian equivalent of our modern
extended middle finger.

10.3   *Honorius/honor/honesty:* a typical Henrician wordplay of a sort much more ubiquitously evident in the Latin text than it can be in translation.

10.32   *bishop of Ostia:* Ugolino was cardinal bishop of Ostia before election to the papacy as Gregory IX, Henry's dedicatee, in 1227.

11.12   *Hananiah, Azariah, and Mishael:* Dan 1:6, 3:52–90. (The latter passage is apocryphal.)

12.17   *so that Martha might not distract:* Luke 10:38–42. The typology of Mary and Martha as representatives of contemplative and active religious devotion, respectively, is standard in medieval biblical exegesis.

12.64   *like an ox threshing while muzzled:* Deuteronomy 25:4.

12.87   *concluding from Solomon:* Sirach 38:1–8.

13.21   *Ugo:* see the note on 10.32 above.

13.42   *the spirits:* as in Henry's other medical digressions above, the spirits in thirteenth-century medical theory were a rarified material substance, rather like a gas, produced by the digestion of food and drink, that moved freely through the arteries and veins.

13.112   *With my voice:* Psalm 141.1 (Vulgate numbering).

14.37–39 *the blind, lame, deaf, and dumb:* the topos of mutually witnessed cures is a hallmark of Henry's hagiographical poetry, found also in the *Life of Birinus* (653–54), *Life of Fremund* (398–400), and *Life of Edmund* (562–69).

LIFE OF OSWALD

1   *My intention (In noua fert animus):* Henry's opening line directly borrows the first four words of Ovid's *Metamorphoses*.

2   *number, measure, and weight:* compare Wisdom of Solomon 11:21.

20   *the praise of Caesar:* Lucan's equivocal praise of Caesar in the *Pharsalia* was a critical commonplace in the Middle Ages (as it remains in modern times).

49   *you for wine, them for ales:* on Henry's low opinion of the latter, see the sometimes independently quoted lines 253–56 of the *Life of Birinus.*

72   *Roger, you who bear the rose:* Henry plays untranslatably on Rog-

er's name and the Latin for "bear the rose" *(rosam geris)*. Compare the pun on Cadwallon's name at line 312 below.

78   *dispose yourself favorably (da michi te placidum):* Henry here borrows from Ovid, *Fasti* 1.17, as he does as well in the *Life of Francis,* at 1.24.

86   *Typhis/Palinurus:* Palinurus was Aeneas's helmsman; Typhis the pilot of the Argo on Jason's quest for the Golden Fleece. The "sudden mutability of things" presumably refers to Simon recently vacating an office now held by Walter.

116   *had conferred their last banquet:* Geoffrey of Monmouth records the tradition that the English mercenaries engaged by Vortigern slaughtered their British hosts by prearranged signal amid a banquet.

117   *Ida, descended from the oldest of the Germans:* the meter of the Latin line is irregular.

132   *natural succession:* the genealogy recorded here, based on that in a life of Oswald by Reginald of Coldingham (ca. 1165), diverges from the more standard version supported by the Anglo-Saxon Chronicle and Bede's *Ecclesiastical History.*

227   *the Irish:* translating here, and throughout the text, "Scotos," according to the usage of Bede; what is now "Scotland" was in the eighth century inhabited by other peoples.

357   *Rightfully did one fall:* John 18:14.

364   *O Cross mighty in battle:* several passages in the meditation on the Cross that follows reappear verbatim in Henry's firmly attested poem, the *Versus de corona spinea* of ca. 1242. The shared lines are the best internal warrant we have for attributing the *Life of Oswald* to Henry.

366   *O tree truly surpassing all trees:* Henry here evokes Venantius Fortunatus's hymn *Pange lingua.*

397   *death and life in equal contest:* Henry here borrows from the Easter sequence hymn *Victimae paschali.*

503–4 *who took his name from giving aid:* Henry's pun probably plays on Norman French: the first appearance of the word "aid" in English occurs considerably later, according to the *Oxford English Dictionary.*

528   *being made all things to all people:* 1 Corinthians 9:22.

588   *love itself that conquers all:* compare Virgil, *Eclogues* 10.69.

599   Prior to this line, the longer version of the *Life of Oswald* recorded in B inserts a passage of twenty-three lines adapted from the life by Reginald of Coldingham.

642   *Jove's tree:* that is, an oak.

648   *Lycurgus:* see Ovid, *Metamorphoses* 4.22. Driven mad by Dionysus, Lycurgus hacked his own wife and child to pieces with an ax.

665   The B version of the text inserts here a passage of twenty-two additional lines.

675   Prior to this line, B includes a passage of some 316 lines treating posthumous miracles of Oswald.

684–85   *Four seasons/four elements:* this catalog, bald as it is, reads almost like a versified (and deliberately incorporated) gloss. It suggests once again the preoccupation with permanence and mutability foreshadowed by Henry's initial allusion to Ovid's *Metamorphoses* in the opening line.

708   Hereafter B inserts a further thirty-three lines.

737–38   *the index finger, thumb, and middle finger:* that is, the hand is set in a gesture of blessing.

LIFE OF BIRINUS

1   *I both blush and confess (Et pudet et fateor):* Ovid, *Tristia* 5.7.57.

4   *who sings of Priam's fortune and his noble war (fortunam Priami cantans et nobile bellum):* Horace, *Ars poetica* 137.

6   *Hercules:* translating "Tyrintius heros," more literally, "the Tyrian hero," since Hercules was associated with a Phoenician hero, Melquart, of similar career.

6–10   *worthier of exaltation (dignior attolli . . . uictus eodem):* compare *Life of Oswald* 21–27.

17–18   *Peter, bishop of Winchester:* Peter held the see of Winchester from 1225 to 1238. He departed on Crusade in the summer of 1227 shortly after his dismissal as advisor by the young Henry III.

29–30   *of whom you first commanded me to write:* Peter appears to have asked Henry for a life of Martin, which Henry has postponed at

his own discretion. It is unclear whether Peter in fact asked for a
life of Birinus at all.

32   *I shall walk, run, leap, and then fly:* the translation of the lines that
follow significantly recasts Henry's Latin, which indulges in a
notable example of the rhetorical device of polyptoton, whereby
a word is repeated in a range of differently inflected forms.

35   *Birinus traverses the sea on foot:* see line 291 below.

39–41   *I shall follow these guides in fixed order:* there is no evidence for
any further continuation of the series beyond the present text.
Peter's departure on Crusade in 1227 might serve to explain the
abandonment of the project.

136–54   This long passage has no parallel in Henry's prose source and reflects the synthesis of active and contemplative lives in the new
mendicant orders.

162   *one of the sixty strong men of Israel:* Song of Solomon 3:7.

187   *reason represses pleasure:* compare Gregory the Great, *Moralia*
20.3.

214–17   *A city set on a hill . . . :* Matthew 5:14–15.

221   *Honorius, pinnacle of nobility and honor (nobilitatis apex et honoris,
Honorius):* compare *Life of Francis* 10.3, "culmen honestatis et honoris, Honorius."

226   *Asterius, bishop of Genoa:* Asterius was in fact archbishop of
Milan. The inaccuracy is inherited from Bede's account in the
Ecclesiastical History.

227   *to exalt the horns of the just:* a phrase drawn from Psalm 74:11 in
the Vulgate version, here referring to Birinus's anointing as part
of his consecration as bishop.

289   *the body of Christ:* that is, the consecrated and so transsubstanti-
ated Host.

368   *so far as a Balearic sling casts its spinning shot:* Strabo (*Geographica*
3.5) and Livy (*History of Rome* 28.37) mention the slinging skill of
the people who inhabited these islands off the coast of Spain.

399   *the penny of the preceding Law:* this elaborate conceit refers to the
supersession of Torah by Gospel in medieval Christian typology.

417–18   *nor will his glory be greater: Versus de corona spinea* 244–45. These
lines (and ll. 485–90 below) reappear verbatim in Henry's firmly

attested poem the *Versus de corona spinea* of ca. 1242. The recurring lines are our best internal evidence for attribution of the *Life of Birinus* to Henry. See also the note on line 364 of the *Life of Oswald*.

429   *matter . . . form . . . being:* the corresponding words of the Latin text (*hyle, idea,* and *ousia,* respectively) are common Greek loanwords in medieval philosophical texts.

445   *the first-made man:* translating *prothoplausti,* a common Greek loanword in medieval theological writings.

485–90   *O dumbstruck Nature . . . : Versus de corona spinea* 112–17.

552   *necessity makes an old woman trot:* Henry here incorporates a medieval proverb.

594   *transformation by God's right hand:* Psalm 76:11.

654–55   *the blind can see the lame run . . . :* the topos of mutually witnessed cures is a hallmark of Henry's hagiography, seen as well in *Life of Francis* (14.37–39), *Life of Fremund* (398–400), and *Life of Edmund* (562–69).